W9-BSU-294

Voices of the Civil War

Voices of the Civil War · Shenandoah 1862

By the Editors of Time-Life Books, Alexandria, Virginia

Contents

THE SHENANDOAH VALLEY
Lying just west of the Blue Ridge and south of the Potomac River, Virginia's Shenandoah Valley was the setting for Stonewall Jackson's masterly 1862 campaign. Shown here in this artist's rendering, this vital region was prized both for its agricultural bounty and for its strategic location.
Valley Turnpike
Mount Jackson
New Market
MASSANUTTEN MOUNTAIN
Harrisonburg
Luray
South Fork of the Shenandoah River
To McDowell
Valley Turnpike
Thornton's Gap
Cross Keys
Staunton
Conrad's Store
Port Republic
Fisher's Gap
Swift Run Gap
Brown's Gap
BLUE RIDGE MOUNTAINS
Rockfish Gap
Stanardsville
Virginia Central Railroad
Rapidan River
Charlottesville

N
To Romney
Martinsburg
Williamsport
Winchester
Shepherdstown
Kernstown
Strasburg
Charles Town
Harpers Ferry
Shenandoah River
Front Royal
Snicker's Gap
Ashby's Gap
Manassas Gap
Leesburg
Chester Gap
Potomac River
Manassas Gap Railroad
Warrenton
Manassas Junction
Orange & Alexandria Railroad
Culpeper
Alexandria
Rappahannock River
Potomac River

To Defend the Valley

Thomas Jonathan "Stonewall" Jackson was seldom given to making strategic pronouncements. But he nevertheless laid it down as law that "if this Valley is lost, Virginia is lost." The valley in question was, of course, the Shenandoah in northwestern Virginia, and it was, militarily, a crucial gateway into the Old Dominion. The corollary of Jackson's law was also stark: If Union troops charging south through the Valley conquered Virginia, the South might quite abruptly lose the war.

It fell to Jackson in spring 1862 to defend the Shenandoah and turn back the first Federal attempt to force the gateway. He did so in one of the most agile and inventive campaigns of the Civil War, or any war. It was a classic campaign of movement in which Jackson bewildered the Federals with swift, surprising marches and sudden, unexpected assaults. In one period of 48 days, Jackson marched his troops an astonishing 646 miles.

Jackson's Valley operation was one of the conflict's smaller campaigns. His army never numbered more than 17,000 men, the battles were not large, and the casualties were relatively light. But it had monumental effects. Not only did Jackson's campaign save the Valley but it also drew off at one point some 40,000 Federal troops needed elsewhere to help prosecute a large Union offensive aimed at Richmond—and doubtless contributed to that thrust's eventual failure.

The Shenandoah, a verdant, 150-mile valley running between the Blue Ridge Mountains and the Alleghenies, angling northeast from the town of Lexington to the Potomac River, was a strategic linchpin. Confederates in possession of the Valley posed a direct threat to President Lincoln and his government in Washington, D.C., only 50 miles from the Valley's northern tip. It was a natural invasion route—and would be used twice later in the war by Robert E. Lee for thrusts into Maryland and Pennsylvania.

If Federal troops controlled the Valley, they could then cross the Blue Ridge by any of 11 passes to invade Virginia's Piedmont region—and head straight for the Confederate capital

This painting by Louis Guillaume depicts Stonewall Jackson at the climactic moment of the Battle of Winchester in May 1862. According to an eyewitness, the general hauled back on his horse and then "in a blaze of triumphant passion" waved his men forward.

of Richmond only about 100 miles away. Almost as serious, Federals reaching Staunton would cut what was perhaps the South's most important railroad, the Virginia & Tennessee, which linked Richmond with the Confederate west as far as the Mississippi River.

The Shenandoah was also important for its provender, the fruit of flourishing farms with barnyards full of hogs and chickens, and fields of corn, oats, rye, and wheat. "The horses and cattle were fat and sleek; the large barns were overflowing with gathered crops," wrote a Confederate soldier in 1861. The Valley was "a perfect stomachic Elysium," enthused another Rebel after packing in a breakfast that included hotcakes, eggs, syrup, butter, freshly baked bread, and boiled ham. Later, after four years of war when one army after another had tramped through, the Valley would be all but stripped, its livestock—the few that had survived—very lean indeed. But until then it remained a prime source of what Virginians, and their embattled armies, had to eat.

Jackson seemed at first glance an unlikely savior of the Valley, despite his bold and timely stand at the Battle of First Manassas, which had helped turn the tide for the Confederates and earned him the sobriquet of Stonewall. Lean and unimposing, he was as graceless in action as he was abrupt and sparing in speech. In a day of peacock generals, he wore an old uniform topped by a battered forage cap, faded by sun and rain to a dingy yellow, that he pulled down low on his brow. On his oversized feet he wore a shabby pair of flop-top cavalry boots. Only his eyes were startling. Blue and piercing, they glittered, observers swore, in the midst of battle, earning him the soldiers' nickname of Old Blue Light.

When astride his horse, a small, nondescript creature named Little Sorrel, Jackson seemed even less impressive. The beast was, an aide said, "as little like a Pegasus as his master was like an Apollo." Troops in his army seeing Jackson for the first time were often shocked to think that this shabby, undistinguished figure was their commanding general. He had the air, they said, of an itinerant peddler, or perhaps a backwoods farmer out for a ride.

Jackson in fact looked like what he was, a countryman from the Allegheny hills. And he might have remained there were it not for a chance to attend West Point. Born on Virginia's western frontier in 1824 and orphaned at an early age, he grew up on an uncle's homestead, doing farm chores and working in the uncle's sawmill and gristmill. He received the equivalent of only about four years of formal education. Nevertheless, he won an appointment to the military academy, actually reporting a year early when he replaced another appointee who withdrew and headed back home. He managed somehow to pass the entrance examination and then squeaked through the Point's tough first year by cramming night after night by the light of embers in his barracks-room fireplace long after everyone else was abed. "I am very ignorant," he told a friend, "but I can make it up in study." He lived, he said, by a simple maxim: "You may be whatever you resolve to be."

This fierce resolve showed on one occasion when, out practicing drill, his platoon was hit by a furious downpour. The other cadets scampered for cover, but Jackson kept right on marching, resolute, alone, drenched but determined—which boded ill, had they known it, for the troops he would later implacably march through every kind of dreadful weather.

Through ceaseless grinding work, Jackson rose steadily in academic standing, graduating 17th out of a class of 59 in 1846. Throughout he astonished his fellow cadets by his ferocious ability to concentrate. "No one I have ever known," one roommate recalled, "could so perfectly withdraw his mind from surrounding objects or influences, and so thoroughly involve his whole being in the subject under consideration." It was a quality he would demonstrate again and again in battle.

Soon after graduation Jackson, like virtually all his classmates, was sent to fight in the Mexican War of 1846-1848. Once in Mexico he jumped at the chance to join an artillery battery led by an exceedingly combative officer named John Bankhead Magruder, who was sure to seek out the hottest fighting. Jackson proved himself a born gunner, recklessly shoving his cannon forward through enemy fire in three of the war's bloodiest battles. His only fear, he said, was that he "not meet danger enough to make my conduct conspicuous." For his "gallantry and meritorious conduct," he was awarded brevet major and was singled out for praise by the army's top commander, General Winfield Scott.

Exhilarated by combat, Jackson found the postwar army a far duller proposition. He was assigned first to a small post on Long Island, then in 1850 to a worse backwater, a swampy little fort near Tampa, Florida. There he got into a bitter feud with the fort's commander, Major William H. French, a habitual meddler who refused to give Jackson a free hand in carrying out his duties as company quartermaster and commissary officer.

A stickler for military protocol, Jackson was outraged—and retaliated by starting an unseemly investigation of the camp gossip that French was dallying with his family's nursemaid. By the time the mess was sorted out, Jackson had received an official rebuke for behavior not befitting an officer. In August

1851 he resigned from the army and accepted an appointment to the faculty of Virginia Military Institute in the town of Lexington, a job partly arranged for him by a Mexican War friend and future fellow general in the Confederate army, Daniel Harvey Hill. At VMI Jackson soon became somewhat less than popular with the corps of cadets. Memorizing the Institute's rule book, he rigidly applied its provisions on all occasions. When not disciplining students he bored them with his droning lectures on mathematics and "natural philosophy," or physics. To many cadets he was Fool Tom, and student notebooks were full of unflattering caricatures and acid comments about his pedagogy and his strange habits and mannerisms.

Some of these quirks were due to Jackson's internal climate, which was uncertain at best. Since childhood he had complained of stomach ailments, a persistent dyspepsia for which doctors could find no physical cause. Seeking relief, Jackson became obsessed with his health and diet. By the time of the Civil War he had settled on a bizarre menu consisting of white bread or corn bread, raspberries, and milk—and sometimes lemons. To help keep digestive anguish at bay, Jackson always stood and sat rigidly erect, his spine never touching the back of a chair, so that, as he explained, his internal organs would remain properly aligned.

Jackson also became a fervent Christian, taking up religion, like everything else, with furious intensity. At VMI he became a pillar of Lexington's Presbyterian church, and although not overly censorious of others' habits, he refused to smoke, drink, curse, or play cards—on the grounds that "I know it is not wrong *not to do*, so I'm going to be on the safe side."

Jackson believed so strongly that Sunday should be devoted to worship that he even refused to write letters on the Sabbath—although during the war he would fight on the Lord's day if the Almighty saw fit to throw a vulnerable enemy force in his path. While serving as church deacon he started a special Sunday school for black children, which he financed from his own pocket.

This caring and softer side of Jackson, undreamed of by VMI's harassed cadets, also found its expression in marriage. Soon after arriving at the Institute he began courting Miss Elinor Junkin, daughter of the Reverend Dr. George Junkin, president of nearby Washington College, later Washington and Lee. They were married in 1853, the union being, Jackson said, "a great source of happiness."

It was, however, tragically brief. Ellie died in childbirth 14 months after the wedding. Jackson was shattered and wrote a West Point classmate, "I desire no more days on earth." But then in 1857 Jackson married again, once more to a clergyman's daughter, Mary Anna Morrison. This marriage was also happy. "He luxuriated in the freedom of his home," Anna wrote, "and his joyfulness would have been incredible to those who saw him only when he put on his official dignity."

Both teaching and domestic tranquillity came to an abrupt end on April 21, 1861, when, the war having begun, Jackson received orders to march a column of VMI students to a railhead for transport on to Richmond where the smartly trained cadets would serve as drillmasters for green Virginia recruits. Jackson gathered the cadets early for prayer service, then kept them waiting until precisely the scheduled 1:00 p.m. departure time before shouting, "Right face! By file, left march!" At age 37 Thomas Jonathan Jackson was again off to war. He would wage it with the Old Testament fervor of Joshua smiting the enemies of the Lord.

From Richmond, Jackson—newly made a colonel of Virginia volunteers—hurried to take command of the Confederate garrison at Harpers Ferry. Within days he had the droves of unorganized recruits gathered there sorted into units and busy drilling. Then on his own initiative he trapped and hijacked 56 locomotives and more than 300 freight cars on the Baltimore & Ohio rail line running through Harpers Ferry to Washington.

Jackson was relieved at Harpers Ferry in June 1861 by Major General Joseph E. Johnston, the South's senior officer in the region, and shortly found himself promoted to brigadier general and in command of what would become his most renowned fighting unit, the 1st Virginia Brigade. Spoiling for action, Jackson soon led his troops in a sharp little engagement on July 2 with a much larger force of Federals at Falling Waters near Martinsburg, Virginia, northwest of Harpers Ferry. Exhilarated as always when bullets flew, Jackson found, as he wrote his wife, Anna, that he was in perfect health.

Jackson soon fell back to join General Johnston's main force at Winchester, the most important crossroads town in the northern end of the Valley. There, on July 20, word came that a large Federal force was about to attack another Confederate army across the Blue Ridge at Manassas Junction. Johnston immediately sent Jackson's troops and the other brigades quick-marching 20 miles eastward through Ashby's Gap, then piled them on trains bound for Manassas.

Arriving in Manassas, Jackson hustled his brigade off the freight cars and then, without waiting for orders, marched them toward the sound of firing. After being held in reserve, Jackson came up just in time to support a hard-pressed unit led by Brigadier General Barnard Bee. "There is Jackson," some heard Bee yell to his men, "standing like a stone wall." The reinforcements turned the tide and the Confederates sent the Federals in disorderly retreat across a little stream called Bull Run and back toward Washington.

Now and forever Stonewall, Jackson remained at Manassas with the main Virginia army through the summer and into fall 1861. Then orders came from Secretary of War Judah P. Benjamin: Jackson would take charge of the force still stationed in the Shenandoah Valley. By November 5 he was back in Winchester with his small staff, ready to take charge.

What Jackson found was hardly to his liking. His army consisted of 1,650 ill-trained militiamen, many carrying antiquated flintlocks, and 500 equally ill-disciplined cavalry troopers. The horsemen, however, were commanded by Lieutenant Colonel Turner Ashby, a swarthy and luxuriantly bearded 34-year-old Virginia farmer who, it soon developed, had a genius for cavalry operations and was just as pugnaciously ready for a fight as Jackson. In the months ahead he would harry the Federals unmercifully. The only other good news was that the war department in Richmond soon decided to send along Jackson's old command, now called the Stonewall Brigade.

But even reinforced, Jackson was vastly outnumbered by the 18,000 Federals under Major General Nathaniel P. Banks, camped in western Maryland but poised to move southward across the Potomac. In addition, Jackson was also menaced by the Federal forces of the Department of Western Virginia lurking in the Allegheny Mountains with a purported 22,000 men.

Banks' force was well equipped, especially with artillery, and several of the officers were solid professionals, particularly a West Point classmate of Jackson's, Colonel George H. Gordon. Banks himself, however, was a rank amateur, one of the so-called political generals appointed by President Lincoln mostly because of their political clout but also in the hope that their savvy in civilian life would carry over into the army.

Banks was in fact a singularly ambitious and successful Yankee from Waltham, Massachusetts, who had risen from the lowly job of bobbin boy in a textile mill to become Speaker of the House of Representatives in Washington and governor of his home state. He even looked the part of a general, resplendent in natty uniforms with yellow gloves, shiny boots, and every brass button at high polish. "He is splendid, his staff behind him is splendid. All is splendid," wryly noted a dubious Federal soldier. But as a tactician and military leader he would prove woefully unsure and timid—and no match for the confident and daring Jackson.

The soon to be commander of the Federals in the Alleghenies, Major General John C. Frémont, was by his credentials far more formidable. A West Point graduate, he had become famous as the Pathfinder for his 1840s explorations in the Rockies. He had already botched his first wartime assignment, however, as general in charge of the West with headquarters in St. Louis, allowing operations there to drift aimlessly. Pulling Frémont east, Lincoln in early 1862 would put him in charge of a freshly created Mountain Department, where presumably his West Point-learned skills would make him an effective field commander.

Facing two Union forces—either of which properly led could crush his tiny army—Jackson decided not to stand on the defensive but to mount a preemptive strike. The most immediate threat was posed by 5,000 Federals from the Allegheny army that in October had occupied the town of Romney only 40 miles northwest of Winchester and astride undefended roads leading deep into the Valley.

Before moving, Jackson asked for further reinforcements, namely the 6,000-man Confederate Army of the Northwest then sitting in the mountains west of Staunton under the command of Brigadier General William W. Loring. Told by the war department to join Jackson, the prickly Loring, who did not enjoy serving under anybody else's command, took his time about it. Loring complained that he needed to assemble a large baggage train to transport his army's gear.

Jackson, annoyed by waiting and fearful that his troops would molder in their camps, decided to make what amounted to a practice strike. Marshaling the Stonewall Brigade, some militiamen, and Captain William McLaughlin's crack Rockbridge Artillery, he hustled them north out of Winchester shortly before Christmas. The target: the Chesapeake & Ohio Canal, which, running parallel to the Potomac, carried bargeloads of the Appalachian coal needed to keep the Union home fires burning.

The troops, having covered 38 miles in less than two days, managed to tear a hole in the canal's Dam no. 5 despite heavy fire from Union defenders. Then they marched back to Winchester at the same speed, arriving on December 23. "This Gen. Jackson is always doing something to vex the enemy," a clerk in the Confederate war department wrote after hearing of the foray, "and I think he is destined to annoy them more."

On his arrival Jackson was enraged to find that only one of Loring's brigades had reached Winchester. Finally the other two straggled in, bringing the army's total to 9,200 infantry and 650 cavalry. Immediately Jackson marched, heading his small army north out of Winchester on January 1, 1862. As usual with their secretive general, the officers and men had no idea what was afoot. "No one but Old Jack himself knows where, or for what purpose we are going," wrote a lieutenant of the Stonewall Brigade. "If silence be golden," another observer commented, "he was a bonanza." It was probably just as well nobody knew Jackson's plans. The troops were headed off on what would become one of the more harrowing winter treks in military annals.

New Year's Day was unseasonably warm and many of the men shed their coats, flinging them into the army's supply wagons. Soon, however, the weather turned foul, with chill winds that brought a blizzard the next day. Meanwhile, Jackson, seeking surprise—and never one to do things the easy way—marched his column northwest on a rough, rutted track toward the town of Bath rather than taking the solid turnpike directly to Romney.

As the snow swirled down, the troops stuggled on, frozen and half starved because the army's 160 supply wagons carrying their rations and coats had fallen hopelessly behind. On the second night out it was so cold that, one sentry recalled, "the soles of the shoes actually froze to the ground." Noted a lieutenant in the Stonewall Brigade: "If a man had told me 12 months ago that men could stand such hardship, I would have called him a fool."

On January 3 Jackson ignored a shortcut to Romney leading from a crossroads called Unger's Store and kept his brigades marching on the roundabout route to Bath. There were Federals in the town, about 1,400 of them, and Jackson did not want them falling on his flank. In his always combative way, he wanted first to capture the Union garrison—and then go raiding across the Potomac to destroy the Federal supply depot at nearby Hancock, Maryland.

The day's march was again a ferocious ordeal. Finally, on the evening of January 3 the exhausted troops stumbled into the outskirts of Bath. With hardly a pause Jackson sent the militia marching off again, around a ridge called Warm Spring Mountain to sever a road the Federals might use to escape. He then ordered one of Loring's brigades, led by Colonel William Gilham, to immediately advance into the town.

At this point nothing went right. The raw militiamen found the path around the mountain blocked by fallen trees and simply gave up. Gilham's brigade advanced timidly, met some Union skirmishers, and, with General Loring's approval, quickly fell back and camped for the night. The next day the militia tried again and were stopped by a small Federal patrol. Gilham also advanced but slowed at the edge of town when he saw some Union troops in the distance. Finally a disgusted Jackson sent his cavalry galloping into Bath, only to find that the enemy had obligingly departed, most retreating northward toward the Potomac.

Giving up his intention to pursue, Jackson contented himself with burning a nearby B & O Railroad bridge and tearing up miles of track. He then sent his force backtracking to Unger's Store and the crossroads to Romney. The march again was a dreadful nightmare. The temperature often plunged down to near zero and the already rough road became covered with a treacherous combination of ice and drifting snow. The men slipped and slithered and fell, their bodies "hitting the road," one soldier recalled, "with a thud like that of a pile driver." The horses dragging the guns tumbled so many times that icicles of blood hung from their knees.

By the time the little army got back to the crossroads, so many men were sick that Jackson had no choice but to call a halt and give them some rest. Then, on January 13 word came in from cavalry scouts that the Union troops, apparently overestimating Jackson's force, had abandoned Romney. Nothing would do but to march there, with a few men also going to Bath, to establish outposts against any Federal return.

The idea of making winter quarters in Romney, partially ruined by the retreating Federals, was too much for General Loring and his troops, who were quite certain by then that Jackson was demented. Soon 11 of Loring's brigade and regimental commanders dispatched a petition to Richmond complaining that Jackson had already half destroyed the army and that wintering in such a godforsaken place would be suicidal.

Secretary of War Benjamin agreed, ordering Jackson to concentrate his force around Winchester and winter there. Angry at this interference with his command, Jackson threatened to resign his commission. The affair was ultimately patched up, Jackson staying in the Shenandoah and Loring being reassigned—angry but no doubt thankful to be through with Stonewall—to a post at Norfolk, Virginia, and then farther south.

The tempest over, Jackson reassembled what was left of his army in Winchester as ordered. There in one of the thriving town's comfortable brick mansions he settled down with his wife, who had come to join him for what was, she said, "as happy a winter as

CHRONOLOGY

November 1861	*Jackson assumes command of the Valley District (November 4)*
December	*Actions at Dam no. 5, C&O Canal (December 8-12)*
January 1862	*Beginning of Jackson's winter campaign (January 1)*
	Skirmishes at Bath and Hancock (January 3-5)
	Confederates reach Romney (January 10)
	Jackson and his army return to Winchester (January 23-30)
February	*Union forces reoccupy Romney (February 7)*
	Banks' Federals cross the Potomac into Virginia (February 24-26)
March	*Winchester abandoned by Jackson and occupied by Federals (March 11-12)*
	Battle of Kernstown (March 23)
	Valley army begins retreat (March 24)
April	*Union forces follow up to Edinburg (April 1-2)*
	Banks assumes command of the Department of the Shenandoah (April 12)
	Federals reach Mount Jackson and New Market (April 17)
	Jackson falls back east to Swift Run Gap (April 19)
	Union troops occupy Harrisonburg (April 22)
	Jackson sets out toward Staunton; Ewell's division enters the Valley (April 30)
May	*Battle of McDowell (May 8)*
	Shields' Federals recalled from the Valley; Banks begins withdrawal to Strasburg (May 12)
	Union of Jackson's and Ewell's commands at New Market (May 20)
	Battle of Front Royal (May 23)
	Banks retreats to Winchester; Jackson pursues (May 24)
	Battle of Winchester (May 25)
	Confederates reach Harpers Ferry; Frémont and Shields converge on Strasburg (May 29)
	Jackson falls back to Harrisonburg (May 30-June 5)
June	*Engagement at Harrisonburg; death of Ashby (June 6)*
	Battle of Cross Keys (June 8)
	Battle of Port Republic (June 9)
	Valley army crosses the Blue Ridge toward Richmond (June 18)

ever falls to the lot of mortals on this earth."

This blissful state was soon interrupted, however, by General Nathaniel Banks. By the end of February, Banks' army had grown to about 38,000 men, and he was pushing some units across the Potomac into the lower, or northern, end of the Shenandoah. By early March the Federals had reached Charles Town, then the village of Bunker Hill only a dozen miles from Winchester.

Finally, on March 12 Banks' advance guard, still moving cautiously, reached the outskirts of Winchester itself—only to be stopped in a stiff little fight with Turner Ashby and some of his horsemen. When the Union troops at last managed to enter the town they found that Jackson's infantry had filed out heading south the previous day. Some of the Union officers professed disappointment, complaining that Jackson had gotten away without a fight. Colonel George Gordon, Jackson's old classmate, was not worried. Stonewall would soon, he said, give the Federals all the "entertainment" they could handle.

Jackson was, in fact, eager to fight even though his army had shrunk over the winter to only 3,600 infantry, 600 cavalry, and 27 guns—about one-tenth of Banks' total. Even with that tiny force, he informed Richmond, "a kind Providence may enable us to inflict a terrible wound."

For the time being, Jackson retreated about 40 miles up the Valley, to Strasburg, to Woodstock, and then to the village of Mount Jackson on the west side of Massanutten Mountain, a long ridge that ran lengthwise down the Valley and would soon provide Stonewall with a valuable blind for his maneuvers. Jackson's orders were to keep Banks busy pursuing so that he would be unable to detach any units and send them east across the Blue Ridge to join up with the main body of the Army of the Potomac, clearly getting ready for an advance on Richmond.

Jackson was satisfied all was going well until March 22, when Ashby and some of his cavalry scouts galloped in. One of Banks' divisions, they reported, was heading east toward the Blue Ridge and another was falling back in the same direction.

This was just what Jackson was supposed to prevent. By dawn on March 22 the Valley army was racing back northward. The next day—a Sunday, as it happened—the troops would smash into Banks' remaining division commanded by Brigadier General James Shields near the village of Kernstown, four miles south of Winchester. Shields, a tough Irish-born midwesterner, had also been a successful politician, but unlike Banks he had gained valuable military experience in the Mexican War and would prove now and in the months ahead to be a more formidable opponent.

The Kernstown fight would not be a ringing success for Jackson and his outnumbered troops. But it served notice that an exceedingly active and combative Confederate general was on the loose in the Shenandoah. President Lincoln, overriding his army chief, Major General George B. McClellan—who wanted every man he could get for the Richmond offensive—immediately ordered Banks back into the Valley and also dispatched another division to the army under Frémont in the Allegheny foothills. Jackson would soon give those Federals a full measure of the entertainment Colonel Gordon had predicted.

ORDER OF BATTLE

CONFEDERATE

January 1862

Valley District Jackson

Garnett's Brigade
Valley Militia (3 brigades)

Cavalry Ashby

Army of the Northwest Loring

Anderson's Brigade
Gilham's Brigade
Taliaferro's Brigade
Johnson's Brigade

March 1862

Valley District Jackson

Garnett's Brigade
Burks' Brigade
Fulkerson's Brigade

Cavalry Ashby

May-June 1862

Valley District Jackson

Jackson's Division
Winder's Brigade
Campbell's / Patton's Brigade
Taliaferro's Brigade

Army of the Northwest Johnson (merged with Ewell's Division in late May)

Conner's Brigade
Scott's Brigade

Ewell's Division
Taylor's Brigade
Steuart's Brigade
Elzey's Brigade
Trimble's Brigade

Cavalry Ashby

FEDERAL

January 1862

Army of the Potomac (part)

Banks' Division
Williams' Brigade
Abercrombie's Brigade
Hamilton's Brigade

Department of Western Virginia (part)

Landers' Division
Kimball's Brigade
Sullivan's Brigade
Tyler's Brigade

March 1862

Army of the Potomac (part)

V Corps Banks

Williams' Division
Donnelly's Brigade
Abercrombie's Brigade
Gordon's Brigade

Shields' Division
Kimball's Brigade
Sullivan's Brigade
Tyler's Brigade

Cavalry Hatch

May-June 1862

Department of the Shenandoah Banks

Williams' Division
Donnelly's Brigade
Gordon's Brigade

Cavalry Hatch

Department of the Rappahannock (part)

Shields' Division
Kimball's Brigade
Ferry's Brigade
Tyler's Brigade
Carroll's Brigade

Mountain Department Frémont

Schenck's Brigade
Milroy's Brigade
Cluseret's Brigade

Blenker's Division
Stahel's Brigade
Koltes' Brigade
Bohlen's Brigade

Cavalry Bayard

LIEUTENANT JOHN H. GRABILL
33D VIRGINIA INFANTRY, GARNETT'S BRIGADE

In October 1861 General Thomas J. Jackson was assigned an independent command that would send him back to the Shenandoah Valley. He bade farewell to the troops of his first command, the Stonewall Brigade, near Fairfax Court House on a raw late-autumn afternoon. Lieutenant Grabill, a 22-year-old Valley native, recorded Jackson's speech verbatim in his diary—not realizing that the brigade would reunite with Jackson in Winchester one week later.

Nov. 4th. The regiment was called out to-day and Gen. Jackson delivered his farewell address to his brigade.

Gen. Jackson and his staff officers road up in front of the brigade, after we had formed on the hillside, and looked up and down the line. He then slowly raised his cap and said, "Officers and soldiers of the first brigade, I am not here to make a speech, but simply to say farewell. I first met you at Harper's Ferry, in the commencement of this war, and I cannot take leave of you without giving expression to my admiration of your conduct from that day to this, whether on the march, the bivouac, the tented field, or the bloody plains of Manassas when you gained the well deserved reputation of having decided the fate of that battle. Throughout the broad extent of country over which you have marched, by your respect for the rights and property of citizens, you have shown that you were soldiers, not only to defend, but able and willing, both to defend and protect. You have already gained a brilliant and deservedly high reputation, throughout the army, and the whole Confederacy, and I trust, in the future, by your deeds on the field, and by the assistance of the same kind Providence who has heretofore favored our cause, you will gain more victories, and add additional luster to the reputation you now enjoy.

You have already gained a proud position in the future history of this, our war of independence. I shall look with great anxiety to your future movements, and I trust, whenever I shall hear of the first brigade on the field of battle, it will be of still nobler deeds achieved, and a higher reputation won.

In the army of the Shenandoah, you were the *first* brigade; in the army of the Potomac, you were the *first* brigade; in the second corps of this army you are the *first* brigade; you are the *first* brigade in the affections of your general, and I hope by your future deeds and bearing you will be handed down to posterity, as the FIRST brigade in this, our second war of independence. Farewell!

Mary Anna Morrison Jackson favored this image of her husband because it caught "more of the beaming sunlight of his home look." Stonewall posed for the portrait in photographer Nathan Routzahn's studio in Winchester in November 1862. Jackson was told that the image would be marred because a button was missing. He pulled the button from his pocket, borrowed a needle and thread, and hastily sewed it back on. It is visible halfway up the left breast of his uniform.

CORPORAL JAMES E. HALL
31ST VIRGINIA INFANTRY, JOHNSON'S BRIGADE

In the fall of 1861 the 31st Virginia was serving in the Allegheny Mountains as part of General William W. Loring's Army of the Northwest. Corporal Hall's complaints about life in the field bespeak the disillusionment that overtook many soldiers recruited early who began to realize that the war was not going to be a brief and glorious affair. Hall was later wounded and captured at Gettysburg and only returned to his regiment in March 1865.

Oct. 29 . . . I hardly know what to say or think, anymore. I even yet, can scarcely realize my circumstances. What have I now to live for? The most flattering anticipations of a bright future, and a successful career in a business life are forever gone. I am wasting my most precious time. I only have one hope or desire to live—on account of my cherished friends at home. For them I only wish to survive, but if I should not ever again meet them, I hope they may think of me only as

"Not to save the life of Gen. Loring, and all the sons of bitches in the Confederate Army, would I volunteer again!"

giving myself for them, and that I glory in it. May the young men hereafter, in the North, think of the responsibilities of making war upon an innocent people who never did them harm, before they embark in such an enterprise again. Is conscience dead? Is reason dumb?

Nov. 6 This is a very disagreeable day. The mountains in the distance are covered with snow. I expect we will have to winter here. If they do keep our Regt. here they will never get another Western Va. volunteer. We have been badly treated. I will have various scores to settle after the war is over.

Nov. 13 I feel like never writing any more. I have quit hoping to ever see our subjugated county as it was once. I feel more like throwing down my gun and cursing the hour I was born to witness such a condition of affairs, than of doing anything else. Unless there is some action soon, I will answer to my name—at a distance! I have a strong idea of getting drunk tonight. I would sure, if it was to be had this side of

632 HARPER'S WEEKLY. [October 5, 1861.

RECRUITING FOR THE CONFEDERATE ARMY AT WOODSTOCK, VIRGINIA.

THE BIVOUAC FIRE AT THE OUTPOSTS OF OUR ARMY ON THE POTOMAC.

These early camp and recruiting scenes appeared in the October 5, 1861, edition of Harper's Weekly. Confederate enlistments rose dramatically as a result of the Rebel victory at Manassas. Lincoln's call for 300,000 three-year troops also spurred recruitment in the South.

Yankeedom. Will and Mike are off somewhere on the sick list. I feel somewhat indisposed myself—every time there is a fight on hand! But I have not gone yet! Bud and I console ourselves over a large two-gallon bottle we keep on hand, but which is empty nearly all the time. I wonder if they at home ever think about us. But I wonder more, what they would think if they were to see me with my large vial filled with whiskey!

Nov 18 Whew! How cold it is this morning! . . . It is now night. We have received marching orders. Our destination is undoubtedly fixed for the top of Allegheny Mountain. Not to save the life of Gen. Loring, and all the sons of bitches in the Confederate Army, would I volunteer again! Not many know where we are going, but I—being a *high private,* find out many things. Bud and I are going to back out in the morning—but not until we get our large bottle filled!

Edward C. Shephard poses in the West Point-inspired dress uniform that he wore as a cadet at the Virginia Military Institute. VMI, founded in 1839 and staffed by West Pointers, provided the Valley District army with disciplined and military-educated officers. Shephard served as a lieutenant in the 2d Virginia Infantry, part of the Stonewall Brigade.

The banner of the 2d Virginia Infantry was produced by Richmond merchant George Ruskell. The seal was emblematic of Southern sentiments about the war.

LIEUTENANT SAMUEL J. C. MOORE

2d Virginia Infantry, Garnett's Brigade

Moore, a Charles Town, Virginia, lawyer before the war, was elected captain of Company I eight days after he penned this letter to his wife, describing the Stonewall Brigade's return to Winchester. Injured at Second Manassas in August 1862, Moore spent much of 1863 in hospitals before returning to the Shenandoah Valley in 1864 to serve on General Jubal Early's staff.

My Dearest Ellen,

You have heard no doubt, that the 1st Brigade has come to the Valley. We are now encamped about 2 1/2 miles above Winchester, on the Turnpike leading to Strasburg. . . .

We had a miserable time coming up—on Friday evening we marched in the mud from Centreville to Manassas, where we took the cars (open burden cars) and proceeded to Strasburg, arriving there at about 2 1/2 in the morning—we then got along the best way we could until breakfast time, got something to eat wherever we could, and soon after breakfast started in the rain for this place—and such a march in the rain I never had in all my life. I am happy to say however that I went through with it all, even to sleeping in the woods on the ground all night, and am now as sound as ever, except sore feet from the long march on the Turnpike. Some of the officers of the Regiment, being too much of parlor soldiers to march at their posts, procured hacks at Strasburg and rode to Winchester, where they took lodgings at the Hotels. the next morning, however, when they were pitying us poor fellows who had slept in the woods, and felicitating themselves upon their superior tact in getting good quarters, an order was handed them, putting them all under arrest for leaving their posts; so that I think the few that were faithful have got rather the best of the bargain. Deahl is one of the arrested ones—he passed us on the road, quite grandly, in a hack; but seems quite cut down at having been put under arrest by General Jackson.

Our company behaved abominably on the march, as indeed did nearly all the companies in the Regiment—most of our men went home, leaving me not more than 30 here. Col. Allen sent a troop of Cavalry for them this morning—I am sorry to say that there are many men in the Company who are not influenced by principle, a sense of shame, of decency, of respect for themselves, their Company, or their Country. Now don't repeat this to anybody, as such a speech if known would perhaps effectually prevent me from writing "Captain" before my name.

PRIVATE CHARLES W. TRUEHART

Rockbridge (Virginia) Artillery

Enlisting in October 1861 as a cannoneer, Truehart, pictured here with his wife, Mary, participated in the attack on Dam no. 5 two months later, an expedition conducted by Jackson to keep his force active in the winter season. In 1863 Truehart became a hospital steward and later served as a surgeon.

You have doubtless heard of the famous partizan leader of the Potomac border, Colonel Ashby. I believe I failed to mention some particulars of the expedition under his conduct, which may prove interesting to you all. We have been on the march from Charlestown since 1 o'clock the previous night, and had halted at a village, (some few hundred yards from the river) called "Hardscrabble," or "Scrabbletown" —Ashby being first in front of our column, then behind—in short, popping up everywhere along the line of our marching column with the most restless, watchful manner, mounted on his splendid Black stallion, and followed by a number of his mounted body guard. But although all his men seemed pretty well fagged, and disposed to rest themselves by stretching full length on the grass, he still road about, peering over the river from behind the trees on the hill, at a larger Yankee camp. He had been up the lane on one of these reconnoitres, when he came dashing down the road exclaiming as he came in hearing, "Ten men follow me." In an instant the whole company of troopers were mounted and dashing off after their gallant leader. Some three hundred yards, just over a hill from us, there stood a house in an old field, near which the Col had discovered eight of the enemy, armed to the teeth. A fence, some four or five feet high stood between our position and the house; he cleared the fence with the greatest ease, and outstripping all his men dashed up to the Yankees, who fired volley after volley at him as they retreated toward the house, where they at last took refuge and kept up the fire on our troopers. But it soon became too warm for them, and they rushed out of the house and they made an attempt to get to the river. But Ashby with a loud voice and his six-shooter leveled at the Yankee Captain's head, commanded them to surrender. They sang out loudly for quarters. And in a minute or two the whole party, Capt. and all were astride behind our troopers, and borne in triumph down to where we were stationed, amid the shouts of our men. One of the prisoners a six-foot-four fellow and large in proportion, who proved to be a Kentuckian, was mounted on a small horse behind a diminutive boy of fifteen, and cut a most ridiculous figure, his legs hanging down near the ground, and head reaching far above the little fellow's head. Numerous were the questions put to the Yankees, who seemed not at all put out at what had befallen them;—one of the rascals with a good-natured laugh, called for a chew of tobacco before he would do any talking. Only the Captain seemed at all gruff. . . .

. . . We regulated march so as to reach a woods in the neighborhood of the Dam where we bivouaced for the night on the bare ground with our blankets only. The upper blankets were stiff with frost when we arose at daybreak in morning. During the night a large force of the Infantry, under cover of the darkness, threw up a stone wall, that entirely protected them from the riflemen of the enemy; besides doing a large amt. of work in the destruction of the Dam. We remained at the work of pulling down the dam some five or six days. And we did the work pretty effectively too. We were engaged in skirmishing with the enemy every day, both with Artillery and riflemen. Genl Jackson by his admirable strategic movements, entirely deceived the Yankees, making them think he had a large force some six miles down the river, by sending the 1,500 Militia down there and making them keep up a large number of fires during the night and attempt to cross the river during the day. But at last, just as we were completing the work on the dam, they brought up some of their Artillery from below to play upon us, and a large force of Infantry. But here again Old Jack fooled them completely. He had the wagons with the boats (Old Jack's fleet, as the soldiers called it) brought in sight on their way up the river to a point of some five or six miles above the Dam, conducted by a considerable display of troops as tho' we were going to effect a crossing up there. No sooner did the out witted Yankees discover this new and apparently formidable and important movement, than off they posted with their whole force up the river leaving us just where we wanted to be left. Without opposition, to prosecute our designs on the Dam.

The Yankees tried hard to shell our Camp, but Jack had out a strong piquet so that no spies could approach and discover our positions. And then he made us move our positions once or twice during the 24 hours; had fires kindled in different positions, of a night, so as to entirely deceive the rascals. Many were the iron messengers sent over to discover our location to them; some of which burst quite near us, so that we picked up the fragments of shell etc. But thanks Almighty God they did us no harm.

Colonel Turner Ashby presented a striking appearance as unforgettable as his flamboyant cavalry feats. The 33-year-old's exploits moved an adversary to admit, "He is light, active, skillful, and we are tormented by him like a bull with a gad-fly."

Sharpshooters in the Mill.
Rebel Artillery.
Rebel Artillery.
Sharpshooters.
Union Troops in Canal Locks.
Rebel Artillery.
Lock-keeper's House.
THE CAMPAIGN ON THE POTOMAC—UNSUCCESSFUL ATTEMPT OF THE REBELS TO DESTROY DAM NO 5, ON THE UPPER POTOMAC, NEAR WILLIAMSPORT, MARYLAND, DECEMBER 1861.—FROM A SKETCH BY CAPT. HENRY BACON OF THE 13TH MASSACHUSETTS VOLUNTEERS.—SEE PAGE 134.

With Confederate artillery firing from the Virginia hills in the distance, Stonewall Jackson's infantry attempts to destroy Dam no. 5 on the Potomac River near Williamsport, Maryland. Captain Henry Bacon of the 13th Massachusetts sketched the scene showing his company on the near shore. Working in icy waist-deep water overnight, Jackson's men breached a part of the dam early on December 21. The Federals repaired it a few days later.

LIEUTENANT JOHN H. GRABILL

33D VIRGINIA INFANTRY, GARNETT'S BRIGADE

After Jackson's reassignment to command the Valley District, the Stonewall Brigade, including the 33d Virginia, came under the command of Brigadier General Richard B. Garnett. Evidence of soul-searching is apparent in Lieutenant Grabill's year-end reflections of a stormy 1861. Dropped from the 33d Virginia's officer rolls in June 1862, Grabill finished his Confederate service as a cavalryman. Born at Mount Jackson in the Valley, he died at the age of 82 in nearby Woodstock.

As I sit in my tent this evening everything seems quiet. The old year is gradually dying. As I take a retrospective view of the past, the great thought of my mind seems to find expression in the exclamation, "What an eventful year!"

Last year Peace reigned throughout our undivided country. We were then under the government of our fathers, and the Union, though tottering, was still standing as a monument to the labors of patriotic hands. The constitution framed by the illustrious men of "76" though threatened, was still exerting its strong power in defense of the rights of the people of the Union. How sad the change! That union so revered, so loved, and so precious to us all, having been degraded from the proud position which it occupied has fallen to pieces and the constitution which was once our shield now lies impotent at the feet of a despot. Many, who began this year in the full enjoyment of health and of the prospect of a long life, are now lying cold and silent in their graves. Many a noble youth who volunteered to defend his native land against the tyranical and wicked invasion of a heartless foe, has sacrificed his life's blood upon the altar of his country. I might here mention the names of a number of my friends which shall be held dear through life. A. Dyer, A. Rench and a number of others of our fraternity have sacrificed their all in defense of the principles espoused by the people of the Confederate States. A year ago, we had no national existence now we look forward to be ranked as one of the nations of the world. May God grant that we may be blessed with prosperity equal to that which has been lavished upon us in the past. May the Lord be with us as a people and as individuals and may His name ever be honored and revered by our new Nationality, and when this life is over may we who are sharing the turmoils of a soldier's life be crowned with immortality at his right hand.

LIEUTENANT HENRY K. DOUGLAS

2D VIRGINIA INFANTRY, GARNETT'S BRIGADE

Douglas suspended his law practice to enlist at home in Shepherdstown, Virginia. He spent his first year under Jackson as an infantryman, but later he was assigned to Stonewall's celebrated staff. Douglas marched in his second winter expedition beginning on January 1, 1862.

It was the most dismal and trying night of this terrible expedition. It had been and was still snowing lightly, and the small army was in uncomfortable bivouac. A squad of soldiers in the Stonewall Brigade had built a large fire and some of them were standing and some lying about it wrapped up in their thin and inadequate blankets. The sharp wind was blowing over the hills and through the trees with a mocking whistle, whirling the sparks and smoke in eyes and over prostrate bodies.

A doleful defender, who had been lying down by the fire, with one side to it just long enough to get warm and comfortable, while the other got equally cold and uncomfortable, rose up and, having gathered his flapping blanket around him as well as possible, stood nodding and staggering over the flames. When the sparks set his blanket on fire it exhausted his patience and in the extremity of his disgust he exclaimed, "I wish the Yankees were in Hell!"

As he yawned this with a sleepy drawl, around the fire there went a drowsy growl of approbation. One individual, William Wintermeyer, however, lying behind a fallen tree, shivering with cold but determined not to get up, muttered, "I don't. Old Jack would follow them there, with our brigade in front!"

There seemed to be some force in the objection, but the gloomy individual continued, "Well, that's so, Bill,—but I wish the Yankees were in Heaven. They're too good for this earth!"

"I don't!" again replied the soldier behind the log, "because Old Jack would follow them there, too, and as it's our turn to go on picket, we wouldn't enjoy ourselves a bit!"

The discomfited soldier threw himself to the ground with a grunt, and all was quiet but the keen wind and cracking flames. . . .

While encamped near Berkeley Springs, if it can be called a camp, I was sent out one night in the direction of Hancock with my company to guard against any curiosity the Yankee cavalry might have to investigate us during the darkness. Some cavalry pickets were in front of us who assured me that there was no danger of such an attempt. I thought it safe, therefore, after throwing some rifle men to the front, to let the men lie down in a field which commanded an advance on either road and go to sleep. It was cloudy but not cold for the season. In the middle of the night I felt moisture on my face, and covering myself from head to foot in a blanket I slept soundly. In the early light I awoke and found myself oppressed with heat. Rising up and throwing off my blanket, I scattered to the air and ground perhaps five inches of snow that had fallen on me.

The scene before me was a weird one. Great logs of men were lying in all directions, covered over with snow and as quiet as graves. Now and then one would break out and look about him with amazement. Suddenly all were aroused by the strident voice of Bill Wintermeyer, the wag of the few nights before, who jumping to his feet, cried out, "Great Jehosophat! The Resurrection!" After that night I knew what the Bible means when it speaks of snow as wool,—I often wished we could make durable blankets out of it.

Lonely sentinels from the 4th Ohio stand guard outside Romney. Jackson wanted to capture and hold Romney in order to threaten the B & O Railroad.

SERGEANT HARVEY S. WELLS

84th Pennsylvania Infantry, Kimball's Brigade

Sergeant Wells of the newly formed 84th Pennsylvania routinely contributed letters to his hometown paper, the Muncy Luminary. Without weapons, Wells and his regiment left their Harrisburg training camp on New Year's Eve and arrived at Hancock, Maryland, two days later. Using the pseudonym A Volunteer, Wells describes his first action in the war.

The next day after our arrival in this place the regiment received their arms (Belgium Rifles), and before they had time to clean, and prepare their guns for use, were ordered to march for Bath, a small village about 5 miles up the Potomac; intelligence having been received that the enemy were attacking the Union Forces at that place. Capt. Flack's Co. having been put on guard through the day, did not go along with the regiment, which went up one evening and back the next, without meeting the enemy except in small squads that would fire on them from behind trees.

Union men living in the vicinity of Bath came in and informed Col. Murray that the rebels with a force of between 5 and 10 thousand men were endeavoring to surround him—in consequence of which he came back to Hancock, and before he had crossed the river the rebels commenced shelling the town. The first few shells were thrown at a fire around which our Company were cooking their suppers and came into pretty close proximity to our heads. . . .

. . . About this time General Lander arrived in town upon his way to join General Kelly's command, and being informed of the position of affairs he immediately took command. The enemy, however, did not trouble us during the night, but, in the morning came over with a flag of truce to warn the inhabitants to leave in one hour, as they intended to burn the town. Now commenced the melancholy scene of men, women and children leaving their homes, their all, and going forth in the cold to

Head Quarters, Valley Dist
Opposite Hancock
Jany 5 1862

To the Officer Comdg
the United States Forces
in & near Hancock. Md

Sir, It is my purpose to cross the River & take possession of the town of Hancock.
If in opposing the execution of this purpose, you make use of the town of Hancock, or the Citizens of the town aid you in your opposition, I will cannonade the town.
If neither of these things is done, I will refrain as far as practicable from firing upon it.
An immediate reply to this communication is required.

T. J. Jackson
Maj. Genl. P.A.C.S.
Comdg Valley District

On January 5, 1862, Stonewall Jackson sent Turner Ashby across the Potomac River to deliver an ultimatum (above). Upon reading it, Frederick Lander bristled: "Colonel Ashby, give my regards to General Jackson and tell him to bombard and be damned! If he opens his batteries on this town he will hurt more of his friends than he will of the enemy, for this is a damned Sesech place anyhow."

seek shelter; it is indeed a painful sight, and one I hope never to be compelled to witness again.

At the stated time, the rebels commenced their work, and in less than 1 hour, and before they had succeeded in doing any damage, they were completely silenced by our artillery, some additions to which came in through the night, and they were driven entirely from their positions. Their location is of such a nature that it would be injudicious to pursue them, although we were all eager to meet them, and give them a severe castigation. General Lander's said to the soldiers as he passed down the street: "Soldiers, do your duty; there is work for you today; meet it bravely; if I am killed, somebody will take my place." There was something about the appearance of the man that indicated he was equal to his station, and there was not a soldier looked upon his countenance, but that felt confidence in his ability. There was no loss on our side, while that of the enemy was about 20 killed and wounded. You can look for stirring news from this quarter in a short time.

Brigadier General Frederick W. Lander fearlessly opposed Jackson throughout the 1862 winter campaign. Lander showed great promise for the Union army, but he died unexpectedly on March 2 from an infected wound received at Ball's Bluff.

SURGEON CHARLES M. CLARK

39th Illinois Infantry, Sullivan's Brigade

On January 6 Stonewall Jackson pulled his troops from Bath and headed southward to Unger's Store. Dr. Clark, a New York native, joined a Federal detachment sent across the Potomac to reconnoiter the Virginia side. Clark began as a regimental physician and finished the war as chief surgeon of the XXIV Corps.

The following day a reconnaissance was made over the river by some of the Thirty-Ninth, who found matters and things at the station pretty badly demoralized. The Swan family had removed, bag and baggage, and no one was found to give us any information. The Swan house, as well as the Orrick, was found to have received the many compliments in shape of shot and shell that we had sent over, and both were badly damaged. The railway had been torn up and the rails twisted and bent with fire, and all the railway property destroyed. Where our medical dispensary had stood there was nothing but a mound of ashes. All was ruin and desolation.

Proceeding up along the road to Bath we found a number of newly-made graves, and several of them were occupied by soldiers who had perished from cold, for the weather had been exceedingly severe and the men in Jackson's command from Georgia, Alabama and Arkansas had suffered extremely.

Many notes addressed to the Thirty-Ninth were found. Some were couched in terms of bitterness and hostility, some complimentary and conciliatory, but all exhibiting evident respect for the pluck and fighting qualities of Western men.

Here is a sample copy of one that was addressed,

"To the Boys over the Way."

"We are about to leave you, and our comfortable quarters to your tender mercies. If you should happen to pick up anything lying around here, I expect that you will want to keep it as a slight token of your regard, or send it home. How much better it would be for the 'liberty boys' if they would go home themselves and leave us poor rebels to enjoy freedom in their own way.

Company G, First Reg't Georgia Vol's."

"P.S. We are poor rebels and cannot offer a more valuable keepsake, but hope you will prize it from the spirit in which it was given.

Col. J. W. Ramsey, First Georgia Vol's."

"P.S. Go home, boys! Go home! We owe you no ill will further than result from your efforts to conquer the Freeman of the South. We will go home gladly when we have effectually defended our borders.

Company G."

WILLIAM ALLAN

CONFEDERATE QUARTER-MASTER DEPARTMENT

A resident of Winchester, Allan joined Stonewall's force on its return from Bath, serving as a civilian clerk for Jackson's chief quartermaster. Allan soon received a commission and quickly became chief ordnance officer on Jackson's staff, with the rank of lieutenant colonel.

"The next morning was bitterly cold, so cold that the ink froze in my jacket inkstand as I was writing."

Well do I remember that day's journey and the night that followed. It was cold—snow—but we were well protected and well nourished. . . . At dark we stopped at a farm house where we stayed, Col. H. making the wagon and men camp in the yard. Next day was bitterly cold. We rode on towards Bath and after some time met the army returning. I remember Gen. Jackson was walking leading his horse when Col. H. rode up to report. The roads were covered with snow and ice and the passing of the men and trains soon made them as slippery as glass. Many horses were killed or maimed by the sliding of the wagons and artillery down the steep hills on them. Men could not walk in the road. My horse was smooth and I started forward to Bath to have him roughed but found the road so slippery and was informed that such crowds filled every shop that I turned back and went on with the army. My horse fell and threw me over but no damage was done. I rode through the fields when it was possible. My recollection is that it froze hard all day. At nightfall the army camped along the road, burning fences and trying to keep from freezing. It was a night of intense suffering to the men. We went to an abandoned hut in a field and making a large fire in the fireplace, slept on the floor around it. The next morning was bitterly cold, so cold that the ink froze in my jacket inkstand as I was writing something in the open hut not far from the fire.

Drawn by Confederate artist William L. Sheppard, this sketch depicts Jackson's troops on their miserable trek toward Romney. The two-week ordeal knocked more than 1,000 sick men from the ranks.

SERGEANT RICHARD W. WALDROP

21st Virginia Infantry, Gilham's Brigade

Subfreezing temperatures gnawed at Jackson's exposed soldiers while they were encamped for one week at Unger's Store. Colonel William Gilham, the 21st Virginia's commander, was charged by Jackson with "slowness of movement" during the Bath expedition. Gilham resigned to return to his teaching position at VMI. In a letter written on January 19, Waldrop describes the miserable conditions the soldiers endured on the trek to Romney.

Dear Father. . . .

. . . I have gotten so lately that it is almost impossible for me to write a letter with any ease or comfort to myself and I dare say any pleasure to anyone else. I must make an effort, however, to do something in that line while we are here for it seems more than probable we are to have very little leisure this winter.

We left Unger's Store last Monday not knowing whether this place or Winchester was to be our destination, but hoping the latter would. After marching about 200 yards we were stopped by wagons in front of us & had to stay there all day. We unloaded & pitched our tents about Sundown & soon after dark it commenced snowing & snowed all night. The next day we made another start & though we were on the road from early in the morning until late at night we made only 5 miles owing to the bad condition of the roads & slow progress of the teams. As usual it commenced snowing again at dark & during the whole night we had a delightful mixture of snow, rain & hail. The next day we made about the same distance & the following day, the twenty-one-sters having the track (the front of the column), we pushed right through. We are about 2 1/2 miles from Romney which they say is entirely deserted by everybody except the soldiers & maybe at some time will be the subject of another poem.

There is (or rather was) about 2 miles back of us a little village called Frenchtown, which the Yankees burnt about a month ago. I never saw anything so completely destroyed there is hardly a *chip* left. They have burnt nearly all the houses on the roads for several miles back & those they didn't burn they knocked to pieces. I suppose they would have destroyed Romney when they left if they hadn't been in such a hurry. The people about here say they never saw such a frightened set of men in their lives. The miserable wretches hearing that Jackson & Ashby (as terrible to them as Marion was to the British) were coming, actually *cried* & the cavalry were so much alarmed that they didn't take time to untie their horses but *cut* the halters & ran off as if "old nick" had been after them. They left a large number of tents & some commissary stores all of which fell into our hands. Those of us who thought our expedition to Bath was a wild goose chase have changed our opinions for without any fighting scarcely Jackson has pretty well run those fellows out of this country, though I fear he has lost more men than he would in a big fight, for about 2,500 have been sent back to Winchester sick & others are leaving every day. We have had a rough time & our suffering has frequently been quite severe. My feet have been wet every day from the time they first touched the ground in the morning until night & it has been so cold that our beards would be covered with frost & ice & we would have to sit up by the fires all night to keep warm.

I am almost without socks, the toes & heels being worn away & I know of no place where I can get any. I don't know how long we are to stay here, but some seem to think that Jackson intends to attempt to

A native of Massachusetts, Wells J. Hawks came to the Valley almost penniless in 1837, but by 1861 he had become Charles Town's foremost businessman. The 43-year-old major was well suited for the position of Jackson's chief commissary.

push on . . . but, as he tells his plan to no one that is mere conjecture.

The weather now is miserable it is & has been raining for two or three days with occasional intermission & as it always rains all day Sunday when it rains in the morning of that day, I confidently expect it to rain all of today. . . .

. . . unless some arrangement is made before long by our Quartermaster I shall be in as bad condition as Marion's men, worse in fact for they were in a warm climate, while it is as cold here as Xmas.

I don't believe there is anything else I have to say so I had as well come to a stop. . . .

Hoping to hear from you all before long
I remain
Yr Aff Son
Richd W Waldrop

SERGEANT ALEXANDER BARCLAY

4th Virginia Infantry, Garnett's Brigade

"Ted" Barclay enlisted with the Liberty Hall Volunteers, a Washington College company that served as Jackson's headquarters guard. Returning to Winchester from Romney at the end of January, Barclay explains to his sister on February 1 the circumstances surrounding Stonewall's resignation, which he rescinded one week later.

When we left Romney, Jackson, as I told you in my last letter, left Loring's force there and brought his old brigade to Winchester. Then Loring, without saying anything to Jackson, sent three of his brigadiers to Richmond and had Jackson's order countermanded and his, Loring's, force ordered back to Winchester by order of Sec. of War Benjamin, in consequence of which Gen. Jackson has resigned and his men swear that they will not serve under Loring.

What the consequence will be I cannot tell. But if the orders of such a man as Jackson are to be disregarded by such trifling people as Loring and seconded by Benjamin, I think the Southern Confederacy is in a bad fix. But enough about that. I guess you will hear more in a day or so for I never saw a more unsatisfied set of men than the Stonewall just now. I hear that Loring's men are just as much attached to their general as we are to ours, so would not be surprised to hear of a bust up soon. . . .

> "For without any fighting scarcely Jackson has pretty well run those fellows out of this country."

What a good thing it is to be at headquarters now, but how long we will be there I do not know. Gen. Jackson still keeps us. As we are the only soldiers quartered in town, we get along finely, especially among the ladies, who think there is nothing equal to the L.H.V.'s or as we are called Jackson's bodyguard. . . .

Try and get me a gray coat if you can. Anything rather than brown or blue, a light gray if possible.

Brigadier General William W. Loring ran afoul of Jackson during the Romney expedition but ended the war as the senior major general on active field duty in the Confederacy. Injured severely at Chapultepec in the Mexican War, he had his amputated arm buried there with the hand pointing toward Mexico City.

"Harper's Ferry was a fitting place to begin an advance against the rebellion."

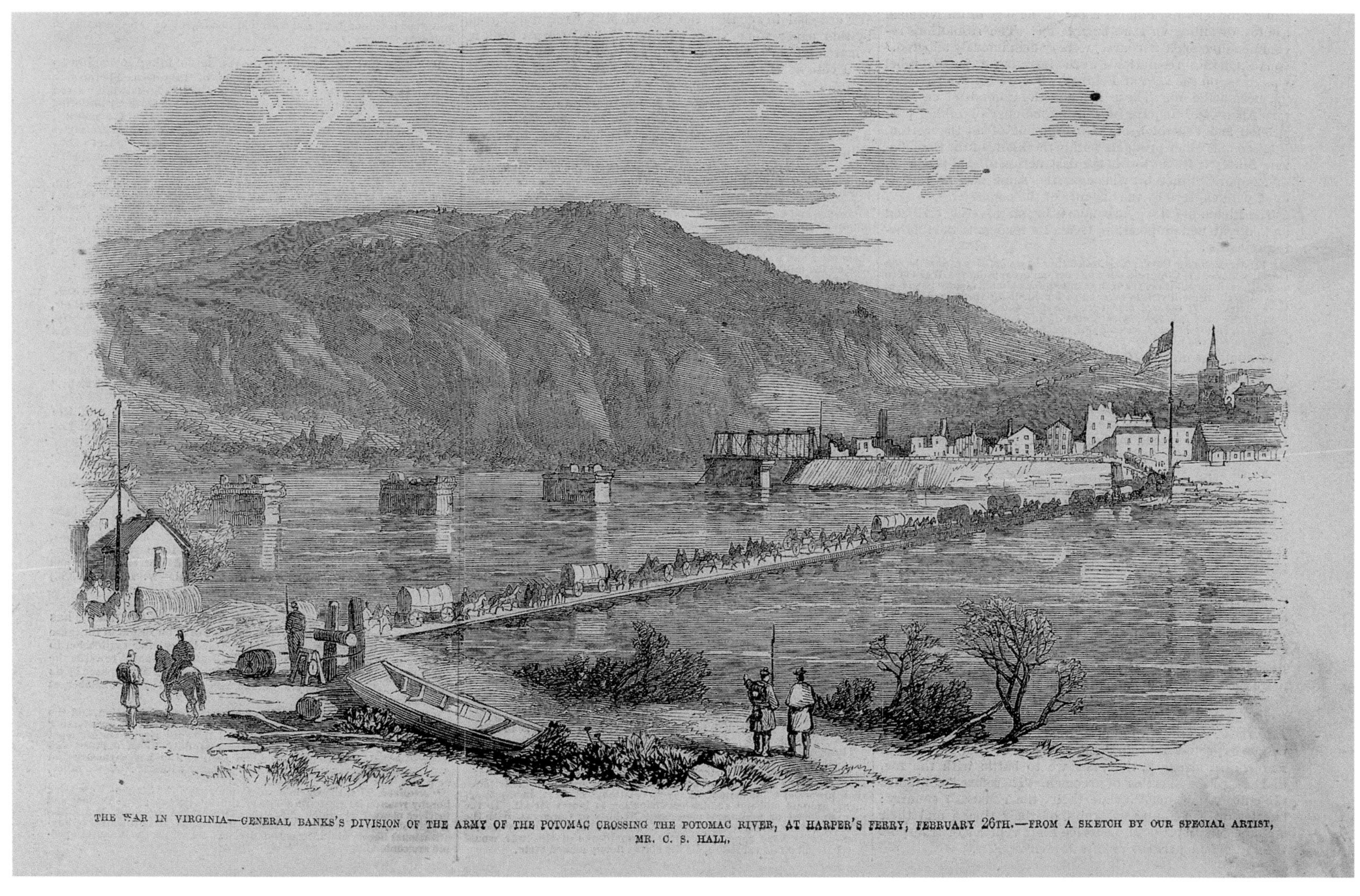

THE WAR IN VIRGINIA—GENERAL BANKS'S DIVISION OF THE ARMY OF THE POTOMAC CROSSING THE POTOMAC RIVER, AT HARPER'S FERRY, FEBRUARY 26TH.—FROM A SKETCH BY OUR SPECIAL ARTIST,
MR. C. S. HALL.

On February 27 Banks' division entered Virginia by crossing the Potomac River at Harpers Ferry on a pontoon bridge erected by the Federals. "Harper's Ferry is truly the most charming and romantic place that I ever visited," raved a blue-clad officer. "No description that I ever read gave half the sober reality."

CORPORAL EDMUND R. BROWN

27TH INDIANA INFANTRY, HAMILTON'S BRIGADE

Brown entered the Shenandoah Valley as a 16-year-old foot soldier in one of only two "western" infantry regiments in Banks' division. The Hoosiers took one company into Virginia that boasted 80 men who stood over six feet tall. Their lieutenant, 380-pound David Van Buskirk, stood one inch below the seven-foot mark.

On February 26, we crossed the Potomac into Virginia. This we regarded as an event of great importance. We were at last upon insurgent soil. We were familiar with the habit among boys of giving a dare by making a mark upon the ground and challenging the other fellow to cross it. Something of the same method had obtained thus far in the war. When the boundary of a state which had declared its separation from the Union was crossed it was understood to mean that hostilities had begun.

The crossing was effected on a pontoon bridge. Needless to say we had never seen one before. This was said to be the first one used in real war, in the United States. Either the event of our using the bridge, or the one that we were moving into the enemy's country, was of sufficient importance to bring General McClellan up from Washington, with his immense retinue of staff officers and orderlies. He stood upon the stone coping of the canal lock, near the end of the bridge, where we had an unobstructed view of him in passing. This was the first time most of us had seen the then much adulated "Little Mack."...

Harper's Ferry was a fitting place to begin an advance against the rebellion. It was a rebellion solely in the interests of slavery. Though it was recognized in the constitution and protected by numberless laws and court decisions, the friends of that institution were not satisfied. Crazed by certain incidents (prominent among which was the wild escapade of John Brown) they had decided to break up the government. If it was right to suppress his lawless act, how much more was it right to suppress their's?

LIEUTENANT ROBERT G. SHAW

2D MASSACHUSETTS INFANTRY, GORDON'S BRIGADE

One year before before he took command of one of the first regiments of black troops, Shaw participated in Banks' plodding ascent up the Valley. On March 9 Shaw wrote home to his sister providing a tongue-in-cheek explanation of how he and other Federals procured some of the spoils of war.

We have had possession of this town for nearly ten days, and a wretched hole it is. I don't know what it was in its palmy days, but now the inhabitants are the most avaricious, grasping set of people I ever saw. They expected when we came that we should burn the town, but finding that their property is respected & no harm done them, they have become very impertinent and exacting & think it a great hardship to have our men quartered in the unoccupied parts of their houses. Genl Banks has issued strict orders against the men's taking any private property & I don't believe the inhabitants have lost anything since the first day. On that day several companies of the 2 Mass were attacked by a large body of pigs, turkeys, chickens & ducks, and as some of those secession animals & fowls met their death in the affray, it was no sin to eat them. One of our company was also assailed in broad day light by a fine cambric shirt, whereupon he gave battle & fortunately came off victorious, taking his enemy prisoner.

Last week all the troops in town were sent into camp with the exception of 4 companies who remain here as Provost Guard. One of these is ours and we have part of a large house on the main street for ourselves & men. When we first took possession the old hag who owns the house was very glad to have us as protection against stragglers, but now there are no more in town she wants to get rid of us & says we are ruining everything.... When we go off I shall try to have one of the Indiana Companies put in here so that she may perceive how lucky she was to have had a quiet set of New Englanders instead of Western men.

LIEUTENANT ALEXANDER S. PENDLETON

Staff, Major General Thomas J. Jackson

At the age of 16 in 1857, "Sandie" Pendleton was already a college graduate fluent in Greek and Latin. Four years later the fair-haired prodigy dropped his graduate studies at the University of Virginia to join General Jackson's staff. Pendleton wrote his mother on March 2 to describe the state of affairs in the Valley District army.

The activity just infused into the various departments and the sending of surplus stores and sick to the rear has set speculation all agog here. People do not reflect that spring is opening and the game of chess beginning, and that the pieces must go from spot to spot as occasion demands, to enable us to checkmate the enemy. What will be done I have no idea. That Winchester will be left, I doubt not, for it ought, but I am equally certain this part of the state is not to be abandoned, and that Genl. Jackson will not leave without some fighting. When or where this fighting is to take place I know no more than you.

The first burst of surprise at the Fort Donelson victory is over, and our people find that a defeat of that sort, though a sad thing, is not the utter destruction of our cause, and finding this they are, I think, beginning to take heart again. At any rate we that are in the field must nerve ourselves to the determination to withstand to the uttermost, and have, notwithstanding odds against us, no more surrenders with arms in our hands. And the men at home must get ready to step into the breach and take the places of those who must fall during the ensuing campaign, while the women by their prayers and exhortation keep up our courage to the most determined resistance. What is life worth, if it brings not freedom and happiness?

PRIVATE JOHN APPERSON

4th Virginia Infantry, Garnett's Brigade

"At last the crisis is upon us," admitted one of Jackson's staffers. As Banks' V Corps, 25,000 strong, appeared on the northern outskirts of Winchester on March 11, Jackson's 3,500-man army could do little to counter the threat. The citizens hid their valuables and despaired over a future of uncertainty. Apperson, a 29-year-old medical steward in the Stonewall Brigade, had been encamped in Winchester for four months. His diary entry for the day expresses his feelings on giving up the town.

This morning we were ordered to pack up. After packing up and lying around for some hours, or until 2 o'clock, we were summoned to take the field. Reports came that the Yankees were marching upon us very rapidly. Cannons were heard in [the] direction of Berryville. Our lines were thrown out across the Valley below Winchester so as to guard the Martinsburg road. Soon, however, the 4th Reg't. was ordered upon the hill west of the road where a battery stood; from this place we could see very plainly all that passed below—the maneuvers of our men just below us and the shifts and changes of our cavalry at the edge of the woods.

Just before night the enemy made its appearance about two miles from us. The pickets could be seen advancing and ours falling back. Two regiments were seen to enter the woods on our left and I presume went into camp as smoke soon ushered out. Further on our left in a field the enemy's bayonets were seen glistening in the evening sun. . . .

Night came on. Two premises were made by us. One that we would remain till morning and give battle, the other, that a retreat would be effected beneath the cover of night. The latter was correct. About dusk we left the field. Taking the road we passed through Winchester but not through the main part of the town. Loud shouts were heard in Main and Market Streets. The soldiers seemed somewhat animated rather than depressed. This animation was from the effect of the excitement of the evening and of the present moment of the moving. I knew many felt sad at heart to leave a place which we had been protecting for the last 12 months, and now looked upon as almost home. Some had ties that bound them to the place, the ties of love had fastened upon them.

But it was to no avail. They had but to bid their sweethearts good bye, take one last kiss and leave them to their fates. This was sad indeed. Many expressed themselves that they would sooner fight than leave those endearments behind.

I did not from the first think that Gen. Jackson would give fight with his small force; but after leaving Winchester, I thought it probable that we might return next morning and have a round or two [with the enemy]. . . .

We marched within two miles of Newton and camped at the house of a Mr. Barton. The farm and improvements were equal if not superior to any on the road. Plank fences, stake fences, and stone fences laying out his farm in good lots; but [when] the enemy comes his plank and stake fences will be all in ashes. Capt. Gibson and myself went into the kitchen and got a bite of victuals. I was proud to get some sour milk of which I drank about a quart. I then lay down in the ambulance to sleep.

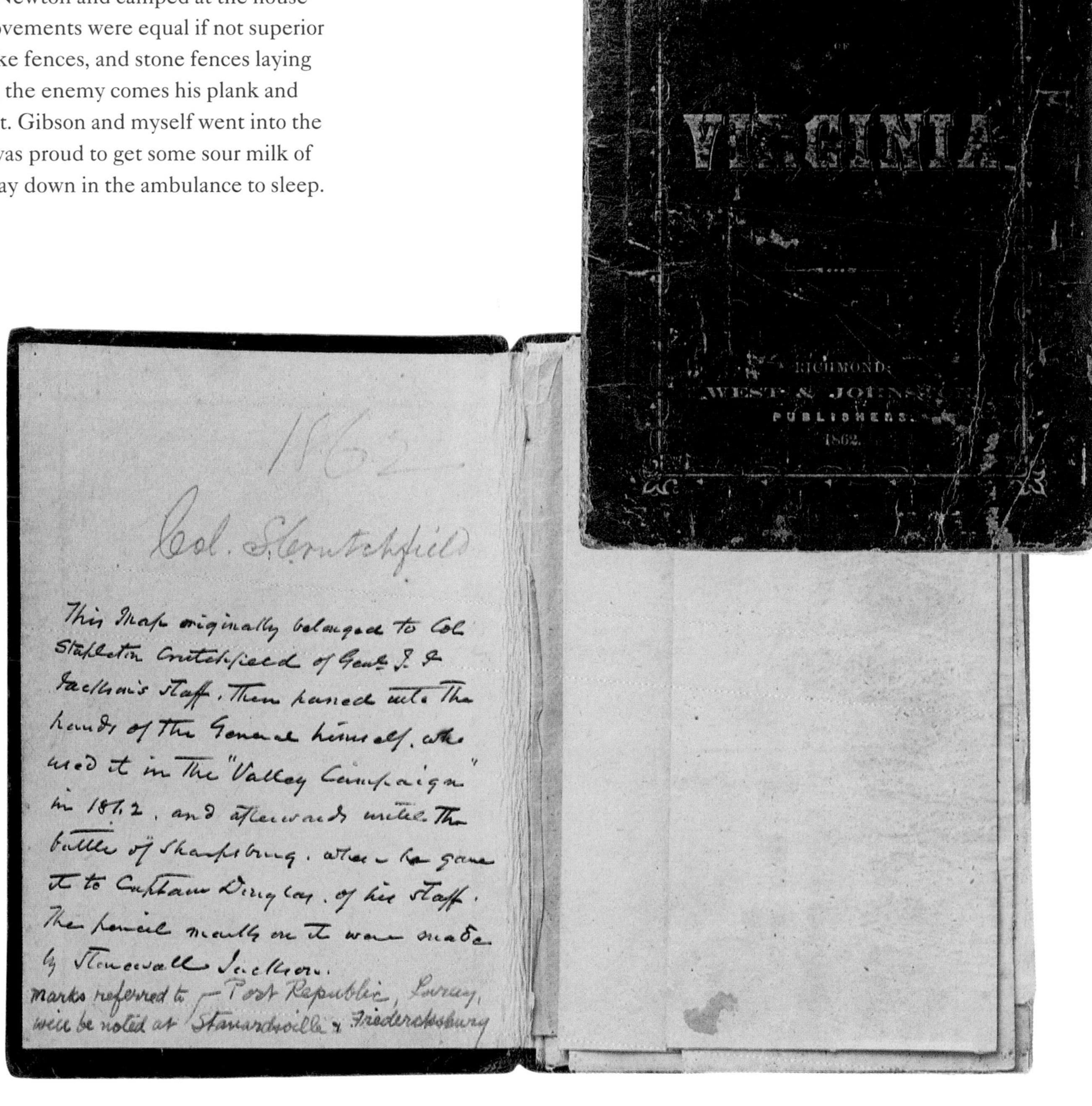

The history of this map's ownership is recounted on the inside cover by Henry K. Douglas. The map originally belonged to Colonel Stapleton Crutchfield, Jackson's chief of artillery. He gave it to Stonewall, who used it for much of the Shenandoah Valley campaign. Late in 1862 Jackson obtained detailed maps from Jedediah Hotchkiss, his expert cartographer. Stonewall parted with Crutchfield's map by passing it along to Douglas, his aide.

"We took a hasty leave of the ladies, and just then the enemy came around the corner and fired quite a volley at us."

CAPTAIN HARRY GILMOR

7TH VIRGINIA CAVALRY

The only organized Confederate force remaining in Winchester on March 12 was Colonel Turner Ashby's 7th Virginia Cavalry. Gilmor, who led one of Ashby's companies in 1862, was captured early in 1865 and held in Boston Harbor for five months. During his confinement he wrote his recollections of the Valley war, including the close call described below.

On the morning after the evacuation had been commenced, Colonel Ashby passed through the town with the rear guard. I was sitting on my horse, as was my brother, before the Taylor House, with four or five of my men, having sent the rest of the company toward Strasburg the night before. The colonel, as he rode by, said to me, "Gilmor, you had better move away as soon as possible; the enemy are coming into the town at the other end." I, with my brother, dismounted, and went into the saloon of the hotel; wrote some letters, which we intrusted to the care of Dr. ——, of the place. On remounting, I found that all the men, except my brother and McAleese, had gone on. On looking along Main Street, I saw the head of the enemy's column then passing by the Virginia House, which was but two squares off. We rode slowly up the street, occasionally turning to converse with the ladies or to give the enemy a shot. I sent my brother, who was my sergeant, to the left, toward the dépôt, to picket, while McAleese and I went to the house of Mr. ——, to bid adieu to the young ladies. We dismounted and entered the house, saw the young ladies, and ate some cake with them. One of them kept a careful look-out for the enemy.

Very soon after my brother rode up and reported that the enemy were coming along Main Street rapidly. Mr. ——'s house is situated on a cross street only two doors from Main Street. We took a hasty leave of the ladies, and just then the enemy came around the corner and fired quite a volley at us, but without doing us any harm. We immediately took to our heels and made off for the country; but, as soon as we got clear of the town, we turned off to the right into an open field, designing to ascertain, if possible, what force was coming into the town on the other side. They were coming on in three columns, the middle one going down Main Street. We rode across this lot, which was bounded on three sides by stone walls; the side next to the turnpike having a board fence, most of which had been torn down and burned. We soon found that the enemy coming on behind us had made more speed than we had anticipated, and therefore we could not get back to the turnpike where we had left it, and which was now in their possession. It became necessary, therefore, for us to jump the stone fence, which was new and of the ordinary height. I was riding an old cavalry horse, and went over first, clear. My brother's horse, a colt which he had purchased the day before, refused the leap, whereupon he dismounted, threw off a part of the coping, remounted, and, charging the wall, went over in fine style. McAleese came next, but his horse would not take it. He was about to dismount and abandon him, but I persuaded him to try it again.

During all this time they were closing on us and firing briskly. McAleese drove his horse up to the fence again, but as he was rising at the leap, he was shot through the shoulders, just in front of the saddle-skirts, and fell with his chest against the fence, throwing his rider over it.

McAleese leaned over the fence and snatched the bridle from his dying horse's head; then, assisted by my foot, he threw himself upon the croup of my horse.

Now the lot which we had just left was filled with the enemy, evidently chagrined that they had not caught us in this stone trap.

They followed us rapidly, and for a while closely; indeed, so close were they upon us that my horse had to take three other fences, not high ones fortunately, which he cleared in capital style, notwithstanding he had a double load on his back.

ADVENTURE OF ASHBY AT WINCHESTER.—Page 71.
"Ashby seized him by the throat, dragged him from his saddle, and putting spur to his horse, bore him off."

Although Ashby was most likely the last Virginia soldier to leave Winchester during the Rebel evacuation, no eyewitness accounts confirm the confrontation detailed in the sketch at left. By 7:00 a.m. on March 12, the city of Winchester (shown in a post-war photograph below) belonged to the Federals. According to entries by the town's diarists, Winchester changed hands 95 more times over the next 30 months.

PRIVATE WARREN H. FREEMAN

13TH MASSACHUSETTS INFANTRY, ABERCROMBIE'S BRIGADE

On a warm late-winter day, Brigadier General Alpheus Williams' division was the first to enter Winchester and raise the Stars and Stripes. Freeman was part of a brigade that left the Valley 10 days later. Captured at Gettysburg, he was paroled and finished the war with the 39th Massachusetts.

At three o'clock the next morning we were turned out, and were ready to move at daylight. Companies A and D of our regiment were then deployed out as skirmishers; we were thrown forward about half a mile in advance of the main body. The road to Winchester runs along a valley, with hills on each side. The width of this valley, or from hill-top to hill-top, was about two miles, and the skirmishers, about five paces apart, extended this whole distance. We had not advanced two miles when we came upon a very large earthwork for artillery, with a rifle-pit nearly a quarter of a mile long in front. Now I thought we were to have a battle. We knew before leaving Martinsburg that the enemy were in force in this vicinity, so we closed our ranks and waited for our regiment and the Fifth Connecticut regiment to come up. We then marched directly up in front of the fort to within about fifty yards, gave a yell and dashed forward into the fort; but lo! the rebels had fled, leaving only some pickaxes, shovels, etc., behind. The forward march was continued toward Winchester; a contraband came in and informed us that the main body of the rebels had left during the previous night. We continued our march and soon captured quite a number of rebels who had lingered behind; they were taken by our cavalry. We reached Winchester about noon, and entered the barracks just deserted by the rebels. We were soon ordered out to scour the country for rebels; we went through fields, over fences, small streams of water, etc., for about four miles in one hour. It was very warm, and I never sweat so much in my life before.

Winchester is a large and beautiful town, and, you may recollect, was the residence of the rebel Mason; his house is among the largest in town. Some of the houses that had been vacated by the richer classes had their doors and windows removed so as to render them uncomfortable to us if we had been disposed to occupy them.

Our Colonel Leonard has been appointed provost marshal, and we are now doing guard duty in the town. I have got a lot of trophies, but have no way to send them home.

Soon after our arrival some of the people of the town desired to trade with our sutler. There is some good money left among them, and if they are loyal to our cause we shall at once extend to them all the rights and privileges which we enjoy.

CORNELIA PEAKE MCDONALD

RESIDENT OF WINCHESTER

The wife of cavalry colonel Angus McDonald, Cornelia endured the Union seizure of Winchester with her younger children in their home at the western edge of town. In 1863 the McDonalds fled and relocated in Lexington, where Angus was captured one year later. He died within days of his release. In 1873 Cornelia moved to Kentucky, where she died in 1909.

I felt so thankful that we were still free, and a hope dawned that our men would come back, as no enemy had appeared. We were all cheerfully despatching our breakfasts, I feeling happy in proportion to my former depression; the children were chatting gaily, Harry and Allan rather sulky at not having been permitted to leave with the army, as they considered it degradation for men of their years and dimensions to be left behind with women and children. Suddenly a strain of music! Every knife and fork was laid down and every ear strained to catch the faint sounds. The boys clap their hands and jump up from the table shouting, "Our

"Take your hand off my head, you are a Yankee."

men have come back!" and rushed to the door; I stopped them, telling them it must be the Yankees. Every face looked blank and disappointed.

I tried to be calm and quiet, but could not, and so got up and went outside the door. Sure enough that music could not be mistaken, it was the "Star Spangled Banner" that was played. A servant came in. "They are all marching the town, and some have come over the hill into our orchard."

I made the children all sit down again, and began to eat my breakfast, but felt as if I should choke with anger and mortification. Now, as I look back and recall this scene, I can be amused at the expression of humiliation on the small faces around me.

Tears of anger started from Harry's eyes, while Allan looked savage enough to exterminate them if he had the power. Kenneth looked very wretched, but glanced occasionally out of the window, as if he would like, as long as they had come, to see what they were like. Nelly's face was bent in the deepest humiliation on her plate, as if the shame of defeat was peculiarly hers. Roy's black eyes were blazing, as if he scented a fight but did not exactly know where to find it. While Donald, only two and a half years old, turned his back to weep silently, in sympathy I suppose with the distress of the rest. Presently a trampling was heard around the house, loud voices and the sounds of wheels and horses' hoofs. Suddenly a most unwonted sound! A mule braying; Nelly looked up from her plate where her eyes had been fixed in shame and distress: "Even their very old horses are laughing." That was irresistible. I was compelled in spite of all to join the horses in their laugh.

I was obliged to attend to my household affairs, and in passing to and fro on the porch and through passages, encountered them often, but took no notice, just moved on as if they were not there. Donald was sitting on a step very disconsolate looking, when one blue coat passed near him, and laying his hand on his head, said, "How d'ye do Bub." He did not look up, but sullenly said, "Take your hand off my head, you are a Yankee." The man looked angry, but did not try to annoy us because the small rebel scorned him.

LIEUTENANT COLONEL WILDER DWIGHT

2D MASSACHUSETTS INFANTRY, GORDON'S BRIGADE

Dwight helped George Gordon organize the 2d Massachusetts. A disciplinarian, he had been known to gag unruly soldiers and tie them to trees. Dwight noted the differences between the opposing Valley forces, admitting, "Jackson and Ashby are clever men. We are slow-w-w!" On March 15 he wrote home about it.

I think more and more, though I am unwilling to write about it, that we missed the cleverest chance at cutting off and bagging Jackson and his force that ever fell in one's way. Caution is the sin of our generals, I am afraid; but military criticism is not graceful, and I will waive it for the present. Yet if you knew how we ache for a chance at fighting, how we feel that our little army corps out in this valley has no hope of it, you would not wonder that a leaden depression rests heavily upon us, as we think of our hesitating and peaceful advent to Winchester. And now why we do not push on upon Jackson at Strasburg passes my limited conjectural capacity to guess. I presume the reason to be that his evanescent tactics would be sure to result in his evaporation before we got there. . . .

This morning a few companies of cavalry, four pieces of artillery, and five companies of infantry, Massachusetts Thirteenth, went out on an armed reconnaissance, and chased Colonel Ashby's cavalry several miles. The cavalry were too quick for them, and our own cavalry has no more chance of catching them than the wagon train has. They are admirably mounted and thoroughly trained. Where our men have to dismount and take down the bars, they fly over fences and across country like birds.

General Banks has just gone off to Washington. Conjecture is busy, again, with "why"? My guess is, that we have outlived our usefulness in the Shenandoah Valley, and that we shall make a cut through the path of the Grand Army. At any rate, nothing more can happen this side the mountains, and I certainly hope we shall not be absorbed into any force that is to be handled by General Frémont.

KATE S. SPERRY

RESIDENT OF WINCHESTER

Beautiful and intelligent, this 18-year-old daughter of a Confederate quartermaster clerk shared her grandfather's Main Street home with her two sisters during the early years of the war. Kate married Dr. Enoch Newton Hunt, surgeon of the 2d Mississippi Infantry, in December 1864. She raised six children in her husband's home state and died there at the age of 43.

I take it every way (I mean the Yanks being here) sometimes I'm very *philosophic*—endure it in silence and contempt—the next minute I'm ready to *cuss* the whole herd and piously wish them in *Hades.* The enemy brought in 6 men this evening, some or all of them were dead—they've been skirmishing with Ashby's men ever since the first came in town. Ashby is staying near here to keep them back from Strasburg until our Army gets everything away from there—the Yanks are the greatest fools not to go after them, but they're afraid and Ashby will keep on making them afraid. . . .

. . . The enemy have swung out a Union flag at the little brick office next to the Kellers. None of the girls in the neighborhood will walk under it, they go out in the mud *round* it and on the pavement again—it makes them furious, the horrid cut-throats—I'm sure they'll stretch one across the whole street. . . .

. . . Went down street today for first time for over a week—walked *round* the flag and the soldiers—it sticks in my throat to call such fiends by such an appelation—it's only applicable to Southerners—cursed me as far as I could hear them and they see me. Went to Jo's—she came down street with me—went in Mr. Danny's store—John Burgess there and little Dr. Stewart—we had a regular secession meeting—when we got to Bell's corner I saw that the Northern rebels had flung their

"The enemy have swung out a Union flag at the little brick office next to the Kellers. None of the girls in the neighborhood will walk under it."

largest sized flag all the way across the street—the small one was still hanging out of the little brick office (one of the sutlers has a shop there) and another of some size on the opposite side of the street at the 3 story brick that used to be our Hospital—so we walked round the back street and the whole gang of them hissed and cursed us to everything—we paid no attention to their remarks only held our clothes close to us to keep them from the pollution of *their touch.*

New York-born Edwin Forbes sketched Winchester as viewed from the east, with the North Mountain chain in the background. In the foreground (labeled 3) are some of the fortifications erected by both armies that would ring the town. Forbes was hired by Frank Leslie as a pictorial war reporter for his newspaper. Although many of his drawings received Union-wide distribution in Frank Leslie's Illustrated Newspaper, this sketch was never published.

LIEUTENANT COLONEL THOMAS CLARK

29TH OHIO INFANTRY, TYLER'S BRIGADE

Clark, an avowed teetotaler, was presented his officer's sword from the Sons of Temperance of Cleveland. A devoted husband and father of three, he wrote daily letters to his wife, Cordelia. On March 19 a disgusted Clark described the previous day's reconnaissance to Strasburg and criticized the conduct of some soldiers.

I'm sick of the service tonight. I've seen lots of men this Eve that only lack bristles to make them hogs. Some of them would steal a bit of sausage from a blind Puppy. About every 5th man in the 110th Pa Regt had a hen stolen from an old widow's coop. There were about a half dozen left & I have stationed a guard near with directions to shoot the next man that attempts to steal one. I am again detailed as Officer of the Day. But all of the Brigade but the 29th Regt has been ordered to move over to the other side of the town. . . . My little wife would like to know the results of the Battle that didnt come off very much. The enemy were undoubtly a portion of Jacksons force covering their retreat & burning bridges after them. The results to our force are as follows. One Leg shot off of one of the marching cavalry & 2 horses killed by the secesh. 4 horses killed & one man's hand torn to pieces of the same cavalry by the shells of our own Artillery. The cavalry were ordered to charge on the Secesh from a position they had taken in the woods & just as they rode out for that purpose some blunder-heels of the artillery let fly 8 shells at them damaging them as above. It was provoking. There are some women at home one in particular I know of who if she had not a little bright eyed boy baby requiring her care would be better calculated to wear shoulder straps than some who have been intrusted with important commands. I hope there will be skirmishing of the Army hot before long. I think a Phrenologist once told me I had not the organ of veneration very large, and I rather think so far as that would have reference to respect for superior Officers. It is growing smaller and beautifully less. I have yet had no collision with any of them & no cause for any in our own Brigade. I wish however the 110th Regt could be swapped off for a team of unserviceable mules & then condemned & shot. It is not much of a Regt. Well Corrie we've seen a small secesh force, have heard their balls whiz through the air & seen their shells burst. But it has not very much disturbed the usual quiet that is now removed a few miles back from the Potomac.

LIEUTENANT ALEXANDER S. PENDLETON

STAFF, MAJOR GENERAL THOMAS J. JACKSON

Pendleton was considered "a very fine young man—a gentleman in every way" by an admiring fellow staffer. On March 21, shortly after eating a large breakfast in the home of Israel Allen, a prosperous farmer living near Mount Jackson, "Sandie" wrote his mother to explain the chess match occurring between Jackson and Shields. Pendleton was unaware that Shields' men had marched back to Winchester the previous day.

Another letter goes from me this morning, but not in answer to anything received. We are carrying on an independent war here —we hear nothing from the outer world, and rely solely upon our own strong arms and Providence. And in one aspect this is beneficial for it keeps our whole attention fixed on the enemy in front of us and pretty well this seems to be telling on them, for they have stopped their advance [up the Valley] and we have begun ours [down the Valley]. I will go ahead and write the news, for I take it for granted that our letters reach you, though we get no mail. We can send our letter by private hands to some Post Office, and there is no disarrangement at the end of the lines where there is no enemy. . . .

But the army news you want. We fell back to this point last Monday, and yesterday started to move our stores further to our rear and were falling back further, but yesterday afternoon the order was countermanded and today we are marching toward the enemy. They are in Strasburg under Shields about ten thousand strong, I believe, and if we can get reinforcement, as the militia are turning out pretty well, we will drive them back near to the Potomac and possibly across it. At all events they have come as far up the Valley as they can without a fight. And if a fight does come they will undoubtedly be sorry for it, as we have the choice of position and will hazard everything upon success.

"I am twenty-one years old today. Strange, don't it seem! I hope I may never pass another birthday in the army."

SERGEANT GEORGE W. PETERKIN

21st Virginia Infantry, Burks' Brigade

The morning after he penned this letter, Peterkin marched 26 miles northward as Jackson attempted to close the gap with Banks' corps at Winchester. Against his wishes, Peterkin passed three more birthdays in the army. After he surrendered at Appomattox as a lieutenant, the Maryland native attended the Virginia Theological Seminary, and in 1878 became the Episcopal Bishop of West Virginia.

Camp, Beyond Mt. Jackson
March 21st, 1862.
Dear Mother:—

We reached this camp yesterday evening and pitched our tents in a driving rain; our day's march was something like our Valley Mountain experience, but with all that experience to help us we did not mind it so much. We kindled a little fire in our tent to dry it off, made a pot of coffee, ate the bread and hard-boiled eggs we had in our haversacks, and spreading down our oilcloths and blankets, committed ourselves to as gentle and refreshing a sleep as visited the eyes of any of the denizens of your gay city. We are now about three miles on the Staunton side of Mt. Jackson, what we will further do no one can tell; we may have to continue our retreat, or we may be able to make a stand here: it is a very fine position. Surely our retreat has been conducted in the most masterly manner. We have now more men than we had when we left Winchester, owing to recruits and re-enlisted men coming in, and our army is in better spirits, and better organized and prepared in every way. *No demoralization* at all has taken place, we are more capable now than we have been for two months. Too much praise cannot be rendered to Colonel Ashby for his gallant and brilliant movements in face of the enemy's overwhelming force: he has opposed them at every step, and with such success that we have been able to move with perfect leisure, and thus far to bring off everything. I am twenty-one years old today. Strange, don't it seem! I hope I may never pass another birthday in the army. We are now under orders to march, and are only awaiting our wagons which have gone off to help to haul stores.

Kernstown

On March 21 Stonewall Jackson and his tiny army were camped around Mount Jackson on the Shenandoah River when the general received an ominous report from his scouts: Large elements of Major General Nathaniel Banks' Federal V Corps, 40 miles away around Winchester, were on the move—heading east out of the Valley. Banks' troops had already begun to file through Snicker's Gap in the Blue Ridge.

The Federal maneuver threatened to compound the danger facing the main Confederate army under Major General Joseph E. Johnston on the other side of the mountains. Twelve days earlier, Johnston had begun withdrawing his entire army from Manassas back toward Richmond to defend the Confederate capital. Already confronting daunting odds, the Rebel commander was desperate to keep Banks from reinforcing the growing Federal force arrayed against him.

The prospect of this unwelcome development weighed heavily on Stonewall Jackson. In fact, it was precisely what he had been ordered to prevent. Johnston had instructed him: "It is important to keep that army in the valley." Never mind that Jackson's forces—about 4,000 men—were outnumbered by Banks 6 to 1.

On March 22 Stonewall got his own troops marching northward on the Valley Pike toward Winchester. Twenty-six miles later, his footsore and weary men bivouacked at Strasburg, where Jackson received a dispatch from his cavalry commander, Colonel Turner Ashby. Intelligence sources had informed Ashby that only four Union regiments remained at Winchester. Thinking that he could sweep away this force, Ashby attacked Federal pickets at the southern outskirts of the town late on March 22 but was driven off by enemy artillery and infantry.

In fact, Ashby had been misinformed. A Federal division, about 7,000 strong under Brigadier General James Shields, had been assigned to stay around Winchester to protect the northern end of the Valley. Shields, who had replaced General Frederick W. Lander, had been on the scene during the skirmish with Ashby and suffered a broken arm when hit by a shell fragment.

The following morning, March 23, Ashby resumed the contest, firing on Federal pickets positioned around Kernstown, about four miles south of Winchester. Colonel Nathan Kimball, Shields' replacement, quickly brought up his forces to counter Ashby's probe. Kimball established his headquarters and 16 cannon on Pritchard's Hill, a commanding elevation just north of Kernstown. By noon the presence of Kimball's brigades and the fire from his artillery compelled the Rebel cavalry commander to pull back.

Jackson, meanwhile, had been rushing his small army toward the sound of the guns. About 2:00 p.m. he arrived on the field and ordered Colonel Samuel Fulkerson's two-regiment brigade to advance against the Federal position on Pritchard's Hill. Fulkerson was easily repulsed; Jackson realized that he had to suppress the Federal batteries on Pritchard's Hill before sending forward any more of his infantry. Thirteen Rebel guns were deployed along Sandy Ridge, a north-south trending hill west of the Turnpike, and by 3:00 p.m. the Rebel guns were firing at the Federal artillery less than a mile away.

The Confederate counterbattery fire proved so effective that Kimball determined to silence the Rebel artillery. He ordered Colonel Erastus B. Tyler's brigade to attack on the Federal right and seize the Confederate guns. Tyler packed his 2,300 men into a tight marching column and directed them southward onto Sandy Ridge from the Cedar Creek Turnpike. Opposing the Union brigade were two Rebel regiments that had been brought up to cover the batteries: The 27th Virginia from General Richard B. Garnett's Stonewall Brigade was placed well forward along the ridge and the 21st Virginia of Colonel Jesse Burks' brigade a few hundred yards to the rear behind the guns. Initially observing no Federals opposite his left, Jackson had ordered the 27th Virginia to probe northward in open order. But when the 27th's skirmishers caught sight of Tyler's five regiments headed their way, the Virginians hustled back to the cover of a stone wall that straddled the ridge.

Tyler's Federals advanced in a narrow-column formation, which allowed only the front ranks to engage the enemy. Thus, when they came within range, the Rebel regiment behind the stone wall savaged the 7th Ohio, leading the attack. Within minutes the 21st Virginia arrived at the wall and added its volleys, which were for the moment keeping the Northerners at bay.

To overcome this obstacle, Tyler shifted one of his regiments to the right and directed it toward what appeared to be an undefended stretch of the wall. But just as the Yankees were approaching their objective, Fulkerson's brigade appeared in the clearing on the far side, and racing forward, reached the wall before Tyler's men and drove them off. In short order the rest of the Stonewall also came up, and over the next hour 1,700 Southerners crowded behind the wall and engaged the Northerners in a maelstrom that one of Tyler's soldiers described as "the most fearful thing you ever dreamed of."

Realizing that Tyler had been stalled in his tracks, Kimball pulled five regiments from his left and hurled them in waves at the Confederates behind the stone wall. The pressure began to take its toll. The Stonewall Brigade was running out of ammunition, and Garnett waited in agony for orders from Jackson—orders that never came. As the sun set at 6:00 p.m., Garnett ordered the Virginians to disengage and withdraw. Now Fulkerson was forced to retreat when his flank was exposed by Garnett's departure. The subsequent retreat was far from orderly. Two Southern artillery pieces fell into Union hands while 235 fleeing Confederates were captured by Northern cavalry. Jackson's losses amounted to 718 men against Kimball's 570 killed and wounded Federal soldiers.

The clash at Kernstown was the first battle waged in the Shenandoah Valley and the largest one fought east of the Alleghenies for nine months of the war. Jackson was bitterly disappointed at his failure to liberate Winchester and placed much of the blame on Garnett for his unauthorized withdrawal. On April 1 Jackson had Garnett arrested for neglect of duty and replaced him with Brigadier General Charles S. Winder.

Kernstown, however, brought an unforeseen bounty to the Confederates. When Shields boasted that he had defeated a Rebel force of 11,000 men—actually Jackson had only 3,600—an alarm sounded in the Union high command. Immediately, some 35,000 Union soldiers were pulled from McClellan's army to counter this phantom behemoth that loomed in the Valley.

Delighted by the Union's reaction, Jackson closed his after-battle report to General Johnston with an optimistic analysis: "I feel justified in saying that, though the field is in possession of the enemy, yet the most essential fruits of the battle are ours."

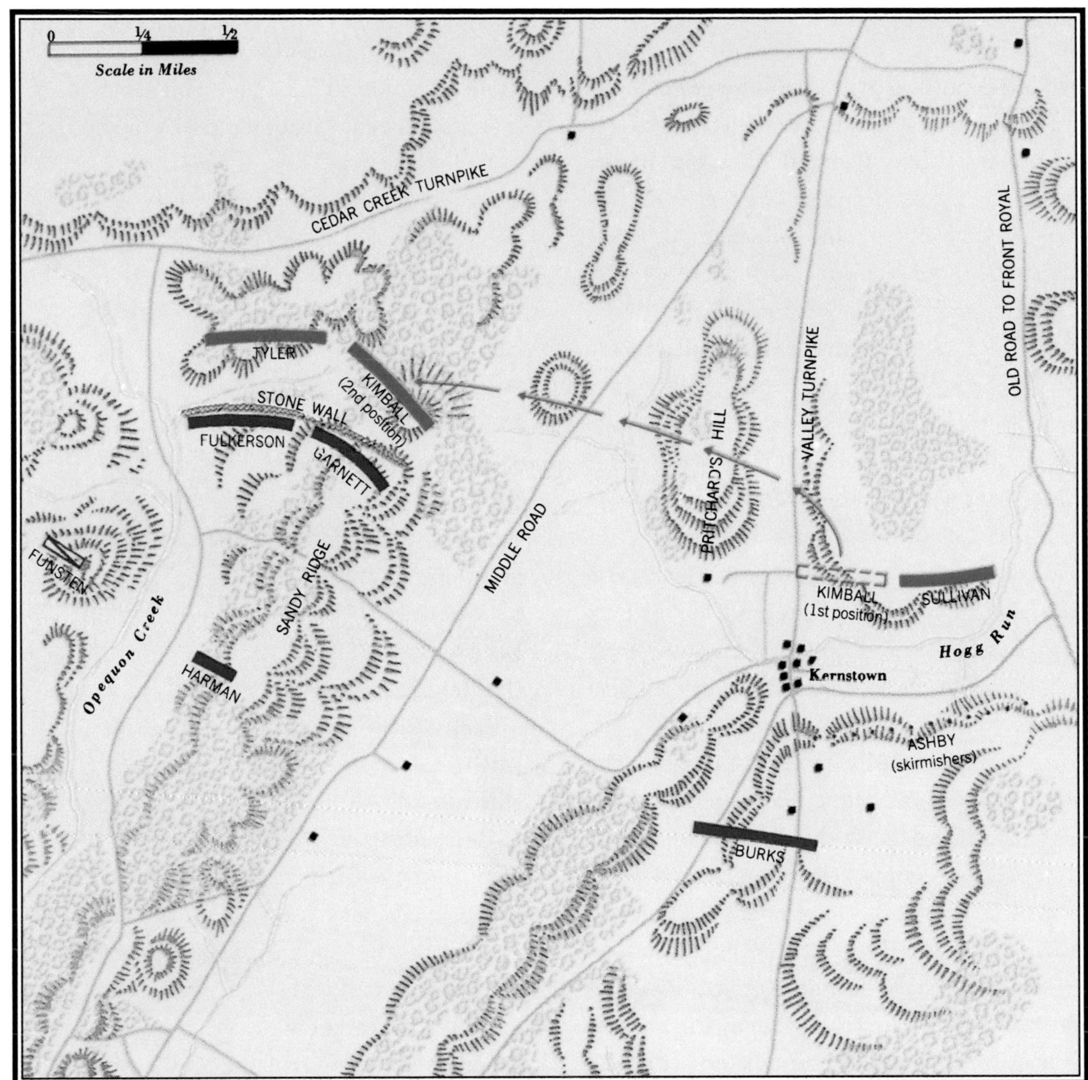

At 9:00 a.m. Sunday morning, March 23, Turner Ashby's horse artillery fired upon Federal pickets at Kernstown, producing a morning-long artillery duel. Jackson arrived four hours later and deployed Garnett's and Fulkerson's brigades along with artillery on Sandy Ridge to outflank the Union right on Pritchard's Hill. The Federal commander, Colonel Nathan Kimball, first sent Tyler's brigade to counter Jackson's move, bringing on a clash with Rebel infantry sheltered behind a stone wall on Sandy Ridge. After Kimball shifted six more regiments to reinforce Tyler, the Confederates, now outnumbered and running out of ammunition, were forced to withdraw at sunset.

SURGEON GEORGE K. JOHNSON
1st Michigan Cavalry

The 1st Michigan was picketing the roads south of Winchester on Saturday afternoon, March 22, when Ashby's Rebel cavalrymen approached the town. Taken completely by surprise, two Federal officers were trapped in a miller's house when Ashby attacked. They escaped, galloped into town, and warned Colonel Thornton F. Brodhead, the 1st Michigan's commander, who in turn brought the news to General Shields.

During the forenoon Ashby's cavalry began to annoy our pickets, and, as the day wore on, became more and more demonstrative. By 2 or 3 P.M. Col. Brodhead of the 1st Cavalry became convinced that the enemy was in force not far away and that his designs were aggressive. He so advised Gen. Shields, but the general discredited and scouted that view. But a little later the cavalry officers on picket, cool, steady, intelligent men, became certain of the imminence of the situation. Again a message of advice and warning was sent to Shields, three miles the other side of the town. Then, with a part of his staff, he came galloping up to the cavalry headquarters, and, still with an air of incredulity, demanded to know where the enemy was who had so disturbed the cavalry. The Colonel, a little nettled at the manner of the general, pointed to a range of hills three-fourths of a mile away, and running directly across the valley pike. The general, still doubting, rode on at full pace toward the hills, accompanied by his staff, Col. Brodhead and myself. When within a short distance of the hill he halted and placed his field-glass to his eyes. He had scarcely done so when a shell from the ridge exploded within a few feet of our group. Gen. Shields fell from the saddle and struck the earth several feet away. In a moment I was at his side and found him limp, blanched, senseless. A fragment of shell had struck his chest and made sad work with his left shoulder. In a few moments he began to revive, and as quickly as possible was removed to Winchester, where for several days he suffered greatly. As he was the only general officer in the vicinity the command devolved on Col. Nathan Kimball, of the 14th Indiana.

Brigadier General James Shields was described by his men as "an Irishman by birth, an American by choice, and a patriot because he could not be otherwise." He once challenged Abraham Lincoln to a duel in 1842 when both men lived in Illinois, but the two resolved their differences. Shields had represented Illinois and Minnesota in the U.S. Senate and would go to Washington as a senator from Missouri after the war. He had commanded Lander's former division for only two weeks when he was wounded at Winchester.

CORPORAL GEORGE M. NEESE
Chew's (Virginia) Battery

Corporal Neese manned the imported Blakely gun, the rifled piece dubbed Ashby's English pet in Chew's three-cannon battery. At 9:00 a.m. on Sunday, March 23, the Blakely fired the first shot of the Battle of Kernstown from high ground south of Opequon Church. The first five hours consisted primarily of artillery exchanges.

The Federal artillery was in position on a range of hills northwest of the town and replied to our opening shot with a vim which at once bespoke that they meant business. In the meantime a body of sharp-

"I for a moment forgot that danger lurked in the black speck that was descending to the earth before me like a schoolboy's innocent plaything."

shooters and two pieces of artillery advanced on our position from the east side of town and a little to right of our front. When the sharpshooters opened on us with their long-range rifles, and the two pieces of artillery commenced firing on us, we abandoned our position and retired under fire. We fell back about half a mile.

The first shell they fired at us from the battery on our right was a twelve-pounder, and I saw it flying in its graceful curve through the air, coming directly toward the spot where I was standing. I watched it until it struck the ground about fifteen feet in front of me. I was so interested in the sky ball, in its harmless appearance, and surprised that a shell could be so plainly seen during its flight, that I for a moment forgot that danger lurked in the black speck that was descending to the earth before me like a schoolboy's innocent plaything. It proved to have been a percussion shell, and when it struck the ground it exploded and scattered itself in every direction around me, and threw up dirt and gravel like a young volcano. Some of the gravel struck me on the arm. Then I left that place instantly, as I did not have any inclination whatever to watch any more shell just then, and my gun had already retired. . . .

The artillery fire now became terrific. Hundreds of shell went just over our heads, howling and shrieking in the air like demons on their way to deal death and destruction to Rebels. Some of their shell exploded over our heads and sowed their fragments and leaden hail in the sod around us. Others exploded close in our rear and thundered like batteries in the air where the furies of battle were fiendishly hissing the weird dirge of death and destruction. Just then I was ready to run without further notice.

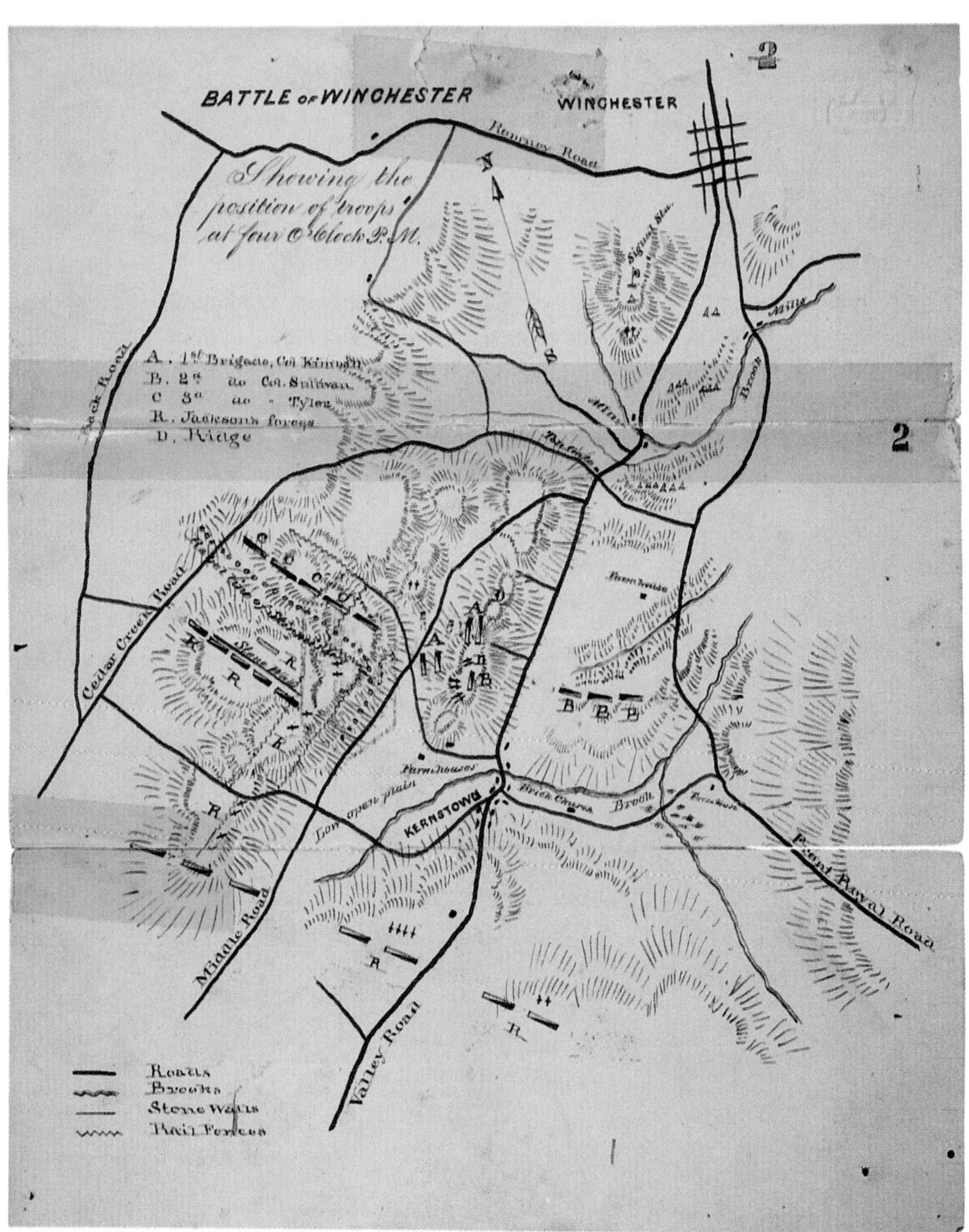

This map of the Kernstown battle by Captain Eddy D. Mason of the 67th Ohio was produced as part of the official report of the action, called by the Federals the Battle of Winchester.

SERGEANT JOHN H. WORSHAM

21ST VIRGINIA INFANTRY, BURKS' BRIGADE

After covering 36 miles in 30 hours, Worsham, the son of a Richmond clothier, and his tired mates from Company F reached the Kernstown battlefield. Entering the largest fight they had seen in the first year of war, the men of the 21st Virginia were ordered to support the Rockbridge Artillery on Sandy Ridge. Later the regiment was sent to reinforce the 27th Virginia, already engaged with Tyler's 2,300-man Union brigade.

We were ordered to double quick; we soon began to run and reached the hills without an accident. F Company was thrown forward as skirmishers, the rest of the regiment following in line of battle a short distance to the rear. The company was soon ordered to join them, and we marched by the flank. A gun or two of the Rockbridge Artillery now joined us. While we marched under a hill, the battery went to the right on top of the ridge. In their movement these guns were occasionally exposed to the view of the enemy's battery. The Yankees fired at them, the shells passing over our regiment. One shell struck one of the drivers of the guns, tearing his leg to pieces, and going through a horse. Both fell. The shell descended and passed through our ranks; it struck a stump not far off and spun around like a top. Before it stopped spinning, one of the company ran and jumped on it, taking it up and carrying it along as a trophy. This is the first man in the war I saw struck by a shell, and it was witnessed by a majority of the regiment.

General Jackson now made his appearance and had a talk with our commander, Lieutenant Colonel John M. Patton. We were thrown forward into line of battle again and marched a short distance to the top of a hill, in full sight of the enemy's line of battle. At this point they were advancing, too. I saw five flags. We opened fire at once and they scattered. In a few minutes I saw only two flags, and soon after only one, which was marched in a field on our right and planted on a pile of rocks. Its regiment gathered about it. Our regiment and the guns of the Rockbridge Artillery had been fighting this force. Our line was lengthened by the arrival of the Third Brigade on our left. A part of our regiment moved to a fence on the right and, facing the enemy, in the field, fired at them. Some of F Company were kneeling down, firing from behind the fence; some were standing straight up. Soon all were standing, and taking deadly aim as they fired. As the excitement increased, many men in F Company mounted the fence and sat on it, loading and firing until every cartridge was shot away.

Edward Lindsay Clarke (far left) and his brother Clordoma were two of more than 700 Confederate casualties at Kernstown. As members of the 23d Virginia in Colonel Samuel Fulkerson's two-regiment brigade, the Clarke brothers advanced toward 16 Federal cannons on Pritchard's Hill early in the fight. Edward was struck in the leg and arm by shell fragments, while his brother suffered a lesser wound. Both survived their injuries and the rest of the war.

CORPORAL SELDEN A. DAY

7th Ohio Infantry, Tyler's Brigade

Day, pictured as a cavalryman later in the war, gained notoriety at Kernstown for capturing one of Jackson's staff officers, Lieutenant George Junkin. Day received a bruise from a spent ball on Sandy Ridge and was wounded more seriously at Port Republic 11 weeks later. He recovered, was commissioned lieutenant, and later fought as a colonel in the Spanish-American War.

As we stood in line behind the hill on which the battery was posted, frequent shots would come over and cut through our ranks. Colonel Tyler of the Seventh Ohio, commanding the brigade, sat on his horse waiting for developments and further orders. He was calm, cool, and patient. I noticed, however, that he was pale, and that he too was feeling the strain of inaction under the trying circumstances. After a while an aide rode up to him from the left and front and evidently delivered an order. The Colonel, when the staff-officer had ridden away, turned to his command, and in a low but far-reaching voice said, "Boys, put on your bayonets;" adding, "you will need them."

The answer to this command must have been gratifying to the leader who gave it, as mingled with the clatter of fixing bayonets a shout of exultation went up from every man in the ranks. The terrible strain of inaction and waiting under fire was over. Column was quickly formed to the right and we marched over in that direction, where double column on the center was afterward formed facing the front, and the advance taken up.

The invisible guns in front of us were still firing to our left at the batteries we had been supporting. Steadily and in silence the brigade moved forward in double column for some distance as if upon the drill-ground. Then coming into a patch of woods, and commencing the descent of a gentle slope, we saw the smoke of the guns through the trees in front of us, on an elevation beyond a stone wall, over which the fire of musketry began to flash. Instantly the artillery was also turned upon us and we got the order, clear and distinct, from our commander, "Charge bayonets!" A rush forward down the slope amongst the trees followed. As the musketry from the wall in front and the canister and shells from the elevation beyond began to tell in our ranks, they were soon broken up and the advance ceased. All began firing without orders, and after that very few orders could be heard at all. C and F of the Seventh Ohio being the right and left center companies, formed the first or leading division of the regiment and brigade, and I, being a corporal in Company C, was of course in the front rank.

When the advance ceased I found myself near the bottom of the hill, but could still see the top of the stone wall ahead of us, on the slope of the opposite elevation, above which were bobbing heads and flashing rifles. More Confederates were running up to it through the grove beyond. Conspicuous amongst these was an officer on a white horse gallantly directing the movements. Some of us singled him out as a target and he was soon brought down.

Men were falling all around me, and glancing backward I saw that the slope of the hill was barely sufficient to enable the men in the rear

Sergeant Joseph Plaisted of the 5th Ohio fought his first battle at Kernstown. He was later accused of cowardice but overcame the charge and became a captain.

to fire safely over the heads of those of us in the front. A sergeant of Company H fell near me, shot through the neck, and I was quite sure it was done from the rear. After my second or third shot at the row of heads above the wall in front of us, as I threw up my rifle to reload, the bayonet went spinning away over my head, shot off near the shank. I replaced it quickly, taking the one from the musket of the sergeant who lay gasping at my feet, and replacing the stub of my own in its scabbard as far as it would go. . . .

Standing on the slope of the hill down which we had come and firing as fast as I could, having loaded my musket, I was holding it at the balance, in my left hand, while feeling for a cap in the little wool-lined cap-box on my belt . . . , and something struck me on the left arm near the shoulder. My gun dropped from the paralyzed hand and I saw that my overcoat was torn and blackened. As I grasped the injured arm with my available hand, Sterry, of Company C, who was standing beside me and firing away, said with a smile, as if it were a good joke, "You have got it, haven't you?" "Yes," I said, and finding that the place was scarcely bleeding, only bruised, added, "but not very bad. . . . "

. . . The air above our heads . . . seemed full of projectiles going in opposite directions. I crept cautiously up the hill until I could see well over the brow, and at one place the slope of the hill beyond, over which more of the enemy were hurrying to the front to reinforce those at the wall and be themselves sheltered as well.

I fired quickly into the advancing men and fell forward on to the slope for shelter while I reloaded. This maneuver I repeated several times, advancing a little before each shot, until I was near the wall, a little below the brow of the hill. At the last advance—on hands and knees—I noticed a short distance farther on and close to the wall, fifteen or twenty feet from it perhaps, a low ledge of rock jutting from the ground, ten or twelve inches above the surface. . . . I crept carefully forward and got into this natural rifle-pit. Though the height of the rock and the depth of the depression were scarcely sufficient to shelter my body when lying flat, the friendly brier-bush screened me from view from the front, and here, with comparative safety, I emptied my cartridge-box, enfilading the line behind the wall down the hill to the right of my position. . . .

While firing down the line, turning on my back to reload each time, I noticed that a fine-looking young fellow whom I did not know, from some other company, had crawled up as near to me as he could get, within arm's length, but not so well sheltered as I. He was firing away as fast as he could. I looked at him as he was loading his gun and preparing for another shot, when he said to me, "Isn't it fun?" I did not reply, and when I looked at him next he was dead.

"I had no sooner gotten into the saddle when the most vicious sounding bullet I ever heard swished by my ear and I thought it had taken a part of it off."

SERGEANT WILLIAM B. COLSTON

2D VIRGINIA INFANTRY, GARNETT'S BRIGADE

At 5:00 p.m. the 2d Virginia, under Colonel James W. Allen, took position at the eastern end of the stone wall, the eighth Southern unit to enter the fray. The Virginians found themselves in the hottest part of the fight, losing five colorbearers in succession before Colonel Allen picked up the standards himself to rally his men. Decades later Colston frankly described to his grandchildren his wounding and his less than heroic escape.

In going into the fight a part of the Stonewall brigade, composed of the 2nd, 27th and 33d regiments, had to cross an open field, which was commanded by one of the enemy's batteries, and it looked like a desperate undertaking, but fortunately they did not quite have our range and the shells flew over our heads, but too close to be comfortable. I remember that the wind from one raised the hair on my head—but that might have been from fright. We did not lose any time in getting across that field, but struck a lively double-quick and got over without the loss of a man. As soon as we reached our position we deployed into line of battle and pitched into the fight.

Just in front of me was a rockbrake and I had to run forward a few steps so that I could see over and get a shot at the enemy. I loaded and fired as fast as I could and was just ramming down my last cartridge when I was struck in the hip and tumbled over. It passed through my mind as I was falling that the bullet had either grazed the bone, broken my hip or gone into the cavity of the stomach, in which case it would have been all over with your grandfather, so as soon as I touched ground I whirled over on my hands and knees to see if my hip was broken and, finding it was not, I commenced to crawl back to the rear. In so doing I passed close to my brother, who called out to me to know if I was shot. I told him yes, in the hip. He ordered two men to take me off the field and one took me by the head and the other by the heels and started down the hill. They did not stand on the order of their going, but they went. We had not gone far before the order was given to fall back and I saw the that men who were carrying me could not get away with their load, so I told them to put me down and look out for themselves. They were just about to do so when Major Lawson Botts, of Charles Town, a warm personal friend of mine, rode by and asked who that was, and, when told, he jumped off his horse and said, "put him on my horse." And then I was guilty of an act I have always been ashamed of. I had no sooner gotten into the saddle when the most vicious sounding bullet I ever heard swished by my ear and I thought it had taken a part of it off. Of course I ought to have taken the kind Major on behind me, but that ball demoralized me and I felt that it was no good place to be, so forgetting all about Major Botts I dashed off over the hill, leaving him behind. Fortunately he got out all right, but no thanks to me.

Artist Edwin Forbes sketched the fighting on Sandy Ridge from behind the men of Tyler's brigade as they attempted to dislodge Jackson's Virginians spread out behind a stone wall 100 yards south of the Federals. Forbes later said he found being a witness to battle was "nearly as dangerous as being a participant."

Riddled by dozens of bullets, the state and regimental flags of the 84th Pennsylvania show the ferocity of the fighting on Sandy Ridge. Conspicuous in the midst of the maelstrom, colorbearers from both sides suffered. More than 15 soldiers who carried flags at Kernstown were killed or wounded.

PRIVATE WILLIAM GALLAGHER

84TH PENNSYLVANIA INFANTRY, KIMBALL'S BRIGADE

An 18-year-old private in the color company, Gallagher was one of 92 Kernstown casualties suffered by the 84th Pennsylvania, whose losses in killed and wounded exceeded those of any other regiment on the field. Writing to his parents from a hospital bed one month later, Gallagher vividly describes the intense action. Struck by friendly fire at Cedar Mountain on August 9, the luckless teenager was transferred to Falmouth, where he died on December 2, 1862.

There was none of our boys hurt during the whole day by the Canons but now comes the most serious Time. We got orders to charge Banots on The Rebles so we let a yell equal to any canon and of[f] we started on a double Quick towards the Enemy a distance of a quarter of a mile a while we was faceing them they was Pouring Bomb shells grape and canester into us like hell however it had not much afect. So on we went untill we got within 30 yards of them when our brave Col. Murray gave the command Halt then we fired a volley into tham which wakened tham which was in the woods and behind the stone wall. There we remained And fired as fast as we could ram cartridges for about one hour when the Enemy returned Almost as fast. If there was one ball past my head I think there was two thousand or more however I ascaped verry well Thank god. I was hit in three places. One through the Middle of my wright hand and one in my left thie and the other in my left shin however the two in my left leg did not anger me anny but the one through my hand has caused me to lay in the hospital for one month. . . . When I was wounded I fell to the Rear of the Regt. In about five minutes after I fell to the rear our Regt. got orders to charge to a stone fence where the Rebles was behind. That was a dreadful charge for our men to do because they had all kinds of advantage on our men. We lost our Brave Col. Wm. G. Murray in that terble conflict. And my Captain Patrick Gallaher was killed shot through the head. The Rebles had a grait spite at our flag. They shot 49 Bullets holes through it But did not kill anny of our flag Bearers. The fifth Ohio Regt. was to the wright of us. They sufered severely. I seen there color Bearer fall 4 times. As soon as one was shot down another would take it up until I seen 4 killed.

Two days before Kernstown, Colonel William G. Murray of the 84th Pennsylvania (inset) received a petition signed by 17 officers requesting his resignation because he had "failed to discover that peculiar genius which qualifies for martial command." During the battle Murray was ordered by Colonel Nathan Kimball to capture Confederate artillery on Sandy Ridge. Murray double-quicked his eight companies onto the eastern slope of the hill, where they were pummeled by Virginia infantry on their front and left flank, as well as by canister-spewing artillery on the crest of the ridge. His horse shot out from under him, Murray ordered the Pennsylvanians to charge. Just then a Confederate ball struck Murray in the forehead. He fell dead near the color guard of his regiment (right). The same officers who had earlier questioned Murray's leadership praised his valor for decades afterward.

Kernstown
Death of Col William Gay Murray - 84th Pen

This German-made, Model 1850 officer's sword was carried on Sandy Ridge by Captain Patrick Gallagher of the 84th Pennsylvania. Shortly before attacking Confederate batteries on the ridge, Gallagher hastily scribbled a note to his family in Hollidaysburg, telling of a premonition of death. After he reached the crest of Sandy Ridge, a Confederate bullet smashed into Gallagher's face and fulfilled his prophecy.

CORPORAL JAMES H. SIMPSON

14th Indiana Infantry, Kimball's Brigade

Barking a "Hoosier yell," the 14th Indiana turned the tide of the Battle of Kernstown, capturing two Confederate cannons in the process and leaving 54 of their own killed and wounded strewn on the field. Corporal Simpson, slightly wounded in the action, relates the scene that unfolded before him as his regiment reached the crest of Sandy Ridge. A heart condition, discovered shortly after the Battle of Antietam, took Simpson out of the service at the age of 21.

We were to take the place of a gallant Pennsylvania regiment, the Eighty-fourth, I believe, which had been literally cut to pieces. The little wood pasture was filled with the wounded of the Eighty-fourth Pennsylvania and Fifth Ohio, who had been able to crawl down from their line on the hill beyond the woods. The bullets rattled like hail in the tree-tops, but in this depression only a few were hurt by glancing balls from the limbs above. As we advanced rabbits sprang up and away, and Tom Thompson ("Old Bustinbinder"), threw a stick at some of them. A dog flew across our front, but he was not after the rabbits, for he carried his tail between his legs. . . . Quickly out of the little wood, we crossed a rail fence. Twenty yards to the top of a hill, in a little field, we came into position upon the left of the Fifth Ohio infantry, a brave regiment that lost five color-bearers killed at that spot. A few men of the Pennsylvania regiment still clung to their old line on the hill. As we appeared over the brow of the hill a perfect blizzard met us. The very air seemed to grow heavy with bullets, which, striking our men, sounded like the dusting of carpets with rods. We scented what I have never seen in print or heard mentioned—the peculiar odor of lead in violent friction. In front of us, across a little level field, but sixty or seventy-five yards distant, stood a substantial stone wall, from behind which Jackson's men were coolly shooting us down. Just back of the wall was a rather abrupt hill, upon the brow of which stood a second line of the enemy also pouring a murderous fire into our ranks. It was a perfect storm of concentrated fire. Already one of our regiments had melted away like snow under the sun. Dead men, with horses here and there, were thick along the line, and I remember thinking as we stood there that this little field came nearer filling my boyish ideas of a battlefield than I ever dreamed of seeing. . . .

. . . As we stood in the withering blast and fired and loaded once we had time to think—and one reasons like a flash at such moments—that one brave regiment had failed after a great loss. Our fire effected but little, while that of the enemy was so deadly that in less than five minutes we should be in the condition of the regiment whose place we had just taken. We felt that it was a waste of life to stand there; that brave men could fall back from such a place without dishonor. We had not been in the roaring place more than a third of a minute—just time to fire and load once—but it was long enough to lose sixty-five men. We must go forward or back. Just at the critical moment out sprang Paul Truckee in front of our line. Waving his gun over his head and shouting, "Come on, boys!" he dashed at the stone wall. It was not much to say, and but few could hear him, but his action was an inspiration. Our regiment charged as one man and the stone wall and the hill beyond was ours almost before the enemy knew what was the matter. . . . On the top of the hill where the second line of the enemy had been we realized how timely was the charge, for we met a large fresh force of the enemy coming up the slope. Had our charge been delayed two minutes we must have failed and been compelled to give up that position; and who can say where the disaster would have ended?

Asa John Wyatt marched toward Winchester on March 23 as a member of the 21st Virginia. "That day I was with the baggage wagons," he remembered about Kernstown, but "at 3:00 p.m. . . . I grabbed my gun and started forward." Wyatt was a bystander that day, but on August 9 he was killed in action at Cedar Mountain.

392 April 26, 1862.] FRANK LESLIE'S ILLUSTRATED NEWSPAPER. [April 26, 1862. 393

THE WAR IN VIRGINIA—THE BATTLE OF WINCHESTER, MARCH 23 DECISIVE BAYONET CHARGE OF THE NATIONAL TROOPS, LED BY GENERAL TYLER.—From a Sketch by our Special Artist, Mr. E. Forbes.

THE WAR IN VIRGINIA—BATTLE OF WINCHESTER—CAPTURE OF A REBEL BATTERY, ON THE ENEMY'S RIGHT, BY THE [illegible] OHIO AND 7TH INDIANA REGIMENTS, MARCH 23.—FROM A SKETCH BY OUR SPECIAL ARTIST, MR. E. FORBES.

THE DECISIVE CHARGE OF THE NATIONAL TROOPS AT WINCHESTER.

In our last paper we gave a general description of the recent Union victory at Winchester. We now illustrate the leading incident of that admirably manœuvred battle, when our gallant men were massed together for that decisive charge which changed the battle into a perfect rout. It will be recollected that, despite the ability and success with which General Shields had drawn the rebel army under General Jackson from its entrenched camp near Mount Jackson to follow him to Winchester, under the belief that the Union army was in full retreat, and that the rebels might re-occupy Winchester—yet, nevertheless, though the rebels fell into the trap, they had managed to choose a most excellent position for their operations. Captain Shriber thus describes the charge of General Tyler's column on the rebels, who had thrown themselves behind a stone wall for protection:

"Gen. Tyler moved his column by the right flank as far as Cedar Creek road, rested his right upon the same, and the left upon the before-mentioned mud road, pushing forward upon both roads some cavalry; changed direction to the left, right in front, and moved silently but steadily upon the enemy's left through the woods for almost half a mile, when, coming upon a more sparsely wooded ground, he made half a wheel to the left and came to the face of the extreme flank of the enemy, who received him behind a stone wall at about 200 yards distant, with a terrific volley of rifled arms; but still on went the regiments without a return fire, and then threw themselves, with immense cheering and an unearthly yell, upon the enemy, who, receiving at fifteen yards our first fire, fell back across the field, thus unmasking two six-pound iron guns, which hurled, on being cleared in front, death and destruction into our ranks with their canister. But still onward we went, taking one gun and two caissons, and making there a short stand. Again the enemy unmasked two brass pieces, which at last drove us, by their vigorous fire, back. But I caused the captured gun to be tipped over, so that the enemy in regaining ground could not drag it away.

"The Fifth Ohio and Eighty-fourth Pennsylvania threw themselves once more with fixed bayonets forward, the former losing four times in a few minutes their standard bearer. Captain Whitcomb at last took the colors up again, and cheering on his men fell also. So, too, Colonel Murray, whilst gallantly leading on his Eighty-fourth regiment. In fact, the ground was strewn with dead and wounded. Gen. Tyler lost his aid, Lieutenant Williamson, of the Twenty-ninth Ohio.

"I hurried back to bring up the One Hundred and Tenth and the Fourteenth Indiana, by a right oblique movement through the woods, and the enemy receiving all the combined shock, retired and left us in possession of our dearly-bought gun and caissons.

"United, onward we pressed, again the enemy's two brass pieces and musketry pouring in their fire. Three companies of the Eighth Ohio reinforcing us, we gained our brass piece and its caisson, and compelled the enemy to fall back."

A spectator, in describing the scene our Artist has sketched, says: "Now approached the decisive charge of the day. A little to the right the enemy were strongly posted in woods and behind a stone wall, and the rebel artillery was posted on eminences on both sides of their left wing. Our whole artillery force engaged consisted of four batteries of twenty-four pieces in all.

"The contest raged furiously till three o'clock in the afternoon, the fighting being done chiefly by the artillery and musketry at a range of not more than three or four hundred yards, and often much less.

"The rebel infantry opposite our right now debouched from the woods and attempted to capture Daum's battery by a charge. The first effort was nearly successful, but the heavy discharge of grape compelled them to retire in confusion. A second and weaker attempt likewise failed, and the enemy fell back, with heavy loss, behind the stone parapet.

"General Tyler now ordered his brigade to charge the enemy's batteries on the left, and a most deadly encounter followed. Twice our men reeled under the storm; but in the third effort they routed the rebels with tremendous slaughter and loud cheering, capturing two of their guns and four caissons.

"Our loss in these struggles was heavy. Out of 300 men engaged in the Eighty-fourth Pennsylvania, 26 were killed and 83 wounded. Colonel Murray fell leading this gallant corps forward, and many other dashing officers were killed or wounded. The Fifth and Eighth Ohio shared the glory and the losses with the Eighty-fourth, and the Third Virginia regiment also suffered. Lieutenant-Colonel Thorburn, commanding this corps, was severely wounded leading it forward to the last charge."

Two engravings by Edwin Forbes of the Battle of Kernstown published in Frank Leslie's Illustrated Newspaper show (top) a largely fanciful rendering of the victorious Federal charge over the stone wall on Sandy Ridge and (bottom) a far more accurate depiction of the Federal advance that resulted in the capture of a Rebel battery on the right of the Confederate line.

BUGLER SAMUEL GILLESPIE

1st Ohio Cavalry

Writing under the pen name Lovejoy, Gillespie contributed his observations to the Fayette County Weekly, a newspaper published in his hometown of Washington Court House, Ohio. He refined and republished the accounts as a history of Company A in 1898. In this excerpt Gillespie describes the active role his company took at sunset on the western end of Sandy Ridge.

The battle had ceased. The sun was fast sinking behind the western hills. —No sound, save the commands of the officers, as they hurriedly rode along the lines, was heard. 'Twas the momentary lull of the tempest; the crouch of the tiger ere the fated spring. We were formed in dense column, in ranks of companies. Slowly and solemnly the remaining three or four hundred yards to the enemy, through the dense wood and underbrush, was half gone over, when the infantry began to go on quick time. Then the yell and rush of the whole column, woke up those old woods again. But we did not get far until the front of the column was one sheet of fire. Then, as if a bunch of crackers had been lighted, or the smouldering coals of a hickory fire stirred, came the reports, only ten times more loud and quick. We were in a little hollow, completely sheltered, but the suspense was painful, seeing only the wounded, and bearing it all. . . .

. . . I was watching the progress of the battle, and looking out for the cavalry from a little rise in the open ground to the right of our columns, when the firing commenced in a new place up the stone wall, to our left, where the enemy's artillery was. The suspense seemed unbearable. Was that the enemy's recruits, or ours? I could not see for the wood and the hill. Then two or three of those drowning reports came—the twenty yards of open space in front of the stone wall at the point of the wood, was strewn with our brave boys, bleeding, dying, dead. Our column trembled. Then as the heavy fire of the 13th Indiana and 84th Pennsylvania came raking down along the fence, the rebels rose from behind it like a flock of quails from a brush-heap. Then Major Chamberlain, of the 1st Virginia cavalry, in command, came galloping up, shouting:

"Cavalry, charge!"

"Where? which way?" replied our Captain.

"Off to the right—there—anywhere! Go in, Captain! Charge on them!"

"Major, will you please go with us and direct the column?" again replied our Captain.

"No I must go and bring up my own boys."

He went, but he nor his boys did not come up. I have not seen them since. Our Captain's horse scared at some dead bodies in a little hollow, through which we passed. He dropped his pistol, and as I turned back to get it, I saw none but our squadron following.

The stone fences were great hindrances to our charge on the enemy. We crossed two fields and passed down a lane a few hundred yards, when we began to call out—"Halt, or I will blow your brains out!" We picked them up for two miles, sending them back by the dozen, in charge of one or two.

Posing with saber and pistol, Private Andrew McGinnis of Company A, 1st Ohio Cavalry, saw action at Kernstown. Five months later he was caught between the lines near Bristoe Station, Virginia, and presumed killed by enemy fire.

" 'Twas the momentary lull of the tempest; the crouch of the tiger ere the fated spring."

LIEUTENANT JAMES H. LANGHORNE

4TH VIRGINIA INFANTRY, GARNETT'S BRIGADE

As the Confederates began to retreat from the stone wall, Langhorne grabbed the flags from the colorbearer and attempted to rally his men to stave off the Federal cavalry. When this failed, he and 250 other Confederates were captured. Writing to his parents from Fort Delaware prison on April 3, Langhorne proudly relates his fearless resistance before his capture. Broken down by prison life, he was released and committed to an insane asylum in Staunton, where he died on May 31, 1864.

Col. Fulkerson remarked to me, as I still held the flag of the Regiment in my hand, that he thought with the mare I was riding that I could save the colors with ease. I told him I knew I could if one of those plagued balls from the enemy's cavalry on our rear and infantry on our left, as were tired, did not make a hole in a fellow's "casemate." Just here the lane turned off at right angles to the right and just at this place, young Durham of the "Pulaski Guards" and Capt. Wright of the "Dare Devils" asked me to let them have my mare that they thought they could make their escape on her. I asked them if they were too badly wounded to save the colors—Durham said he had only a slight wound through the right shoulder and could save himself on foot but for having been broken down by the marches and knew, with my mare, could save both Wright and himself. So I got down and helped them on my mare and I gave Durham the colors, telling him to tear them up if he thought there was a danger of their being captured. He was a cool brave fellow, and a fine horseman—I got over the fence and threw the rider off and then got back on the side they were, took "Annie" by the bridle, drew her back from the fence, and struck her on the side with my hand saying, "Go over Annie."

She cleared the fence beautifully with both of them on her back. I was more afraid of being killed just as I took the rail off the fence than at any time before during the day as the cavalry got within one hundred yards and were firing upon us with their minie carbines—I jumped over the fence and started as fast as I could across the field, but before I got fifty yards the cavalry had got to the fence I had just left and I knew would shoot me in my back, so I drew my pistol and turned and fired at the front cavalry man just as his horse struck the inside of the fence. He threw both hands to his chest but I did not see him fall from his horse. The next man that came over the fence was a Lieutenant. I shot at him just as his horse was riding to leap the fence, as I saw him in the act of drawing his pistol. I think the nail must have passed through his clothes, as I was confident the sights on the pistol covered a blue uniform. He was a bold fellow and fired on me twice. As he advanced my pistol misfired or I would have killed him. He rode right up to me and asked me if I was a "sesech." I told him "No, confound you, but I am a rebel." He then said "You are my prisoner, surrender." I told him I would see him d—d first and struck high guard and thrust with all my might at his abdomen. But that old sword Frizzell made me failed in the first effort and did not get through his clothes. My compliments to Mr. F. and tell him he has mistaken his calling.

To show you how cool the Lieutenant was, as I thrust at him he drew his second pistol and shot me in the side. I thought at the instant, and until the Surgeon opened my clothes at Winchester, that it was a mortal wound, as it knocked me down. Several cavalrymen rode up and seeing that I was leveling my pistol at the front, one of them, who was putting a cartridge in his minie carbine—I tell you he dropped his cartridge the quickest I ever saw. None of these shots struck me; but a fine looking fellow rode up on my right and said, "sesech you might as well surrender, your ammunition is out." I always did hate that word "sesech" and I threw my sword in his face, but the plagued thing was so dull it did not even cut his skin. I put the muzzle of the pistol I had, which belonged to Col. Preston, and which was given him by Colonel Echols—on the ground and succeeded in breaking the stock off. The fellow did not shoot me for this, but just before I snapped my pistol in his face, he shot me. The ball struck the little ring I wore on the little finger of my left hand and drove it down to the bone. But the ring saved the finger from being broken.

The fellow then got down, took my pistol, unbuckled my sword belt, then come around and put his arm under my head, said he was "sorry he did not have some water to give me," and that I was wrong for fighting when I saw such odds against me. He was a brave noble fellow, and I felt it an honor to be taken by such company of men. They were Ohio men attached to Col. Copeland's regiment of Michigan cavalry.

"Mother, Home, Heaven are all sweet words, but the grandest sentence I ever heard from mortal lips was uttered this evening by Captain Chew when he said, 'Boys, the battle is over.'"

CORPORAL GEORGE M. NEESE

Chew's (Virginia) Battery

Attached to Colonel Turner Ashby's 7th Virginia Cavalry, Chew's battery of horse artillery manned their cannons south of the village of Kernstown for the entire 10-hour battle and suffered no casualties. Neese, who remained a corporal throughout the war, was captured in October 1864 and spent the last months of the conflict at Point Lookout prison. He published his war experiences in 1911.

It was nearly dusk when the firing ceased, and Jackson gave up the field, repulsed but not vanquished, defeated but not routed nor demoralized, for his troops are camped for the night around Newtown, not more than three or four miles from the battle-field.

To-day was the first time that I experienced the realities of an actual battle-field, and am willing to admit that to see two armies in battle array is an imposing sight. The glittering flash of burnished arms, the numerous battle flags floating over the forming lines, the infantry marching with measured step in close order taking their places in the growing battle line, with here and there a group of artillery in position, is so inspiring as to almost fascinate even a timid freshman as he stands ready to take his place for the first time in the human shambles. The enchantment act transpired before the battle opened, but when the firing commenced and they began in earnest to pass the bullets, shot, and shell around promiscuously, the fascination and all its kindred suddenly took flight from me faster than forty suns can rout the most delicate morning mist. Mother, Home, Heaven are all sweet words, but the grandest sentence I ever heard from mortal lips was uttered this evening by Captain Chew when he said, "Boys, the battle is over."

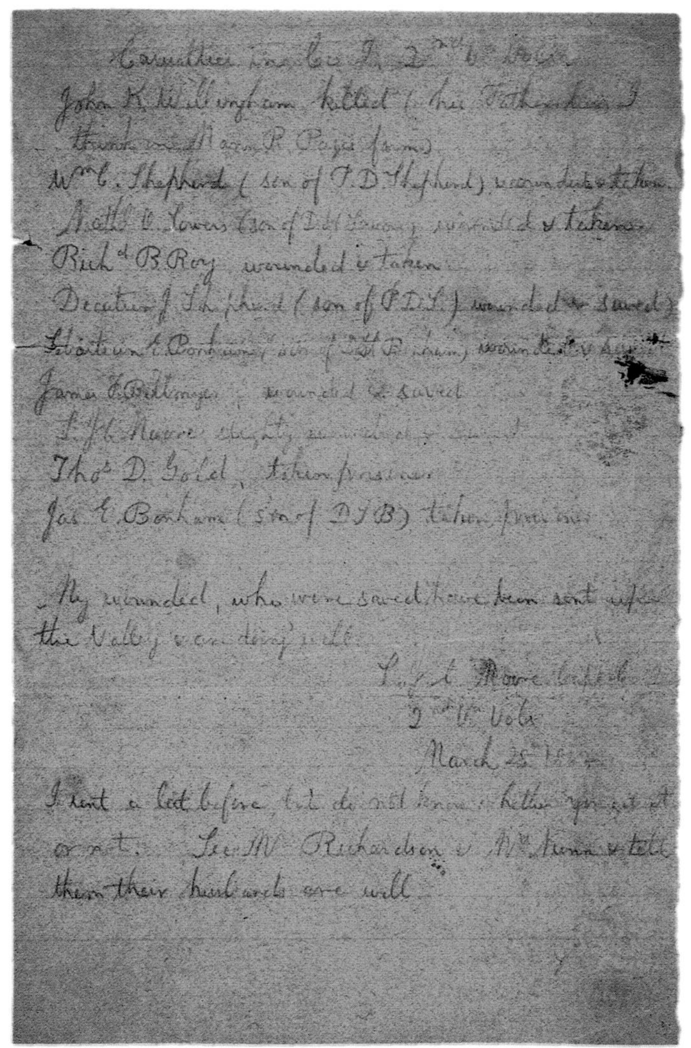

Casualties [illegible] Co. I. 2nd [illegible]

John K. [illegible] killed ([illegible]

[illegible] P. Page [illegible])

Wm. [illegible] Shepherd (son of P. D. Shepherd) wounded & taken

[illegible] (son of [illegible]) wounded & taken

Richd B. Roy wounded & taken

Decatur J. Shepherd (son of P. D. S.) wounded & saved)

[illegible] (son of [illegible]) wounded & saved

James [illegible] wounded & saved

[illegible] Moore slightly wounded & saved

Thos D. Gold, taken prisoner

Jas. E. Bonham (son of D. J. B.) taken prisoner

My wounded, who were saved have been sent up the Valley & are doing well.

[illegible] Moore [illegible]

2nd V. Vols

March 25 [illegible]

I sent a lett before, but do not know whether you got it or not. See Mr Richardson & [illegible] & tell them their husbands are well

Samuel J. C. Moore's March 28 letter to his wife includes a casualty list for Company I, 2d Virginia (above). Moore suffered a bruised back but stoically said, "I am not enough hurt to unfit me for duty." Another bullet scraped the side of his head. The 2d Virginia's 90 casualties amounted to 28 percent of the number engaged—more killed and wounded than any other Confederate regiment at Kernstown.

The stone wall at Kernstown (photographed from the Confederate side in 1885) stretched for 500 yards across the northern segment of Sandy Ridge. In two and a half hours, 900 American soldiers were killed or wounded on the hill. In some places, a Pennsylvanian claimed, "One could walk for rods by stepping from one body to another."

DR. LEVI RITTER

Civilian Physician

Ritter, an Indiana resident, arrived in Winchester one week after the battle to offer his services in a town taxed by overwhelming numbers of wounded soldiers. Although the casualties were removed from Sandy Ridge within two days of the battle, Dr. Ritter strode out to Kernstown on March 30 to view the battlefield. Two days after he penned his observations, Dorothea Dix and her corps of nurses arrived in Winchester from Washington to help the citizens aid the wounded.

On this ridge—which is mostly wood land—the enemy made their stand, keeping a flank out on the right and left, and concealing themselves in the woods in the centre, and on the left flank by stone fences. When our forces drove them from the stone fence they would run into the woods, and on coming to the next stone fence, which usually run through the valley up to the hill where the woods are, would run out along it and make another stand. In the face of these stone fortifications our men had to advance and *did* advance with a coolness and bravery unparalleled in the history of warfare. The woods for a mile are perfectly torn to pieces with missiles. There are but few large trees, but a thick undergrowth, and I could see scarcely a sprout as large as a man's finger, but what was cut by a ball. How any escaped is more than I can see. About the middle of the grounds I was shown the place where 86 rebels were buried the next day after the battle. How forcibly have they realized the truth of the saying of our Savior that "they who take the sword shall perish by the sword." At the point where our troops captured the Rockbridge battery, I saw two horses which were killed by cannon balls passing through their shoulders, making holes of at least 8 inches in diameter—Blood, hats, clothing, and every conceivable kind of equipments are to be seen on the grounds now, just one week after the bloody conflict. A conflict equal in mortality to any in this war in proportion to the forces engaged. I picked up an unexploded shell (or rather dug it up) to preserve as a relic of the battle. Thousands of balls have been cut from the trees already, and the grounds which were perfectly strewn with guns, pistols &c., have been well searched for visitors,—each one carrying away some trophy.

MARY GREENHOW LEE

RESIDENT OF WINCHESTER

A cousin of the famous spy "Rebel Rose" Greenhow, the widow Mrs. Lee shared her home in Winchester with sisters-in-law and three nephews. Mrs. Lee openly expressed her hatred of Yankees. Her flagrant disobedience of Federal edicts sealed her fate in February 1865, when General Philip Sheridan banished her from Winchester. She spent the rest of her life in Baltimore.

I went with Mrs. Barton to the office of Col. Batchelor, the Provost Marshall, to try to get a pass to go to the prisons; Mrs. Barton made a very pathetic appeal, told him a number of sons & relations she had in the battle, & implored his consent, but in vain. He said everything was in such confusion that it was impossible to allow citizens entrance at the prisons. I thought he was very rough to Mrs. Barton, & I told her, before him, it was utterly useless to expect any consideration, & that I would not ask any favours of them; whereupon he commenced apoligising, & promised, that as soon as he had made out the list of prisoners, & wounded, we should have a pass. . . . The Provost' Marshal's list of prisoners was not completed, & Willie Barton's was the only name we recognized. We left the office & joined the rest of our party, at Mr. Sherrard's door; there one of the officers came to me, to say he had ascertained Sergeant Major Barton, was amongst the prisoners. Then we went to the Court House and other places, where they were, & made the Sentinels go on and look for my boys, but we could hear nothing; all this time we were in perfect ignorance as to their fate, & were hoping most eagerly to hear that they were prisoners, as it was the only way we could be assured of their safety; we heard there were some at the Union, & were on our way there when Mary Jones came to us, with a few lines from Ranny, saying he, Bob, Willie, & Bob Bell were safe, well, & at the jail; it was joyous news; the next thing was to collect a breakfast & take them, in spite of the Provost Marshal; Mr. Burwell had joined us, & we all went up to the jail where we found the officers very accommodating; they let us send the breakfast & a little note to the boys; then Mr. Burwell & I went again to the Provost Marshal to make him say when he would give us a pass; he was harassed to death, the room was full of officers, but he was much more polite than he had been to Mrs. Barton, & said he would go with me himself, to the prison at 2 o'clock. . . . We found out about 12 o'clock, that we could see Bob & went up, & were taken to the grating one at a time; the officer let him come into the hall to see some of us, & I got a kiss; I never saw him looking handsomer or brighter; he had marched 24 miles on Saturday; 12 on Sunday; then in the battle all day & at dusk was picked up by the Cavalry; we hear he was in the act of helping some of our wounded but he did not say so himself; I thought I was glad yesterday, that he was a prisoner & out of harm's way, but after the terrific sights I have seen since, I cannot be grateful enough to our Heavenly Father for keeping him out of the dangers of the next few weeks, for I believe the fighting will be done in that time that will achieve our independence. . . . At 2 o'clock the prisoners here marched by our door to the cars enroute for Washington, it is said. They were as bright & joyous as if they were in a triumphal procession; every one came out to tell them good-bye, & to cheer them, & I found myself hurraing . . . for Jeff Davis, in spite of the Yankee officers by their sides, who heard every word we said to them; we had our letters ready for Bob rolled up in a bundle, which Mr. Burwell handed him, & the girls went out in the middle of the street, to give them biscuits, &c. They had more life & spirits, though prisoners, than any of the Yankees who have been here.

Seventeen-year-old Sergeant Major Randolph Barton of the 33d Virginia had his pistol shot from his hand before his capture at Kernstown. Penned in a Baltimore jail, Barton wondered, "Would I ever tread the streets a freeman?" He was transferred to Fort Delaware, where he remained a prisoner for four more months. Once exchanged, Barton rejoined as a lieutenant in the 2d Virginia.

PRIVATE AUNGIER DOBBS

RINGGOLD (PENNSYLVANIA) CAVALRY

The day after the Battle of Kernstown, the Federals pursued Jackson's retreating Confederates into the heart of the Valley. On March 25 Dobbs wrote his wife from Strasburg. His narrative reveals the hardened mentality that he adopted after witnessing death and depredation in a war that had yet to complete its first year.

You have before this heard of our battle with Jackson at Winchester he thought to drive us out but missed it to his injury Our company was deployed as Skirmishers and the fight commenced on Sunday about 10 oclock and lasted till dark I saw the last hour of the fight which was the most violent thing I ever witnessed the enemy was behind a stone fence our boys charged upon them and in the charge many of our best men fell the enemy fled and Oh how they suffered in their flight. . . . we pursued them as far as Strawsburgh killing and wounding several of them Our company was in the advance with the cannon I tell you shells would burst near us but it is strange I never felt like they would hit me. . . .

. . . I now think there will be a good bit of hard fighting to do before this rebellion is Quelled I must say of the Women of this country although they are Secesh they are humane & kind but some of our Soldiers dont use them well They rob them of eggs chickens and milk their cows I think some suffer Notwithstanding our General is doing all he can do to prevent it you know Stealing will go on in a place in time of peace he keeps a Patroll guard all over the country and town who will arrest anyone they find out of camp without a pass yet they strip the country of all the Poultry and it is not for want for the soldiers are well provided with rations & clothing and the Secesh passed through and bought near all they had with a promise to pay now we pass and strip them of the rest and burn their fences and throw open their fields there is one thing in their faviour there will be no Stock left to require a fence my health & spirits is good I enjoy myself as well the last 4 months as the 9 months previous but the time seems short their is about Enough of excitement in it to keep me up when within cannon shot of the enemy I can sleep as sound as if a friendly army was there Soldiering has become a business and I can go out Expecting a fight with more composure than if I was going to a barn Raising the sight of the dead & wounded has no terrors to me dont think I have become hardened I could wait on them as tenderly as a mother but have no Squeamish feelings about it.

SERGEANT RUFUS MEAD

5TH CONNECTICUT INFANTRY, DONNELLY'S BRIGADE

In Winchester on the day after the battle, Sergeant Mead observed the scene when Confederate prisoners taken at Kernstown were marched through the town past the residents, many of whom were related to the captives. Mead served as the regimental commissary sergeant, marching with his unit up through Gettysburg in the east and with Sherman across Georgia and the Carolinas. Mead returned to civilian life as an engineer and surveyor.

Just as I got to town I saw a crowd around the jail where C. H. are and I went up and found 118 prisoners there under guard and any quantity of the citizens many or most of them ladies bidding them good bye and giving them presents of oranges, cakes, pies, gloves, socks, handkerchiefs and etc. in any quantity. While there the Provost Marshal came to take them to the cars to Harpers Ferry and I saw them as they were marched off two by two to the depot. There were 5 Capt's and 10 Lieut's but no two were dressed alike. In the whole they were good enough looking but most were miserably clothed, some hardly decent. There were many tears shed over the poor fellows as they marched along as they were nearly all from Virginia and some from Winchester. Capt Daboll said he never was so troubled in his life as he was during the fight when they were bringing in the prisoners. He said he thought the women would tear him to pieces. They called him every name they could think of.

Confounding the Yankees

The setback at the hands of General Shields' Federals at Kernstown failed to throw Jackson into despair. The night after the battle he was warming his hands by a fire near the Valley Turnpike when a garrulous young soldier approached and commented that "the Yankees don't seem willing to quit Winchester, General," adding that instead of falling back they had been "retreating after us." Without looking up Jackson stiffly replied, "I think I may say I am satisfied, sir."

Jackson in fact had reason to be at least partially content. The Kernstown fight had gone badly, but he had hit the Federals hard and achieved his main object of causing alarm in the Union high command. If Jackson had dared to attack, Federal authorities reasoned, he must have been reinforced. To handle the threat, General Banks was ordered to keep his two divisions in the Shenandoah, while an additional 10,000 men were detached from McClellan's army and sent to bolster Frémont's force in the Alleghenies.

The Valley Turnpike boasted a cement-and-gravel surface, limestone shoulders, and a remarkably straight course. On May 24 the stretch just south of Winchester shown here was packed with Federal troops and wagons fleeing Jackson's oncoming army.

Knowing he had stirred up a hornet's nest, Jackson retreated, marching the Valley army south down the much traveled pike. By mid-April his troops were safely camped south of Mount Jackson on Rude's Hill, a rise protected from surprise attack by a nearby loop in the North Fork of the Shenandoah River.

Banks did not start pursuing until April 1—and then came on slowly, his advance guard plagued at every step by Turner Ashby's cavalry. When at last the Federals had chased Ashby back to Rude's Hill, Jackson headed south again, marching through Harrisonburg on April 18 and then 20 miles east to Conrad's Store near Swift Run Gap.

While keeping out of Banks' reach, Jackson received several crucial messages from Robert E. Lee, who, not yet commanding in the field, was serving as military adviser to President Jefferson Davis. Richmond, Lee reported, was in increasing danger. General McClellan's huge Union army had begun advancing up the Peninsula on April 4, threatening the Confederate capital from the east. Almost as bad, more than 30,000 Federals under Major

General Irvin McDowell were moving on Fredericksburg to come at Richmond from the north.

But instead of ordering Jackson east to help defend the city, Lee suggested a far riskier ploy. Jackson would stay in the Shenandoah and stir up the noisiest possible diversion. With luck this would keep large numbers of Federals busy in the Valley and far from the forces heading toward Richmond. To help, Jackson would get reinforcements, 8,500 men led by Major General Richard S. Ewell. "If you can use Genl. Ewell's division in an attack on Genl. Banks and to drive him back," Lee wrote, "it will prove a great relief to the pressure on Fredericksburg."

The idea of again hitting the Federals in the Valley suited Jackson perfectly. By April 29 Ewell and his division were on their way west, marching fast over the Blue Ridge by way of Swift Run Gap from their blocking position near Stanardsville. Reaching Jackson's camps during the night of April 30, they quietly filed past and set up a bivouac nearby.

Both Ewell and his troops were astonished the next morning, however, to find that Jackson along with his army had vanished, leaving nothing behind but "the smouldering embers of his deserted campfires." Stonewall was already off to hit the Federals as Lee had suggested—and in his secretive way telling his new ally virtually nothing of his plans. Ewell was simply ordered to hold the gap, and if necessary to deal with Banks.

Ewell, a 45-year-old bachelor and West Pointer who had spent years commanding cavalry in the West, was more eccentric in his ways, if possible, than Jackson. Also a chronic dyspeptic, he ate only a concoction called frumenty, made of hulled wheat boiled in milk with sugar, raisins, and egg yolks. He spoke in a high, lisping, birdlike voice—and punctuated what he said with streams of oaths, swearing "in a style," said a fellow officer, "that defies description."

Ewell's fragile digestion was not assuaged by Jackson's secrecy or the conflicting orders he had left behind. "I tell you, sir, he is as crazy as a March hare," Ewell complained to one of his regimental commanders. "I will just march my division away from here. I do not mean to have it cut to pieces at the behest of a crazy man."

Jackson's first objective was to deal with a Union threat to the Shenandoah from the west—the vanguard of Frémont's army, led by Brigadier General Robert H. Milroy, that had advanced out of the Alleghenies to the area of Staunton. Marching his men south from Conrad's Store on April 30, Jackson then headed through Brown's Gap to Mechum's River Station, giving the impression he was quitting the Shenandoah. Once there, however, he piled troops on cars of the Virginia Central Railroad and headed back into the Valley.

Jackson reached Staunton on May 4 and joined up with a 2,800-man Confederate force led by Brigadier General Edward Johnson that had been shielding the town. Stonewall immediately marched the combined force 25 miles into the Allegheny foothills, threatening Milroy's camps near the town of McDowell. Not waiting to be assaulted, Milroy launched a spoiling attack on the Confederates on May 8 but, beaten off, moved his outnumbered force back into the hills toward Frémont's main force at the town of Franklin.

Certain he had discouraged Frémont from further moves on Staunton, Jackson abruptly reversed direction, marching his now larger army back across the Shenandoah. He had received news that General Shields and his division were moving east out of the Valley to join McDowell's force at Fredericksburg, leaving Banks with only 10,000 men around Strasburg. Shields had to be stopped—and here at last was the perfect chance to crush Banks.

Urging on his footsore troops, Jackson headed for Harrisonburg and New Market. So did Ewell, who set out from Conrad's Store on May 19 to join up. Jackson's plan: to march north with all speed down the pike and assault Banks at Strasburg.

But Ewell brought fresh news. The town of Front Royal at the northeastern tip of Massanutten Mountain and on Banks' left was held by only about 1,000 Union troops. Jackson, seeing a golden opportunity to make a surprise attack on the enemy flank, immediately decided to hit Front Royal first. Making a right turn, he hurried the army up the single road that crossed Massanutten, then turned left into the Luray Valley.

Nearing Front Royal on May 23, Jackson swiftly attacked, sending the Union defenders fleeing in panic. With that, Banks, realizing he was both outflanked and outnumbered, immediately abandoned Strasburg, hurrying his troops north. Jackson pursued at once, ordering his infantry and cavalry up three different roads to assault Banks' column and cut it off. Banks slipped past to Winchester the next day, but the Confederates won a sharp little battle outside Winchester on May 25, sending the Federals fleeing through the town and all the way to the Potomac.

The lightning strike and Banks' headlong retreat alarmed President Lincoln, especially when Jackson kept on going to Charles Town, only seven miles from Harpers Ferry. Something had to be done about this wild man in the Valley, and Lincoln himself designed a trap. Shields would march back westward along with some of McDowell's troops, coming in south of the Confederates to cut Jackson's line of retreat around Strasburg. Lincoln also ordered Frémont to march his army from Franklin to tighten the noose from the west. With a total force of 35,000 men, Frémont and Shields would trap Jackson's army and batter it to pieces.

Frémont, cavalierly disobeying orders, marched on a roundabout route to Strasburg instead of taking the quickest way through Harrisonburg, as instructed. Thus slowed, he just missed catching the Rebel column. Jackson managed to speed his army through a gap in the closing pincers on May 31 and June 1. Unperturbed as always, he then moved on south once more, leaving the Federals in his wake. On June 6 Jackson suffered a grievous loss. About three miles south of Harrisonburg in a clash with Federal troopers, his cavalry chief Turner Ashby was killed, victim of a sharpshooter's bullet.

Shields and Frémont pursued with unusual speed, Shields moving his division up the Luray Valley east of the Massanutten to attempt a surprise attack on the Confederate flank. But Jackson and Ewell were ready. Rounding on the two Federal forces beyond the southern end of the Massanutten, Ewell knocked back Frémont at Cross Keys on June 8 while Jackson the next day defeated Shields in the last battle of the campaign, at Port Republic.

In little more than two months, since the setback at Kernstown, Jackson had fought and won five battles, marched the length of the Shenandoah Valley, twice and, most important, had dislocated the Federal master plan for the taking of Richmond. "The campaign in the Valley was the most exciting in this war," said one Maryland Confederate. "Now it is all over, I look back with pride—and for all the world I would not have missed it."

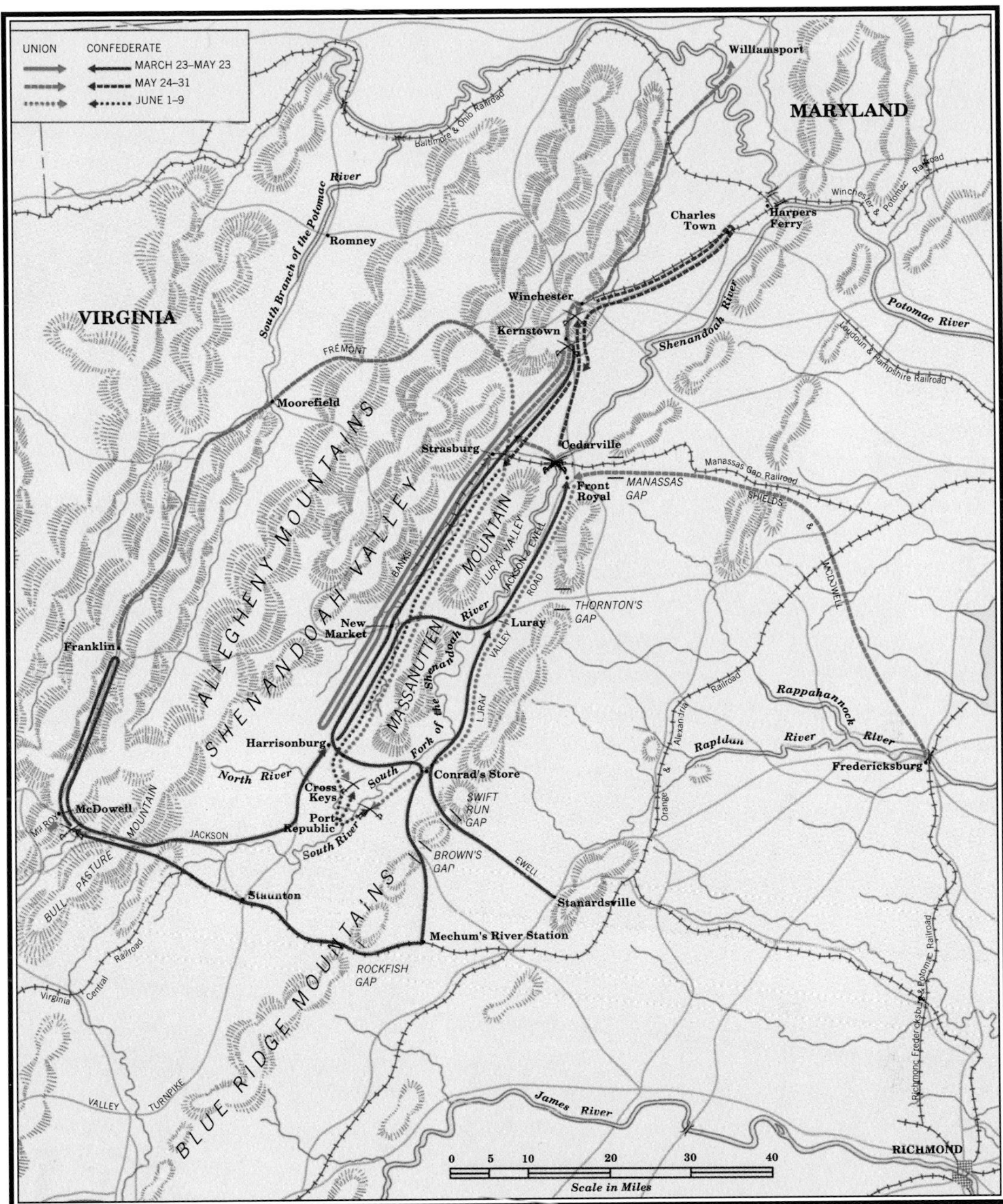

Jackson's campaign to secure the Shenandoah was marked by marching and countermarching up and down its length. After losing the first battle at Kernstown, Jackson took his army on a 100-mile march, falling back to regroup and then heading west to defeat Milroy's Federals at McDowell. Returning, he combined with Ewell's division and marched north to smash Banks at Front Royal and at Winchester. Compelled to withdraw back up the Valley to escape Frémont's and Shields' forces, he turned and defeated them at Cross Keys and Port Republic.

"Vacillation is our name. We cannot take Jackson."

LIEUTENANT COLONEL WILDER DWIGHT

2D MASSACHUSETTS INFANTRY, GORDON'S BRIGADE

Dwight had been detained with his brigade at Berryville while Shields' division fought at Kernstown. Returning to Winchester five hours after the last shot of the battle was fired, Gordon's brigade remained in town for two days, then marched toward Strasburg. Banks slowly advanced four miles south of Strasburg, where Dwight penned his thoughts from camp on March 28.

I have had an opportunity to hear directly from Jackson's camp yesterday. He is a few miles beyond Woodstock. He has no tents, and his wagons carry only subsistence, and are ready to move at a moment's notice. His force is four or five thousand men. He says, "My men have no uniform, they wear multiform." He keeps Ashby in his rear with his cavalry and two pieces of artillery. His game is a winning one even when he loses. With his small force he detains twenty thousand men in this valley. It seems probable that his attack on Winchester was in pursuance of a positive order from Johnson to make the attack at all hazards, to arrest and detain our force from its intended movement to Centreville. In this aspect it was a success. In my judgment our weakness was in turning back. The force left behind was large enough to take care of this valley. But, indeed, it seems as if we had no plan and no courage or decision. Vacillation is our name. We cannot take Jackson. If we mean to hold the valley, we should establish our force in position to do so, take the rest to Centreville, and thus perform our part in the campaign. The life that we have led for the week past is a waste of men and of energy. It quells the spirit of our troops, and destroys the prestige of our leaders. My admiration and sympathy go with the gallant Ashby, and the indefatigable and resolute Jackson. With an equal force, the latter would have beaten us at Winchester. Banks, in his general order, speaks of a *"subtle"* foe, a most unlucky word for a shrewd observer of our movements. As soon as we give him a chance by dividing our forces or exposing a detachment, Jackson may seize the occasion for an attack. While we remain strong in numbers or position, he will do neither, you may be sure.

A former politician, Major General Nathaniel P. Banks became the Union army's fourth-ranking officer—despite his lack of military experience. Although the political influence of the commander of Federal forces in the Valley drew recruits and money for the Union cause, a subordinate officer said, "An operation dependent on plenty of troops, rather than skill in handling them, was the only one which could have success in his hands."

PRIVATE CHARLES W. BOYCE

28TH NEW YORK INFANTRY, DONNELLY'S BRIGADE

After the Battle of Kernstown, five brigades of Banks' corps, including one led by the 28th New York's first commander, Colonel Dudley Donnelly, pursued Jackson toward Staunton. Boyce, a 20-year-old private in the corps' only New York infantry unit, provides a running narrative of events during the last week of March. He was captured at Chancellorsville the following May.

The troops were in motion again early in the morning of the 25th. We passed through Middletown and came within five miles of Strausburg where it was expected the rebels would make a stand, but there was no resistance made to our advances excepting a kind of running, skirmishing fight kept up by a squadron of cavalry under command of Col. Ashby—to cover the retreat of Jackson's main force. We marched into Strausburg and in the afternoon went into camp in the vicinity of the town to wait for the arrival of supplies.

Marched from Strausburg to Woodstock 12 miles. The enemy were known to be in force between these two places, and as a battle was expected, camp and garrison equipage, with all the trains were left behind to wait for further orders. Before noon we passed over the ground on which the enemy had been encamped. Their fires were yet burning. They continued retreating covered as usually by Col Ashby's cavalry. Every bridge in the line of march was destroyed, and every possible hindrance to an advance was placed in our way. Through the day no stream was reached but what was easily forded. So far their efforts to hinder our advances was rendered abortive. We passed through Woodstock. About three miles further up the valley the rebels had set fire to the bridge over Narrow Passage Creek. The bridge was new, and yet in an unfinished state. The timber was green, and not kindling readily, the fire had not damaged it materially, when our advance guard arrived and quickly extinguished the flames—saving this bridge from destruction. A little further on at Edinburg, another bridge, over Stony Creek and old, half decayed, crazy structure was fired and the timber being old and dry the fire communicated rapidly, and when our men arrived it was so far gone that it was impossible to save it. This barred all further progress for the present—at least as the banks were very high and steep and the stream deep and rapid. The whole force went into camp between Woodstock and Edinburg to wait for the construction of a new bridge, and orders were sent back for the trains to come up.

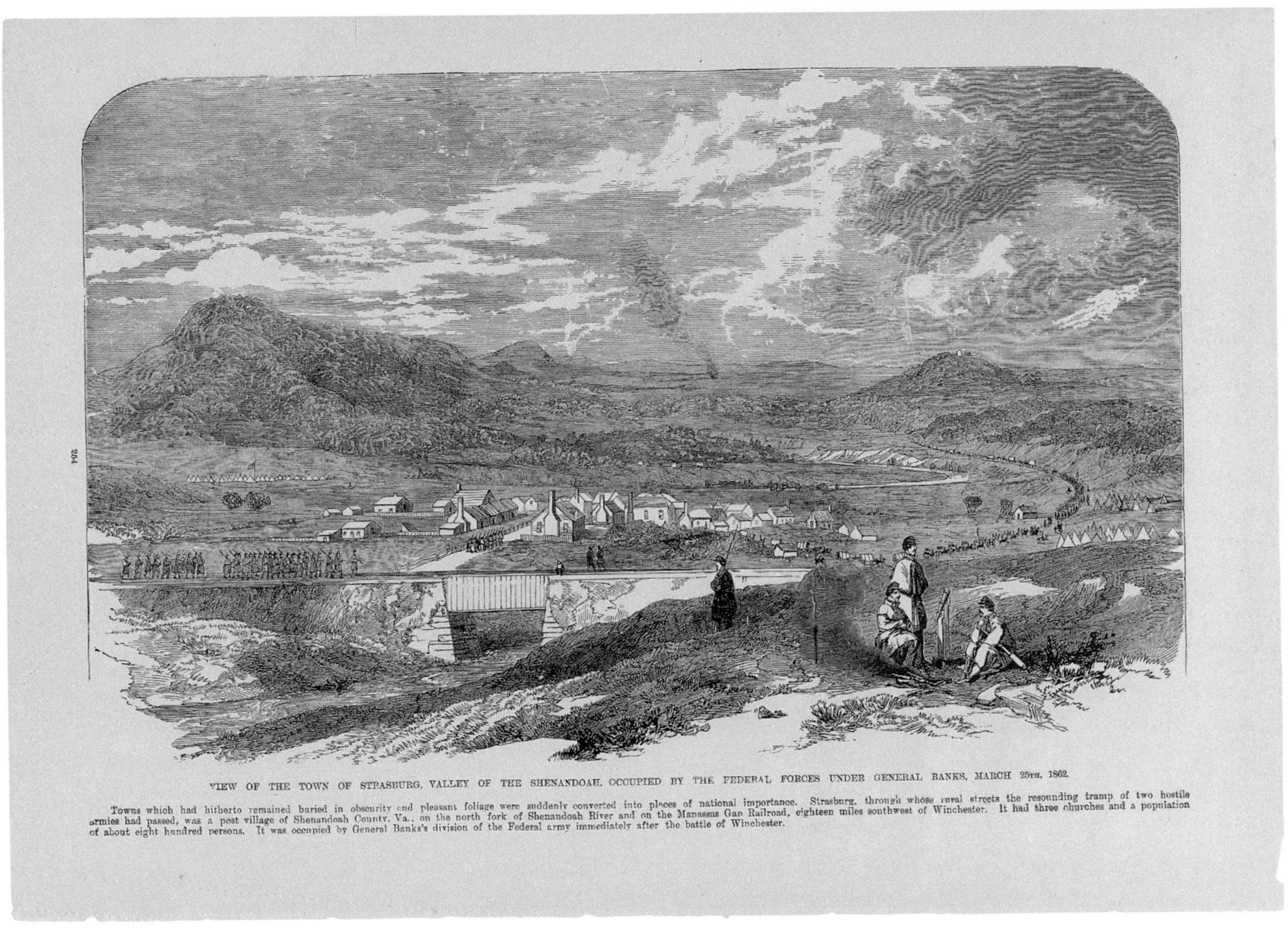
284

VIEW OF THE TOWN OF STRASBURG, VALLEY OF THE SHENANDOAH, OCCUPIED BY THE FEDERAL FORCES UNDER GENERAL BANKS, MARCH 25TH, 1862.

Towns which had hitherto remained buried in obscurity and pleasant foliage were suddenly converted into places of national importance. Strasburg, through whose rural streets the resounding tramp of two hostile armies had passed, was a post village of Shenandoah County, Va., on the north fork of Shenandoah River and on the Manassas Gap Railroad, eighteen miles southwest of Winchester. It had three churches and a population of about eight hundred persons. It was occupied by General Banks's division of the Federal army immediately after the battle of Winchester.

Overlooked by Massanutten Mountain, Federal troops from Banks' V Corps occupy a Manassas Gap railroad bridge and the hills near Strasburg while Union infantry file south in pursuit of Jackson's Confederates. Banks' men controlled the town for much of the spring of 1862.

LIEUTENANT SHEPARD G. PRYOR

12TH GEORGIA INFANTRY, CONNER'S BRIGADE

Pryor spent the war's first winter in Camp Allegheny as a member of Edward Johnson's Army of the Northwest. One month after Pryor wrote this letter to his wife on March 28, Stonewall Jackson brought Johnson's men into his Valley army during his movement to McDowell. Pryor was wounded there and promoted to captain the same day.

In 1896 William Sims wrote to the 28th New York regimental commission, "I will send you my picture [above] that was taken in a snow storm at Woodstock, Va., March, 1862, . . . whilst in camp waiting for the bridge to be repaired, when we were after Stonewall Jackson. . . . I was 30 years old at the time it was taken. My hair was black as a raven, but now as white as wool. Was straight, but now bent over."

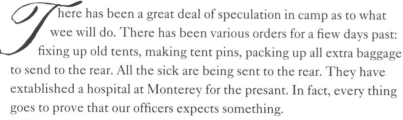

There has been a great deal of speculation in camp as to what wee will do. There has been various orders for a fiew days past: fixing up old tents, making tent pins, packing up all extra baggage to send to the rear. All the sick are being sent to the rear. They have extablished a hospital at Monterey for the presant. In fact, every thing goes to prove that our officers expects something.

From the preparations, I think wee will verry soon evacuate this place and fall back somewhere between here & Staunton. Wee may join Jackson: he is now near Harrisonburg. He had a pretty severe fight over there a fiew days ago, lost some two hundred men killed, wounded & taken prisoners. He was falling back from Winchester, the enemy following him. He stoped & gave them battle. He succeeded in saving all his waggons &co, but I fear got the worst of the fight. He had only five thousand troops, the enemy had eighteen thousand: you see, the odds was too strong against him. These are the reasons I think this brigade will be sent to reinforce him. Then again, it is hardly reasonable that wee should leave this road open from here to Staunton & give them the chance to come around here & get behind us and attack us then front & rear at the same time.

So upon the whole, wee know not what is going to take place [and] neither does our officers: Johnson dont know himself. Our moovement, I think, depends a great deal on Jackson. If he is forced back farther, wee will then be compelled to fall back. I hate suspense & cant know what wee are going to do.

. . . I write you so often that I find it difficult to find anything to write about when I get through with our affairs up here. There is scouts sent out every day or so: if the enemy does anything, wee will be apt to find out before they can do much. I think Gen. Johnson keeps pretty well up with their moovements. He is a stirring old coon, allways on the alert.

The weather here has been verry bad for ten days past, snowing & raining & verry cold [and] disagreeable. It began to moderate yesterday, & today is a beautiful, pleasant day: sun shining. To get on the sun side of the house it is comfortable enough, but I look for more bad weather here yet untwill the first of June. Spring will not open up here on the mountain untwill June. There is parts of Virginia where they have pleasant weather now.

This is one of the last places in the Confederate States & wee cant moove from here too soon to suit me, but I shall expect hard times in our old tents this early in the spring & fear that it will make a great many of our men sick [even] if they are hardened to camp life. [They have] been in those cabins four months now; it will go pretty hard to take it on the ground. That is what I dread most in the service is getting sick in camp. I fear if I was to get bad sick in camp it would kill me.

Our men are standing it verry well now. There is fifty seven in camp now, all well. We have only seventy one in all: I think our company is pretty well drained out now. The balance of them or the most of them will stand it through.

William B. Taliaferro (seated) returned to the Valley to take command of one of Jackson's brigades in mid-April 1862, with a general's commission, for which he had lobbied in Richmond. Taliaferro was no favorite of Stonewall, who had been displeased with Taliaferro's attitude during the Romney campaign. The new general proved an able commander, but Jackson was not one to give up a grudge easily.

LIEUTENANT MCHENRY HOWARD

STAFF, BRIGADIER GENERAL CHARLES S. WINDER

In early April the commands of Jackson's three brigades changed hands. In one controversial move, Jackson had Garnett, the commander of the Stonewall Brigade, arrested and replaced with Winder. Howard, an aide to Winder, vividly recalls his first observations of Jackson and Ashby.

My recollection of Ashby's appearance is not, of course, from my first impression at that time; I saw and was near him very often, sometimes day after day until he was killed two months later. I would describe him as of slender build and somewhat under medium height. His beard, thick and of a very dark brown color, covered the entire lower half of his face, from above the line of the moustache, and was so long as to come to his breast. His eyes were a dark hazel, perhaps some would call them brown, and his complexion also was brown—nothing being light in his appearance but the whites of his eyes. I thought he looked more like an Arab, or the common idea of one, than any man I ever saw. His manner was grave but courteous. Where there were many fine riders, no one was a better or more graceful horseman. Careless of the increased risk, he generally rode a beautiful milk white horse, which was said to be well known to the enemy, and certainly he was very often so close to them as to give them every opportunity of recognizing him.

He presently suggested to General Winder to ride forward and look at the enemy's picket line and we accordingly rode to our outposts a little way in front on the west side of the Turnpike road, and for some time we looked at them, not far off and plainly visible through the thin timber. As we stood there, a small group on horseback, one or more bullets came over to us and I thought it was a needless and foolish exposure. But Ashby paid not the slightest attention to the shots, nor did General Winder, and staff officers had, of course, to simulate a like indifference. I was relieved when we leisurely moved back. General Winder said to Ashby that he would not assume active command of the entire rear unless something occurred to require it, to which Ashby made no reply, but he looked surprised, not being used to receive orders from any except the commanding general.

Presently General Jackson—Stonewall—rode up with part of his staff . . . , and I then saw him for the first time. But I saw him nearly every day after this and was very often close to his side. . . . He was above middle height, compactly and strongly built but with no superfluous flesh. His eyes were a steel blue in color and well opened when he looked straight at one, which he did in addressing a direct remark. His hair was dark brown and the hair on both his head and beard was curly or wavy. The beard was thick and over the lower part of his face but was not long and luxuriant like Ashby's. His nose was well made, perhaps roman in shape, but not prominently large, and his mouth, half seen under the moustache was very firm and the lips usually compressed. The lower part of his face was tanned by exposure, but when his cap was off, the forehead, high and broad, was white. I remember a feature about his face, which I have never seen noticed by others, however, was an unusual fullness of the temples. He wore at this time, if not during the Valley campaign, a dark blue uniform, being, I understood, his dress as a professor and major at the Virginia Military Institute at Lexington. The cap was particularly noticeable, being of the kepi kind, high in make but the upper part not stiff and showing as you faced him the small round top falling over to the front and almost, if not quite, resting on the visor, which was well down over his eyes. He wore high boots, as did nearly all mounted officers.

. . . While very courteous, his words were few and to the point, the voice distinct but rather low and, sometimes at least, a little muffled—but that may be too strong a word—like that of many partially deaf persons; he once told me he was deaf in one ear and could not well tell the direction of sounds. The habitual expression of his face was that of one communing with his own thoughts and others seldom spoke to him without being first addressed. We heard that the colonel of one of the Stonewall regiments had vowed that he would never go to his headquarters again unless sent for, because, on making some remark, Jackson brusquely replied that he had no time to talk on other than military matters. In fact, all the field officers, certainly the colonels, were resenting strongly the arrest of General Garnett—Winder's predecessor—for withdrawing the brigade when out of ammunition at Kernstown on March 23, and I believe the feeling was shared largely by the men. The implicit confidence in and devotion to Jackson came later—after the experiences of the Valley campaign—if not indeed still later.

CAPTAIN JAMES F. HUNTINGTON

Battery H, 1st Ohio Light Artillery

Huntington, an artillerist in Shields' division, faced off against Ashby's men at Stony Creek near Edinburg early in April. It was his second encounter with Ashby, the first occurring in a skirmish the day before Kernstown. Huntington would engage in hotter fights with Jackson's infantry, at Port Republic in June, then at Chancellorsville 11 months later. In both battles he also narrowly escaped capture. Incapacitated by a hernia, Huntington resigned in October 1863.

Ashby's artillerists soon discovered our position and seemed to think they had a chance for a bit of target practice. They daily improved themselves in gunning by pitching shells at us of various descriptions. In return we furnished them specimens of Mr. Shenkle's invention, just then the latest thing out in rifle projectiles. Every morning a fresh regiment of infantry was sent up, as a so-called support. They occupied the wood in our rear in a good place to catch the shots that went over the valley, as many of them did.

One morning the 62d Ohio assumed this duty. The surgeon of the regiment, a very portly gentleman, appeared at my quarters and was anxious to know if I thought the enemy would open on us that day. He really hoped they might, as he had never seen any artillery practice and was longing to do so. The evening before I had posted a section about one hundred yards to the left of our regular position. It happened that when Ashby's battery began to fire the Doctor was looking about on the line of pines. Soon after we began to reply, as I walked towards the detached section, I espied my stout friend prone behind the trunk of a fallen tree, fairly hugging the ground. In reply to my suggestion that he had selected a very poor place from which to observe artillery practice, and had better get from under that log, he muttered something about being a non-combatant, and stayed where he was.

After playing target for a week the battery was withdrawn under cover of the wood in our rear. I call it playing target because our guns were in a fixed position and in plain sight, while Ashby's were concealed behind a crest and moved from place to place. We could only judge of the distance by watching the smoke rising when they fired and timing the flight of the projectile. I imagine we did them about as much harm as they did us, which was just none at all, though we had some very close calls. The immunity was due not so much to want of skill on the part of the enemy's gunners as to the poor quality of their ammunition, as they made good line shots. Their powder was doubtless of uncertain value, a condition fatal to accuracy in firing beyond point-blank range. Their percussion shells very often failed to explode; many of them were so poorly balanced as to come end over end, striking butt first. We built quite a little pyramid of these unexploded projectiles.

The principal damage was sustained by the wrong party. A woman whose husband was serving in Jackson's army, lived in a small house near the river at the foot of our position. One of their shells fell short and passed through the kitchen, incidentally smashing the poor woman's cooking-stove into remarkably small pieces.

The Schenkl shell (above), a 10-pounder rifled missile, was flawed by the tendency of its cotton sabot to swell with moisture and prevent the shell from being loaded—a problem that Huntington would encounter at Port Republic in June.

CORPORAL GEORGE M. NEESE

Chew's (Virginia) Battery

In the first two weeks of April, Jackson's division leisurely withdrew toward Rude's Hill on the road south to Harrisonburg, while Colonel Turner Ashby vigorously contested the Federal pursuit using only his 7th Virginia Cavalry and Chew's three-gun horse battery. On April 17 Ashby, who reveled in feats of bravado, experienced his closest call to date. His gallant but mortally wounded white horse, Tom Telegraph, collapsed underneath him minutes after the encounter that Neese describes here.

April 17—This morning, an hour before day, the same old alarm that has waked us so often in the last month was brought into requisition and sounded in our ears again, "Get up! The Yankees are coming. Pack up and get ready to stand to your guns." This thing of being rear guard of an army and operating on the immediate front of the enemy is a service both active and arduous, full of alarms, hardships, and excitement.

Before daylight we were out on the pike in position, and before sunrise we saw the Yankee skirmish line coming through the fields on our left and their cavalry advancing up the pike at the same time in our immediate front. . . .

The whole Yankee army was advancing, and when they brought their artillery to the front to fire on us, we left and fell back to Rude's Hill, two miles south of Mount Jackson. At the south end of Mount Jackson where the Valley pike crosses Mill Creek our men burnt the bridge, but its destruction offered very little resistance to the progress of the enemy's advance, as the creek is small and there is a very good ford just below the bridge. Consequently, we knew that destroying the bridge would present no serious obstacle to the advancing cavalry, but we thought that it would at least for a while check the column of infantry; but it did not in the least, for I saw the leading regiment of the infantry column march down the hill to the ford in quick time and dashed into the creek and through it without the least hesitation or faltering.

. . . We were on a hill about half a mile from the creek when they crossed, and their infantry was close up with the cavalry, and advancing so determinedly and rapidly that meant business all over, that we did not deem it judicious nor very wholesome to go in position just there and then before a column of cavalry and infantry, backed with batteries of Parrott guns. At the southern base of the hill we were on the turnpike crosses the north fork of the Shenandoah. The bridge was already prepared for destruction. The proper quick inflammable material was all in place ready for the igniting match, but the enemy pressed us so vigorously and dashed so boldly over the bridge that they captured the man who set it on fire and extinguished the kindling flames. When the Yanks rushed impetuously across the bridge like wild men, flushed by the success of its passage, with drawn sabers and firing as they came, our cavalry was rather surprised by the sudden appearance of the enemy in their midst,—as it was a foregone conclusion that the bridge would be destroyed,—consequently our men were incautiously not looking for the unexpected irruption that was so momentously thrust upon them so unceremoniously.

As soon as the front of the column had crossed the bridge the fight commenced in earnest, with saber, pistol and carbine. Our men stubbornly resisted the advancing foe with saber and pistol, and at one time were mixed up with the Yankee cavalry, fighting hilt to hilt. . . .

In the meantime the Yankee cavalry were still coming across the bridge, overwhelming our men in number, who at last succumbed and fled from the field. We were in position with our howitzer on the pike nearly half a mile from the bridge, but did not fire, as our men were mixed up with the Yanks.

When our cavalry began to break away we double-quicked for Rude's Hill, which was a mile away, just about as fast as our horses could travel in an extraordinary emergency. The Yankees were then charging us. When Colonel Ashby galloped past us on his bleeding horse, he called, "Good-by, boys; they will get you this time." I think his remarks were partly intended as an effective incentive to make us run faster, which we surely did. I ran one mile just a little faster than I ever hoofed it before. The Yanks gained on me at first, and I could hear their clattering arms close behind me.

But when Ashby passed us and said, "Good-by, boys," it gave me such an impulse and incitement for running that it really seemed to increase my speed without extra exertion. As we drew near Rude's Hill, which was to us the goal of freedom, the Yanks gave up the chase and we were safe. The Yankee cavalry then retired to the north side of the river, and nothing in the shape of an enemy remained on our side of the river except a few scattering footmen sharpshooters, with long-range rifles, creeping along the fences in derailed chipmunk style, trying to conquer the Southern Confederacy by shooting now and then at a daring careless Rebel.

Captain R. Preston Chew, who turned 19 years old in April 1862, performed admirably under Ashby's command in the Shenandoah Valley, as he did later as a colonel under Generals Jeb Stuart and Wade Hampton. Chew reflected in 1867 that he had "never seen one who possessed the ability to inspire troops under fire with the courage and enthusiasm that Ashby's presence always excited."

MARY GREENHOW LEE

Resident of Winchester

Mrs. Lee and the others living in Winchester—mostly women and children—endured their first month of Union occupation with no promise of Jackson's return. She reveled in making life miserable for the occupying force, proudly citing Secretary of State William H. Seward's "compliment" to the citizens after he visited the town at the end of March: "The men are all in the army and the women are the devil." Mrs. Lee's diary entry of April 17 is marked with both hope and despair.

This day is the anniversary of the secession of dear old Virginia, & here we are, still fighting the battles, which were then inaugurated. If they, the Yankees, continue to make as slow progress in occupying this State, as they have done, taking a year to get as far as Woodstock, in one direction, & to Yorktown in the other, I think they will be bankrupt before they reach Richmond. I forgot to tell yesterday, that our dear old Dr. R. Baldwin was arrested, because he refused to prescribe for the Yankees; I wish I had time to tell you of his conversation with the Provost; your father would be proud of his old friend, though he was one of the last to leave the Union; I could fill volumes were I to tell you all the bold, daring, remarks that the Southern men & women make to these people, who certainly have us very much in their power. . . .

. . . It seems this anniversary has produced another panic, though differing in character from that of last year. Then it was at the departure of our friends—now, at the expected invasion of the most barbarous of our enemies. Mr. Williams has been sounding the tocsin of alarm, about the Germans, who are very near town; it is supposed they will pass through in the morning; their depredations & outrages in Clarke have been dreadful, as their officers say they cannot control them, our *timid* inhabitants are much alarmed; as I do not belong to that class, I give myself no anticipated uneasiness. I shall lock the doors & shut the windows, & trust to the same kind Providence that has protected us heretofore. . . . I went out with Mrs. Barton this morning to look for some supplies, but, as usual, found nothing; starvation is beginning to assume a more real form, than I had ever anticipated. When will our army come back; still I dread that terrible battle. How I wish McClellan would call Bank's division to re-enforce him, at Yorktown. But I must not grumble; I believe our President & Generals know best what is right, & may God prosper their plans, even though we suffer.

HEAD QUARTERS.

Commander of the Post.
Winchester, Va., April 17th, 1862.

Citizens of Winchester:

Upon me has devolved the duty of commanding this Post. My wish and my duty is to afford you all the *liberty* and *protection*, due to *fellow citizens.* The *Government* I represent, is *the same our forefathers established*, to form a more perfect *Union*—provide for the common defence—promote the *general welfare*, and secure to *us and our posterity* the blessings of *Liberty.* We mean truly to represent its Impartial *Justice.*

But no one can expect the privileges of a ***citizen*** and behave as an *enemy.* No one can expect kindness or courtesy who does not extend it to others.

Citizens are reminded that the troops now stationed here are those of *their own Government*, and are *lawfully* here on their *country's soil*—common to all citizens, and that they are here for the *protection* of their fellow citizens—and for the prosecution of their Country's Enemies the "*Rebels.*" Those persons Male or Female engaged in circulating flying rumors and creating false excitements are *particularly warned.*

Our soldiers are to support the ***Rights of all*****, and** were I to permit flying reports and insulting remarks to be made the means of mischief, annoyance, and insult to the service or its servants, they would provoke retaliations and lead to much useless suffering.

I trust, ***Fellow Citizens*****, you will understand and** appreciate the justice of these principles, and by your conduct obviate the necessity for harsh measures.

WM. D. LEWIS, Jr., Col. 110th Reg't. P. V.
Commanding Post.

Members of Captain Charles H. T. Collis' Zouave company are shown relaxing in their camp near Manassas Gap in mid-April 1862. The Zouaves D'Afrique entered the Valley as Banks' headquarters guard, were detached to a command east of the Blue Ridge, and returned to fight as part of Banks' rear guard at Middletown on May 24. Collis' men wore uniforms closest in style to the original French pattern, including the "talma," a hooded overgarment worn by the soldier lying in front.

As provost marshal of Winchester, Colonel William D. Lewis posted this provocative circular (left) warning citizens about possible retaliations for insulting remarks hurled at his regiment, the 110th Pennsylvania. The 110th—which had already set a dubious record for poaching, drinking, and brawling—was ill fitted for the delicate role of guarding an occupied town. Continuous complaints to General Shields soon forced the removal of Lewis and his regiment from provost duty.

PRIVATE JOSEPH F. KAUFFMAN

10TH VIRGINIA INFANTRY, TALIAFERRO'S BRIGADE

In May Jackson marched his men eastward through Brown's Gap and out of the Valley, leaving his troops thinking that they were headed to Richmond. To the soldiers' delight, Jackson ordered his men to board boxcars at Mechum's River Station on May 3 and head westward back into the Valley. Kauffman recorded the first leg of this journey in his diary. He was killed at Brawner's Farm on August 28.

Wednesday (April) 30—We were aroused from our slumbers this morning by the fife and drum beating at 2 o'clock. We left camp at 4 o'clock, and halted in the woods that we were in on the 28th. The whole division came over the river this morning. I still have a pain in my neck. In crossing the river I could see the end of the mountain close to home. I would like to see home once more. "Attention!" shouted our Col. At last every man was up and at his post. Each and everyone was expecting to be off to Harrisonburg, but soldiers are doomed to disappointment, and that was our case this time. We were turned back toward camp, but did not get there. We turned off the Pike at Dr. Jennings' Mill enroute for Port Republic. We traveled about four or five miles from our old camp through mud and rain, and we are soaked to the skin and half starved, and drew 1/2 pound bacon per man for a day's rations. A small quantity for a hungry soldier—with nothing else. A poor part of the country. Still raining and we have no tent.

May 1 (Thursday)—We have just gotten through with our meat. Are waiting for orders to march. I slept soundly last night on a pile of rails. It looks very much like rain this morning. We have just finished our supper—12 o'clock at night. We began our march to Port Republic today. The worst road I ever traveled over. Raining all the time. The mud has no bottom at all. Oh! will it never stop raining. We traveled about 8 or 10 miles today without anything to eat.

Friday 2—It has cleared off this morning and has the appearance of a fine day. We left our camp early this morning and are now lying in the woods. To the left of Port Republic about 1/2 mile, awaiting further orders. Orders came at least. We fell in and began our march and are camped on top of the Blue Ridge at a place called Brown's Gap. I begin to think that Old Jack is a hard master from the way he is putting us thru. We surely see hard times. It is 12 o'clock at night. We had a beautiful day. God knows where we will stop. My feet have given out but still I have to travel on. Oh, how I wish peace would be declared.

CAPTAIN WILLIAM C. OATES

15TH ALABAMA INFANTRY, TRIMBLE'S BRIGADE

A Pike County, Alabama, lawyer and publisher, Captain Oates and his men had milled about for two weeks along the Rapidan River. As Jackson was conducting his march back into the Valley, Ewell's 8,000-man force received orders to cross the Blue Ridge to hold Banks in check while Stonewall set out against General Frémont west of Staunton.

Soon the order came to cross the Blue Ridge; never will I forget that beautiful spring morning. It had rained a little and sleeted a little during the night. The long lines of infantry, four abreast, filled the winding road through Stanard's Gap. On the top of the mountain you could look over the country that lay behind us to the Potomac, and before us lay the beautiful valley of Shenandoah, which in after years the brutal Sheridan boasted that he would make so bare of sustenance that if a crow were to fly across it he would have to take his rations with him to keep from starving; and he came near making his word good in 1864, by the indiscrininate application of the torch to private property. In the midst of that valley the Massanutten Mountain rears his crest into the clouds, and miles and miles beyond the beautiful valley extends to the foot of the Alleghanies. This was the valley in which Stonewall Jackson performed those feats of war which confounded his enemies and astounded the world, and which have been so often justly compared to the archievements of Boneparte in Italy. As the frozen raindrops in icicles hung upon the trees, glistening in the sunbeams as brightly as stalactities, Taylor's Louisiana brigade in the advance, followed by Trimble's, Kirkland in his gay uniform at the head of the Twenty-first North Carolina, Canty following with the Fifteenth Alabama, then Posey and His Mississippians, Mercer and his Georgians, with all the bands playing "Listen to the Mocking-Bird," while Early's brigade brought up the rear, made a scene of unsurpassed granduer.

"On the top of the mountain you could look over the country that lay behind us to the Potomac, and before us lay the beautiful valley of Shenandoah."

Artist and cartographer David English Henderson painted "The Halt of the Stonewall Brigade" depicting General Jackson and his staff taking a break near a watercourse. After a respite to re-form and refit in April, Jackson's men earned their reputation as foot cavalry by completing arduous marches—nearly 340 miles in a 24-day span during May. After brief service in the 2d Virginia, Henderson parlayed his drafting skills to get a lieutenant's commission in the Topographical Engineers.

Bald and bright eyed, Major General Richard S. Ewell reminded many of a bird. The Georgetown native and West Point graduate joined Jackson in the Valley in May 1862. Although Ewell questioned Stonewall's sanity and Jackson took exception to Ewell's profanity, the two earned each other's respect. A leg injury at Brawner's Farm on August 28 took Ewell out of service for a time. Fitted with a wooden limb, Ewell led Jackson's foot cavalry after Stonewall died in May 1863.

CHAPLAIN J. WILLIAM JONES

25TH VIRGINIA INFANTRY, ELZEY'S BRIGADE

Jones passed up a posting as a missionary to China to fight for the Confederacy in 1861. The Baptist minister spent a year in the ranks, earning the nickname the Fighting Parson, before becoming regimental chaplain. As a nephew of General Ewell's chief of staff, Jones observed the general's mounting pique at being left uninformed of Stonewall Jackson's plans. In a memoir, Jones recalled Jackson's legendary reputation for confounding friend as well as foe.

A few days after Ewell's division moved into Swift Run Gap to take the place of Jackson's troops, who were then marching on Milroy, Walker had occasion to call to see Ewell on important business, but found him in such a towering rage that he took the advice of a member of the staff and did not broach his errand to him. But as he was about to leave Ewell called him and abruptly asked: "Colonel Walker, did it ever occur to you that General Jackson is crazy?"

"I don't know, General," was the reply, "We used to call him 'Fool Tom Jackson' at the Virginia Military Institute, but I did not suppose that he is really crazy."

"I tell you sir," rejoined the irate veteran, "he is as crazy as a March hare. He has gone away, I don't know where, and left me here with instructions to stay until he returns. But Banks's whole army is advancing on me, and I have not the most remote idea where to communicate with General Jackson. I tell you, sir, he is crazy, and I will just march my division away from here. I did not mean to have it cut to pieces at the behest of a crazy man." And as Walker rode away he left Ewell pacing the yard of his quarters in no good humor at being thus left in ignorance of the whereabouts and plans of his chief.

Riding down to see General Elzey, who commanded the brigade, Colonel Walker found that officer in an exceedingly irritable frame of mind over an order he had received from General Ewell, and pretty soon he said: "I tell you sir, General Ewell is crazy, and I have a serious notion of marching my brigade back to Gordonsville." Just then one of the conscripts who had been recently assigned to the Thirteenth Virginia (Walker's regiment), bolted in with a paper in his hand and rushing up to General Elzey exclaimed:

"I want you, sir, to sign that paper at once, and give me my discharge. You have no right to keep me here, and I mean to go home."

As soon as General Elzey recovered from his astonishment at the fel-

"We used to call him 'Fool Tom Jackson' at the Virginia Military Institute, but I did not suppose that he is really crazy."

low's impudence, he seized his pistols and discharged two shots at him as the man rushed out of sight. Coming back he exclaimed: "I should like to know, Colonel Walker what sort of men you keep over at that Thirteenth regiment? The idea of the rascal's demanding of me, a Brigadier-General, to sign a paper. Oh! if I could have only gotten hold of my pistols sooner."

"Well," replied Walker, "I don't know what to do myself. I was up to see General Ewell just now, and he said that General Jackson was crazy; I come down to see you, and you say that General Ewell is crazy; and I have not the slightest doubt that my conscript, who ran from you just now, will report it all over camp that General Elzey is crazy; so it seems I have fallen into evil hands, and I reckon the best thing for me to do is to turn the conscripts loose, and march the rest of my regiment back to Richmond." This put General Elzey in a good humor, and they had a hearty laugh over the events of Colonel Walker's visits to division and brigade headquarters.

Somerset County, Maryland, native Arnold Elzey (Jones) dropped his surname in favor of his more distinctive middle name after he graduated from West Point in 1837. After Kirby Smith fell with a neck wound at First Manassas, Colonel Elzey took over his brigade and handled the troops admirably, earning brigadier general's stars the following month. Elzey commanded one of Ewell's brigades in the Valley before suffering an injury at Cross Keys on June 8. Severely wounded at Gaines' Mill one month later, Elzey recovered and later became chief of artillery in the Army of Tennessee.

McDowell

Early on May 7, marching westward from Staunton, Jackson joined forces with General Edward Johnson and pushed into the mountains with characteristic aggressiveness. Jackson's objective: to engage and defeat the Federal troops of General Robert Milroy, who had steadily been pushing back Johnson's Confederates across a succession of steep ridges. Jackson arose before dawn on May 8 and prodded his men briskly all through the spring day. Late that afternoon the armies came to grips at close range on a high ridge above the pastoral village of McDowell. The battle that erupted there raged across the steepest ground Jackson ever fought over in Virginia.

As Jackson approached McDowell, his cartographer, Jedediah Hotchkiss, led him over the hump of Bull Pasture Mountain and onto a spur known as Sitlington's Hill, which reached down to the Bull Pasture River next to the little town. From its dominant position atop Sitlington's Hill, Jackson's artillery could presumably sweep clean the Federal infantry based in the valley around McDowell. But as the Rebels soon discovered, they faced an insurmountable problem: Getting cannon up the craggy slopes of the hill proved impossible. Even foot soldiers struggled to negotiate the narrow, rocky ravine leading up to the plateau that crowned the hill. Furthermore, Confederate infantry was strung out on the narrow Staunton-Parkersburg Turnpike and could only arrive slowly and piecemeal.

After examining his options, Jackson ordered Johnson to spread his regiments around the crest of the hill and sent scouts scurrying in several directions to find practicable routes by which he might attack the enemy flank.

Milroy, meanwhile, knew nothing of Jackson's difficulties. Told by scouts that Rebel guns were heading up Sitlington's Hill, the Federal commander decided that retreat was inevitable. But realizing that the Rebel cannon would maul his retreating columns, he ordered a preemptive assault to pin down the Confederates until nightfall, when the bulk of the Federal forces might get away under cover of darkness.

A little after 4:30 p.m., 2,000 Federal troops crossed the Bull Pasture River on a bridge concealed from view and came charging hard up Sitlington's Hill. And the Battle of McDowell quickly developed into a savage, close-in struggle.

Soldiers defending high ground usually enjoy a tremendous advantage. Sitlington's Hill, however, was so steep that its contours actually proved something of a disadvantage to defenders at the crest. The slope came up so smoothly that Southerners ready to fire at their enemies were obliged to expose a silhouette against the skyline. Particularly vulnerable were the men of the 12th Georgia, positioned at the nose of Jackson's horseshoe-shaped line. The 12th also suffered from enfilade fire because its line, following the lip of the highest ground, projected out toward the Federals.

Supported to their left and rear by the 58th and the 52d Virginia, and to their right and rear by the 44th and the 31st Virginia, the Georgia men bore the brunt of the Federal onslaughts. Captain James G. Rodgers of the 12th wrote, "For three hours did the balls whistle among and around us like so much hail." Rodgers' friend and subordinate, Lieutenant William A. Massey, exulted, "Don't the boys fight nobly!" a moment before a bullet hit his side. "Oh, captain, I am a dead man," he sighed to Rodgers; "send me home to father."

Virginians on the flanks of the horseshoe behind the Georgians came under attack too, but the terrain in their area was more favorable to the defenders. One of them recalled gratefully how, unlike the 12th Georgia's soldiers, they were able to "la[y] low among the rocks and trees, which afforded us ample protection."

Northern soldiers scrambling up the steep slopes—most of them from Ohio regiments—faced a daunting storm of lead. "It was one continual buz of ball past me all the time," one of the Buckeyes wrote home to his mother, "some would go over my head others all round and others plow up the ground at our feet." Most of the attackers hit by musketry suffered wounds to their heads or upper bodies, the result of the steep slope and the Southern angle of fire. The men of the leftmost Federal regiment, the 3d Virginia (U.S.), hailed from the mountains of western Virginia, and many were neighbors of the first Confederate unit they confronted, the 31st Virginia. According to one witness, the Rebels "came close to the 3d, and saluted them, and called them by name, and proceeded with the slaughter."

Stonewall Jackson had little to do with tactical details once the fight opened, leaving "Allegheny" Johnson to manage the battle. That subordinate general was a picturesque leader, notable for the immense ears that he wiggled oddly and for colorful profanity in action. A Virginia soldier of gentler temperament described Allegheny as "a good general and a brave man but one of the wickedest men I ever heard of." When a bullet smashed into his foot at about 8:30, Johnson shouted, "Goddamn that Yankee." Near the time of the general's wounding, Confederate musketry faded as ammunition ran out. Strenuous efforts at resupply kept the line intact, however, and none of the Federals managed to gain a lodgment atop the hill. Darkness finally put an end to the bloodshed.

Nearly 300 Federals had fallen. Jackson lost twice as many men, with the gallant 12th Georgia being the hardest hit regiment. He won control of McDowell, however, and with it the opportunity to press Milroy north toward Franklin.

On May 9 the victorious Stonewall wrote a brief wire report to Richmond. It was typically terse and typically pious: "God blessed our arms with victory at McDowell yesterday." A staff officer riding across Sitlington's Hill saw the temporal cost at first hand in the form of dead and suffering men. "The trees, bushes and twigs are cut all to pieces," he wrote. "The wonder is how any body got off alive." A member of the 31st Virginia estimated that "two acres . . . was almost mowed by the bullets. There was bushes six inches in diameter that was cut by bullets until they fell down."

For the next four days Jackson urged his men onward in Milroy's wake, sometimes through forested byways choked with smoke from burning woods. On May 13 Milroy and Frémont reunited at Franklin. They soon continued northward in joint retreat, thus ensuring the crowning achievement for Jackson: With the enemy's mountain column out of the picture, he could annex Johnson's command, return to the Valley, and join up with Ewell to smash Banks' now outnumbered Federals.

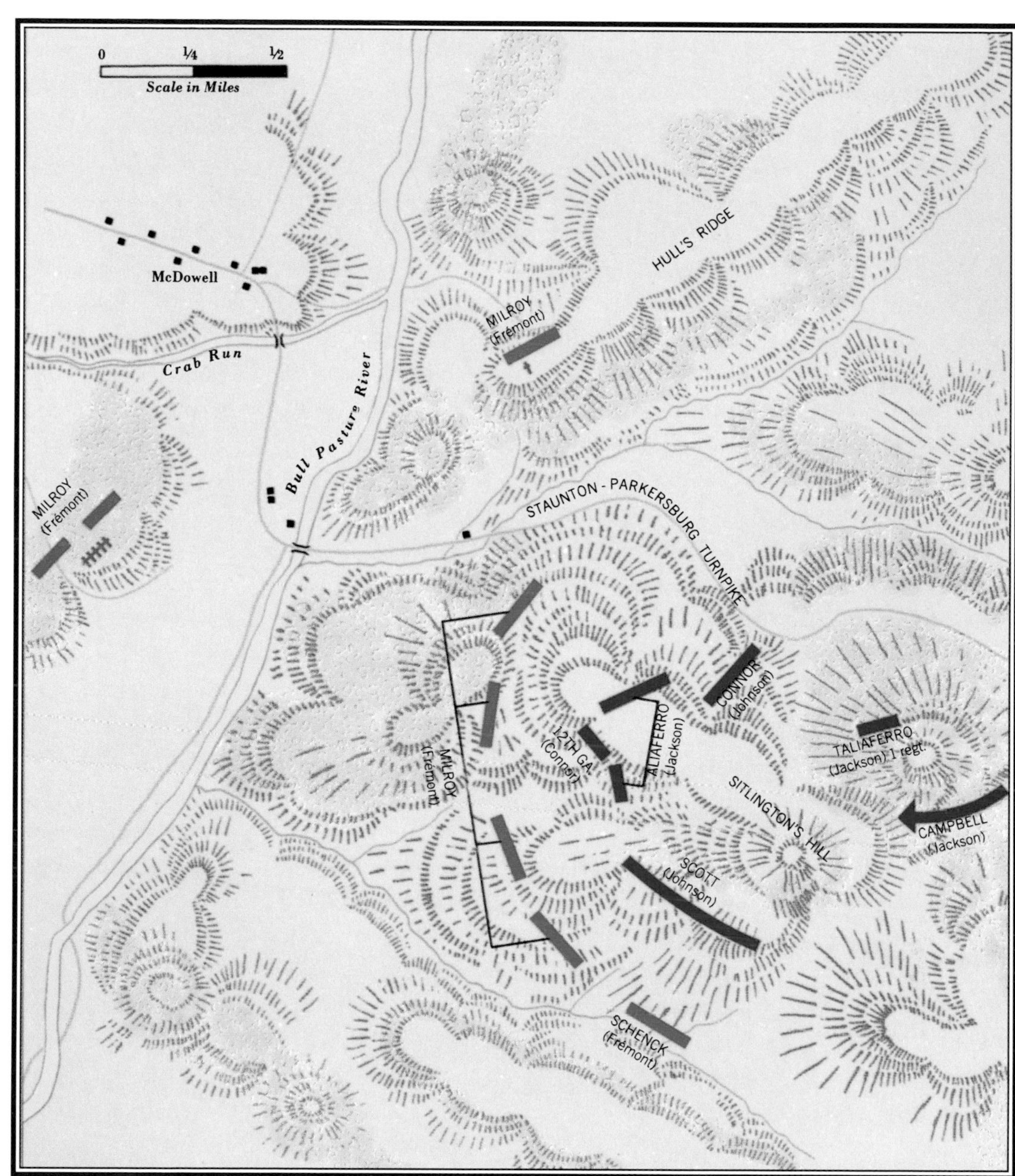

Outnumbered and hotly pursued by the combined forces of Jackson and Edward Johnson, Milroy decided to stage a spoiling attack near the hamlet of McDowell. As the Confederates were filing on to Sitlington's Hill, the Federals attacked, setting off a stand-up firefight that raged until after dark, when Milroy withdrew and fled west.

CADET JOHN OPIE

Virginia Military Institute

Enlisting in the 5th Virginia, 17-year-old Opie was discharged in December 1861 for unruly behavior. Ten days later, Opie entered VMI and in the spring marched toward McDowell with 200 fellow cadets, joining Jackson at Staunton on May 4. The cadets were held in reserve during the battle. Opie left VMI in June and enlisted in the 6th Virginia Cavalry in October. He was wounded at Brandy Station on June 9, 1863, and after the war graduated from the University of Virginia.

When Gen. Edward Johnson occupied Shenandoah Mountain, before the battle of McDowell, a Georgia soldier was placed on the side of the mountain as a vidette. The fellow carried his fiddle with him, and when General Johnson, with two members of his staff, in examining the outposts, walked up to the soldier, he was playing away on his fiddle, with his gun resting against a tree. Johnson, who was very indignant, asked the fellow what in the devil he was. The man, never ceasing his music, replied, "Well, sir I suppose I am a sort of picket. What in the h—— are you?" "Well," said the General, who was a rough, seedy-looking individual, without any insignia of his rank, "I suppose I am a sort of a general." "Well," said the Georgian, "wait till I get my gun and I will give you a sort of a salute."

General Edward "Allegheny" Johnson earned his nom de guerre for holding his position in the mountains of western Virginia in December 1861. Joining Jackson's march to McDowell, Johnson directed the battle for the Confederates until a foot wound forced him to leave the field. His two brigades took the brunt of the casualties in the battle.

CADET BENJAMIN A. COLONNA

Virginia Military Institute

A native of Pungoteague, Virginia, Colonna marched to McDowell as first sergeant of cadet Company D. Although the cadets did not fire a shot in battle in 1862, two years later Colonna, promoted to captain, led his company in a famous tide-turning charge against Franz Sigel's troops at New Market. A civil engineer in Washington after the war, Colonna conducted a topographical survey of the New Market battlefield to help historians interpret the fight.

So the morning passed until a little after sunrise, when we halted at Buffalo Gap near the splendid spring that bursts out about fifty feet below the railroad track. We had covered just what the 21st had covered in the same time thirteen months before, and, of course, I expected to go into camp; but in an hour we were under way again, following the same road we had traveled in 1861. We were taking a short rest now every hour, say twenty minutes, and then resuming our march. In about five hours we came to the very place where we camped in 1861 at the end of our second day out. The log blacksmith's shop that stood on the south side of the road just off a point of woods that was on the north side was there as natural as life. "Now," I thought, "we are about twenty-four miles from Staunton this 8th day of May, 1862, and we will surely go into camp." It was growing monotonous, and, though I did not like to own it, I was getting a little tired of carrying that musket and other toggery. But, no; we were called to attention and soon found ourselves climbing Shenandoah Mountain. The boys were beginning to feel the strain, but none of them so far had fallen by the wayside, though we saw several veterans of the Stonewall Brigade resting by the roadside and looking unhappy. Though I thought it took ages, we finally reached the top of Shenandoah Mountain and to the westward could see the valley of Cow Pasture River. We were now over thirty miles from Staunton, but on we went. It was down grade, and that brought another set of muscles into play, so that we reached Cow Pasture River in better shape. We crossed the river and ascended a hill, where in a pretty little valley near a small rivulet we filed to the left and went into camp along with the brigade. . . . Then we all rolled up in our blankets and went off dozing and dreaming of "the girls we left behind us." It was probably an hour later when the beating of drums all around us called me to my feet. In an instant my clothes were adjusted and I was accoutered to march, for it was the long roll that was sounding. At the last tap of the drum the companies were fallen in and faced to the front. So far as I can remember the cadets were all present, but it was a peaked-looking crowd that faced to the right and took up the march along with the Stonewall Brigade, still to westward. Some of the boys were limping, but, though sore, we were much refreshed by that short rest. The blankets, etc., we were ordered to leave on the ground with the camp guard. The sun was getting low in the west, and I suppose it was about 5 P.M., when we took up the march toward McDowell. We were soon on top of the flat-topped hill that formed the divide between Cow Pasture and Bull Pasture rivers, and could hear continually and distinctly the fire of the infantry and occasionally of a cannon. It seemed to put new life into the boys as we pressed forward, and on reaching the west slope of the hill we heard a band playing; a little later we passed it on the north side of the road. . . . As we progressed the firing gradually ceased; we were halted and a rest ordered, and finally marched back to our camp. I was certainly tired when at about midnight we filed to the right, marched to our bivouac, were given "stack arms," and dismissed. I was about five or six yards from my blankets when I fell to my knees and crawled to my blankets, wrapped them about me and fell asleep.

"It was a peaked-looking crowd that faced to the right and took up the march along with the Stonewall Brigade, still to westward."

LIEUTENANT MCHENRY HOWARD

Staff, Brigadier General Charles S. Winder

Starting from Staunton on May 8, Howard and the Stonewall Brigade conducted an extraordinarily long march to unite with the rest of Jackson's army near McDowell. Arriving too late to take part in the battle, General Winder's staff witnessed the ambulances escorting the wounded to the rear, including the injured General "Allegheny" Johnson. And, along the way, Howard and General Winder encountered a couple of naive young cadets.

Some time in the day we saw along the road two or three cadets of the Virginia Military Institute at Lexington and learned that its corp of students had been ordered out for temporary service and was somewhere ahead. These young stragglers (but I do not apply the term with any sense of reproach,) seemed much exhausted and one of them asked General Winder, "Mister, won't you take me up behind?" and the General helped him up. Presently he asked, "Mister, what cavalry company do you belong to?" "I don't belong to any," the General replied. "Well, to what battery?" "To none." "Well, to what regiment then?" "To none," said the General. "I am General Winder of the Stonewall Brigade." "O, General," said the young fellow, "I beg your pardon, I never would have asked you to take me up if I had known who you were," and he made a motion to slide off. But the General prevented and carried him a long way, the two soon getting into an easy chat. I had taken up another.

This VMI dress uniform coatee belonged to William Gibbons, the younger brother of Colonel Simeon B. Gibbons of the 10th Virginia Infantry, a VMI graduate in 1852. Colonel Gibbons was killed leading his regiment at McDowell, and after the battle his cadet brother escorted the body home to Harrisonburg for burial.

This sketch, drawn by Sergeant Oscar D. Ladley of the 75th Ohio (below), shows the Union camps south of the village of McDowell with the heights occupied by Jackson's troops in the background. The 75th Ohio, charging uphill, suffered 39 casualties in the May 8 fight. Despite Jackson's commanding defensive position, the Confederates suffered twice as many in killed and wounded as the Federals but still won the battle. Ladley, a dry goods clerk from Yellow Springs, Ohio, served for two and one-half more years before leaving the service at the end of his term as a captain.

CAPTAIN JAMES G. RODGERS

12TH GEORGIA INFANTRY, CONNER'S BRIGADE

Fearing that his regiment's sacrifice would go unrecognized, Captain Rodgers wrote his hometown paper in Macon, Georgia, in June to describe the Battle of McDowell. The oldest of nine children, Rodgers participated in 17 engagements, leading the regiment during the Seven Days' Battles. Refusing to leave the field at Antietam after all the fingers were shot off his hand, Rodgers was hit again in the leg and then killed instantly by a bullet to his head.

We got our position on the hill designated, about 4 o'clock in the afternoon, and was ordered to lie down on our arms, to wait the progress of events, but in thirty minutes, the cry was heard, "to arms, the enemy are advancing," instantly every man was on his feet, and his blood bounding with electric speed through his veins, at the speedy prospect of contending with the foe. The 44th Virginia Regiment was on the left flank, and the 25th Virginia on the right flank. The order was given that the 12th Georgia should change its position, and occupy the centre, to which point the enemy was pressing. It was a a small knoll between two large hills, running to a point as it approached the village; it had once been an old field, but had long since been deserted, and had a few shewmake bushes growing on it. We got our position, and sure enough there were the Yankees advancing upon us. Each company, wheeled into position and opened fire and received that of the enemy in return, and then began one of the bloodiest fights of the war, considering the forces actually engaged; the enemy had nine thousand men at three different points, these had been stationed. We had actually engaged, three thousand two hundred, out of which only about five hundred men, viz: the 12th Georgia had through accident, to bear the principal part of the fighting. The members of the Blues fought like tigers, each tried to outvie the other in deeds of valor. We had been fighting about one hour, when poor Sherwood, (than whom a braver and better soldier never lived,) was the first to fall, pierced through the head with a minie ball. The cry immediately went up, "avenge his death," and nobly did they respond to the cry; it was with difficulty, [that I] could keep some of the company from rushing madly at the foe. Next to fall was W. S. C. Rogers. He had nobly done his work, and being much exhausted, he was lying on his side. [I] had just shot his gun for him, and handed it back to be reloaded, when he exclaimed, "Oh, Captain I am shot and dying." I at once examined him, and saw a hole in his coat between the neck and shoulder blade. I told him that perhaps he was only slightly wounded. My attention was then drawn off for about ten minutes, and when I again turned to examine him, he was in the last agonies of death. The next to fall, were the brave uncle and nephew, Joe Wilder and Wm. Hurd, both shot through the head.

Oh, I tell you, it was trying to a Captain's heart to see his brave men being shot down all around him—not enough to kill those brave boys named. [I] had still to suffer in the fall of [my] friend and officer, Lieut. W. A. Massey; for two long hours had he been in the thickest of the fight, cheering by deed and words, the men. He had just said to me—"Don't the boys fight nobly!" and had given a loud cheer to Jeff Davis, when he fell by [my] side, shot through the side; he exclaimed, "Oh, captain, I am a dead man; send me home to father; I am willing to die, for it is a righteous cause." I had him conveyed from the field immediately. He lived about two days, then quietly sank to rest, after continued and repeated assurances of his readiness and willingness to go. Thus died as true a patriot as ever lived—one beloved by all who knew him. But I must again to the battle field, where the fight still rages with increasing energy. For three hours did the balls whistle among and

"The sun went down as though unwilling longer to behold men created in the likeness of God seeking to destroy that life they could not give."

around use like so much hail. During this time four more of our brave men had to be conveyed from the field, badly wounded—Glover, Puckett, Kavanaugh and Bullock freely shed their blood in defence of their country, and long may they live to enjoy the fruits of their valor on that day. The sun went down as though unwilling longer to behold men created in the likeness of God seeking to destroy that life they could not give. The full moon rose in all its beauty to look upon the scene; but still the fight went on.

Lieutenant William A. Massey was one of eight officers of the 12th Georgia who were killed at McDowell. Positioned at the apex of the Confederate center on Sitlington's Hill, the Georgians lost 175 killed and wounded soldiers on May 8, more than twice as many as any other unit on the field. The Georgians "fought like tigers," acknowledged a member of the 31st Virginia.

LIEUTENANT ALFRED E. LEE

82D OHIO INFANTRY, SCHENCK'S BRIGADE

Attacking the center of the Confederate line, the 82d Ohio suffered 57 casualties. Lee, who began the war as a private, was promoted to captain five months after the battle. As a member of the XI Corps in 1863, Lee was present with the 82d to suffer the humiliation of having their flank rolled up by Jackson's corps at Chancellorsville. Two months later at Gettysburg Captain Lee was shot in the right hip. He recovered and finished the war.

To get at our antagonists it was necessary to descend to the bottom of this valley, and climb the heights on its opposite side. Colonel Cantwell, therefore, started his men on the "double-quick" down the mountain, himself leading them on foot. The entire movement had to be executed in full view of the enemy, and it quickly brought us within range of his musketry. With a great shout the regiment rushed down to the turnpike, reaching which, the men scarcely stopped to take breath, before they began clambering up the steep slope of Bull Pasture Mountain.

And now the crash of their Enfields began to resound through the gorge! And, in spite of all the battles which have since intervened, how the bang of those muskets reverberates even yet in the living ears that heard them! The enemy's bullets, fired down the mountains, flew over us in myriads, but were not heeded. The Confederate fire seemed only to add to the exhilaration and *elan* of our charge. Up through the slanting meadows went the blue lines, with colors flying and Enfields crashing! No flinching! forward! Some soldiers fall, and lie motionless upon the grass, but there is no time to pay any attention to that! On the right the Twenty-fifth, Seventy-fifth and Thirty-second Ohio come upon in splendid style, their muskets crashing too! Up, still up go the steady lines, until they arrive within short range of the Confederates. The action is so violent all along the front that Jackson hurries up his reserves.

This 1880s image, taken facing west from Bull Pasture Mountain, offers a view of the McDowell battlefield. Sitlington's Hill (center), the spur on which most of the battle was waged, blocks the view of the lowland area where the village of McDowell lies. The rugged terrain hampered troop deployment, particularly the placement of artillery on the steep heights. Although he won the field, Jackson suffered more losses than his opponent for the second straight battle.

Our men want to go at the enemy with the bayonet, and some of them even make a rush for that purpose, but are called back. It is not deemed prudent to advance the line farther against such superior odds, but the fight goes on unabated until the sun sets, and darkness hides the combatants from each other.

Happening to look to the rear, I saw some men lying on the grass. My first impression was that they had lain down to avoid being hit. But they were motionless. The truth flashed over me—they were dead! I had scarcely noticed, before, that anybody had been hurt, except that a bullet had struck the musket of a man next me, and glancing had wounded him in the wrist.

As darkness came on the firing slackened, and at length ceased. The troops were then recalled. The wounded had all been carried to the rear, but there lay the dead, and it seemed too bad to leave them behind. So two of us picked up one of the bodies, and endeavored to bear it away with the retreating line. But we had not realized until then how fatigued we were! The slain soldier was a young German, who had received a bullet full in the forehead. We laid him down gently by the stump of a tree, with his face upturned to the moonlight, and there we left him. A few minutes later I found myself trying to quench, in a muddy pool at the turnpike, the fever and thirst begotten of the extraordinary exertion and excitement.

Promoted captain one month before he fought at the Battle of McDowell, William Scofield saw three years of service with the 82d Ohio, first in the Alleghenies, and later as part of the XI Corps, Army of the Potomac. When the 82d Ohio transferred to the Army of the Cumberland, Scofield became the provost marshal of Joseph Hooker's XX Corps. After participating in Sherman's capture of Atlanta, Scofield was mustered out in October 1864.

PRIVATE GEORGE W. SPONAUGLE

25th Virginia Infantry, Conner's Brigade

One month after he enlisted at the age of 16, Sponaugle fought at McDowell when the 25th Virginia entered the engagement on the Confederate right. Afterward, Sponaugle deserted his unit, then reenlisted with the 62d Virginia Mounted Infantry. He took up residence in the new state of West Virginia after the war, working as a carpenter. Shortly after his 81st birthday, Sponaugle provided his hometown paper with an account of his first battle.

We were on a hill and had to shoot down at the Yankees, and there was a tendency to overshoot them, while they had us between them and the sky-line and we made a good mark. The timber had been cut down in front of us. This made it harder for them to get up to us, but at the same time it afforded them shelter. There was a long log lay about fifty yards away from us, paralled with our lines, and they were thick behind this log. They were about all killed, too, shot through the head, when their heads would appear above the log.

The first one of our men wounded was Balser Pullin, of Highland county. He was shot in the mouth or face. I did not mind it much though, once I was into it. I was a mighty good shot with a gun, as I had used one ever since I had been big enough to carry one. I fired 23 rounds, and some of them were fired at mighty close range. Every time I saw a head I shot at it. They were concealed by the timber, and it was not long until the hill was wrapped in powder smoke, like a thick fog, and it was hard to see them. I expect I came as near killing some of them as the next one, but it is better that one does not know for certain. It does not weigh so hard on one's mind. . . .

O, yes, there were a lot of my company killed and wounded. I can remember some of them. Charles Dyer, our first lieutenant, was killed instantly, I saw him fall. His brother, Streit Dyer, was shot in the mouth, but he got well. Isaach Hartman, a brother of the late Jesse Hartman, was shot through the body, and died the next day. Jacob Rexrode, a son of Harman Rexrode, was killed, as was also Michael Skiles. Abel Wimer, cook of our mess, was wounded in the hand and side. George W. Smith had his shoulder cap knocked off by a cannon ball. Jehu Johnson was wounded. . . . I wish I could remember all their names, but it has been so long, lots of things have escaped my mind.

This first-pattern national flag, the Stars and Bars, was carried by Company A of the 25th Virginia. Initially held in reserve, the regiment was ordered to take position on Sitlington's Hill in midafternoon. The Virginians tallied 76 casualties in their short action, second only to the luckless 12th Georgia for losses on the field.

CAPTAIN THEODORE F. LANG

3D VIRGINIA (U.S.) INFANTRY, MILROY'S BRIGADE

Participating in their largest engagement to date, the Union 3d Virginia first faced off against the Rebel 31st Virginia along the Staunton Turnpike. One company from the Confederate regiment and three companies from the Federal regiment hailed from Stonewall Jackson's boyhood home of Clarksburg. Seeing some of their prewar neighbors, the 31st members saluted their Federal counterparts, called them by name, and then opened fire upon them.

The enemy were protected by a natural position on top of the mountain, while the 3d West Virginia regiment was partly in an open field and partly (say one company) in a wood, our whole front not being over 100 yards from the enemy. The fight in our front was peculiar in this, that the enemy fired by regiment, and in this order: when they were ready to fire, they would advance quickly to the top of the mountain, exposing just enough of their persons to enable them to discharge their guns; when the volley would be fired, they would as quickly retire from view. In that manner the 3d West Virginia regiment was engaged with at least two, perhaps three, regiments of the foe.

This must have been so, for the time that would elapse between volleys was not sufficient to enable one regiment to reload. But our own boys soon got the hang of it, and awaited each time the coming of the exposure; our men loaded and fired at will.

As we were in an open field, without breast-works or other protection, we must have suffered greatly but for the fact of the haste with which the enemy fired. The leaden hail went mostly over our heads, and that part (the left) of the regiment referred to as being in the wood, verified this assertion by their appearance when they left the field after the battle, for their caps and shoulders were covered with the bark and buds and twigs of the trees.

Called brave and reliable by one of his peers, Robert Milroy recalled his men only after they had depleted their ammunition. "My boys were anxious to hang on and send for more," Milroy explained to his wife on May 13, "but I deemed it prudent in their exhausted condition to withdraw them down to camp." Milroy's active field service ended with a defeat at the hands of Richard Ewell's corps at the second Battle of Winchester in June 1863.

SERGEANT WATKINS KEARNS

27TH VIRGINIA INFANTRY, WINDER'S BRIGADE

A member of the Shriver Grays recruited from Wheeling, Virginia, Sergeant Kearns and the rest of the Stonewall Brigade arrived too late to take part in the fight at McDowell. But he was there in time to witness some of the sadness and horror of a battle's aftermath. Kearns could not move with his regiment the following morning, "being so much in need of sleep that I can scarcely stand."

A great many wounded are coming down the mountain. Col. [Gibbons] of the 10th Va is killed. Gen. Ed Johnston is slightly wounded. We pass many a wounded man who asks us to hurry on. It is late in the night when we arrive at the scene of action. The moon is partially obscured by clouds and casts a pale and sickly glow upon the field as though its purity [is] offended by these dreadful scenes. Gen. Jackson is here—cold—collected—impenetrable—saying but little—watchful—thoughtful. The firing has altogether ceased and far below in the plain beyond McDowell shine the camp fires on the enemy. We watch them for some time but at last . . . the body compels us to lie down on the cold grass and endeavor to sleep. Waken up cold and stricken as with an ague fit and march back to Shaw Fork to cook. Soldiers are bearing their wounded comrades off the field by the light of torches and here & there the dark outlines of a form "covered" with a blanket mark where one of our brave boys sleeps the unchanging sleep of death. It is a melancholy and never-to-be-forgotten spectacle.

As the 12th Georgia pulled back from its exposed position, Colonel Simeon B. Gibbons (right) was ordered to bring up his 10th Virginia. Brandishing his sword (below), Gibbons marched his men to the front and secured the ground given up by the Georgians. A captain in the 12th Georgia recalled that Gibbons' advance "was one of the handsomest affairs that I witnessed during the war." Gibbons was shot and killed on Sitlington's Hill before night enveloped the field.

"Soon after being shot I was seized with the most intense craving for water I had ever felt. It seemed as though my insides were burning out."

PRIVATE MARTIN W. BRETT

12TH GEORGIA INFANTRY, CONNER'S BRIGADE

A farmer from Dooly County, Georgia, Brett boarded a train in May 1861 and traveled to an instruction camp around Richmond. One month later he was on his way to the mountains of western Virginia, where his regiment spent the first year of the war. Brett avoided the frostbite that afflicted many of his comrades at Camp Allegheny during the winter, but he did not escape the casualty list at McDowell. His wound took him out of the ranks for 10 weeks.

About nightfall, I received my first wound by a minie ball through the left arm. It was a new experience to me. Soon after being shot I was seized with the most intense craving for water I had ever felt. It seemed as though my insides were burning out. I stood several minutes watching other men fall near me. I heard others calling for water. I did so too, but there was no one to supply our wants. I watched the blood spout freely from my arm. Very soon the gray mountain rocks turned green. The mountains seemed to spin around in the air like a boy's toy top. My desire for water overcame all pain caused by the wound, and I staggered back about fifty paces to a little branch we had fought over about an hour before. The water was cool and refreshing and I drank my fill.

A doctor who was working among the wounded found me there and applied a wad of raw cotton to my arm where the ball had entered and also one where it passed out, and bound it up very tight to stop the bleeding. I had no other attention or advice then, and did not know that it was proper to keep the bandage wet. It soon got thoroughly dry, and I suffered untold misery until the next day, when the doctor came and gave me temporary relief. I was then, with many other wounded men, sent on to the hospital at Staunton, and while there suffering from my wound I came near losing the arm. The doctors in charge said that in order to save my life it was absolutely necessary to amputate, and actually had me on the table for operation. I fought against it in every way I possibly could. If I had consented, they would have cut it off.

CAPTAIN HARRY GILMOR

12TH VIRGINIA CAVALRY

Born into an upper-class family near Baltimore, Gilmor lived briefly in Wisconsin and Nebraska before returning to Maryland to train in a militia company at the outbreak of hostilities. Joining Ashby's command on August 31, 1861, Gilmor was commissioned captain of Company F of the new 12th Virginia Cavalry in March and fought in that regiment for the rest of Jackson's Valley campaign. The 24-year-old cavalryman relates an incident from May 11, 1862.

On the Sunday morning after the battle of McDowell, while the whole of the Stonewall brigade were deployed on the front as skirmishers, General Jackson's adjutant, Robert L. Dabney, preached a sermon, surrounded by the army. The place selected was an open bottom, well up to the front, for every shot could be heard distinctly, and occasionally a stray bullet would come whizzing by. Mr. Dabney stood on the ground uncovered; General Jackson a few paces in front, resting on one foot, with his hat off, shading his face from the sun. I watched him closely, and saw not a muscle change during the whole service. The sturdy soldiers, browned in many a hard-fought field, were lying around on bunches of hay, taken from the stacks near by; and although an incessant skirmish fire was going on, all listened attentively, with every eye fastened upon the great chief. Few have I ever seen with such unflinching nerve, and it was his iron will that won for us many a stubborn fight. While sitting near him the day previous, with my company in rear to act as couriers, a shell came crashing through the trees, and cut asunder a large white oak within a few feet of the general. It fell, but fortunately it fell *from* him, otherwise he must have been crushed to death.

"My gracious! general," I exclaimed, "you have made a narrow escape."

He was then a little hard of hearing; and thinking he had not heard me, I repeated, "You have had a narrow escape, sir."

"Ah! you think so, sir—you think so." And, turning toward my men, "You had better shelter them in a ravine near by," but did not move himself until he was called to another part of the field. Fear had no lodgment in that man's breast.

I do not think Jackson intended pursuing them any farther; for, while our advance was skirmishing at very close quarters, the whole army was falling back to McDowell, and next morning our cavalry alone were left. The enemy, thinking us still advancing, were drawn up in line of battle, and continued shelling the mountains on all sides during the whole day. All the time my company were burning the wooded ridges in the vicinity, to make them believe there was a large force of infantry encamped near.

By Telegraph
from
McDowells May 9th
via Staunton Va. 10th

Mrs T. J. Jackson
Care James B Irvin

Yesterday God crowned
our arms with success
The enemy is retreating
T J Jackson

11 Collect 200

Giving credit to the Almighty, Jackson informed his wife of his victory at McDowell. Jackson's success on May 8 was a rare bright spot for the Confederacy in the first five months of 1862.

Jackson carried this Presbyterian prayer book throughout the Shenandoah Valley campaign. The Reverend Robert Graham, who quartered the Jacksons in Winchester, maintained that Stonewall's "simple, earnest, Scriptural faith in God" formed and strengthened his character.

PRIVATE EPHRAIM HUTCHISON

82D OHIO INFANTRY, SCHENCK'S BRIGADE

A farmer from Marion, Ohio, Hutchison left behind a wife and infant son to fight for the Union in December 1861. Over the next 19 months, Hutchison experienced bloodbaths at Manassas, Chancellorsville, and Gettysburg—battles in which his regiment lost heavily. Hutchison first fought at McDowell, where six of his comrades were killed and 50 others were wounded. Writing to a neighbor on May 21, Hutchison graphically describes the casualties in the 82d Ohio.

I had the pleasure of giveing old John C *Fremont* a smile the other day. he visited our hospital, the Doctors were not present at his call, I showed him the wounded Soilders in my ward, he examined every man[,] he viewed them with a look of sorrow, but urged them not to be disheartened but keep their spirits revived, he is a plain looking and plain spoken man, he looks like a man that had stradled the Rocky Mountains and scratched into the gravel of California's Cliffs, he is somewhat swarthy, of course, caused by his constant exposure[.] he has a keen eye not a large man, I think he would have moved toward Staunton before now if he had transports[.] The force he brought with him have wanted for provision[,] as they did not have teams enough to bring provision with them. . . .

Gen Fremont will not leave this place untill he has his troops well suplied for and enough to take them through a march, there is some probability of us staying here several days yet. . . .

The[y] generaly overshot us[,] their officers could be heard commanding their men to fire low, but our wounded and killed were generaly shot in the head, about the breast and in the arms[.] Many of the boys had their guns shot to pieces[.] A ball would strike the stalk and shitter it, driveing the splinters into their hands and faces, they would pick up another gun that would be handy by and go to work as usual. 5 or 6 of our regiment were killed[,] 5 certain as it is supposed the 6 might [have] been taken prisiner. Two of our comp. were killed, Christ Solce from our place and George Watson of Marion, 13 or 14 were wounded[,] some of them very seriously[.] both of our Lieutenants—were dangerously wounded[.] The first[,] G. H. Berry was shot across the head about 2 1/2 or 3 inches above the eare[,] the ball entered the skull bone and came out about 3 inches from where it entered, The wound was cut open the other day and several pieces of fractured skull taken out[;] pieces nearly as large as [a] dime, his brain can eaisily be seen[.] I can almost put a hen egg into his head, he . . . is entirely blind [and] crazy, he is a little better today but I am afraid he will never recover. The 2nd Liut. was shot in the neck[.] Charles Diebold[,] the ball missed the large artery in his neck about 1/8 of an inch, the ball entered his chest[.] The Drs could not extricate it as they could get an ins[t]riment to reach it, he is doing very well but I am afraid it will eventualy kill him.

One young man of our Comp. will die tonight, The ball entered his shoulder and passed through his left lung and was taken out close to the backbone just below the ribs, he has suffered a great deal[;] he is know bleeding at both wounds. Three have died from wounds received at that fight of our regiment and more will die.

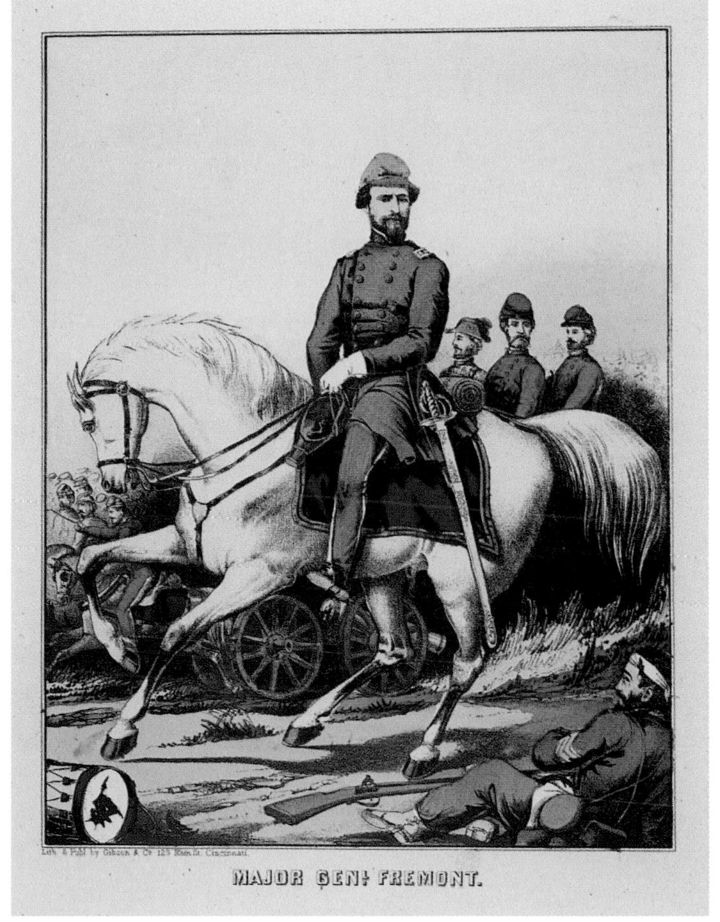

John C. Frémont fell well short of expectations as commander of the Federal Mountain Department. Frémont's vacillation allowed the Confederates to push Milroy's men all the way back to Franklin and remove any threat to the Valley from the west for nearly a month.

BRIGADIER GENERAL RICHARD TAYLOR

BRIGADE COMMANDER, EWELL'S DIVISION

Taylor brought the largest brigade of Confederates into the Valley. His Louisianans played a key role in the culminating phase of Jackson's Valley campaign. Stonewall's practice of marching 50 minutes and resting 10 minutes was adopted from Taylor's efficient marching style.

"Every man seemed to think he was on a chessboard and Jackson played us to suit his purpose."

At nightfall of the second day in this camp, an order came from General Jackson to join him at Newmarket, twenty odd miles north; and it was stated that my division commander, Ewell, had been apprised of the order. Our position was near a pike leading south of west to Harrisonburg, whence, to gain Newmarket, the great Valley pike ran due north. . . . That night a pioneer party was sent forward to light fires and repair the road for artillery and trains. Early dawn saw us in motion, with lovely weather, a fairish road, and men in high health and spirits.

Later in the day a mounted officer was dispatched to report our approach and select a camp, which proved to be beyond Jackson's forces, then lying in the fields on both sides of the pike. Over three thousand strong, neat in fresh clothing of gray with white gaiters, bands playing at the head of their regiments, not a straggler, but every man in his place, stepping jauntily as on parade, though it had marched twenty miles and more, in open column with arms at "right shoulder shift," and rays of the declining sun flaming on polished bayonets, the brigade moved down the broad, smooth pike, and wheeled on to its camping ground. Jackson's men, by thousands, had gathered on either side of the road to see us pass. Indeed, it was a martial sight, and no man with a spark of sacred fire in his heart but would have striven hard to prove worthy of such a command.

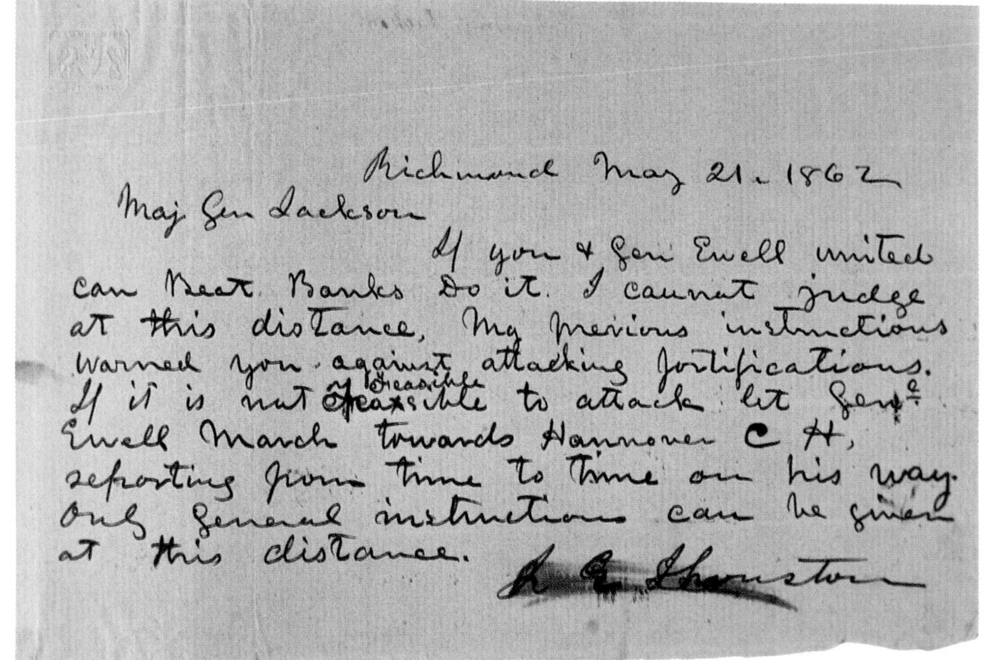

Richmond May 21. 1862

Maj Gen Jackson

If you & Gen Ewell united can beat Banks do it. I cannot judge at this distance. My previous instructions warned you against attacking fortifications. If it is not ~~feasible~~ feasible to attack let Genl Ewell march towards Hannover C H, reporting from time to time on his way. Only general instructions can be given at this distance.

J. E. Johnston

General Joseph Johnston's telegram to Stonewall Jackson allowed him full discretion to attack Banks in the north end of the Valley. One day earlier Jackson had learned that General Ewell's division had been ordered to join Johnston at Richmond. Jackson suspended the order and subsequently received Johnston's endorsement.

SERGEANT SAMUEL D. BUCK

13TH VIRGINIA INFANTRY, ELZEY'S BRIGADE

One of eight children born to a wealthy Warren County farmer, Sam Buck was a clerk in a Winchester dry goods store in 1861 when the war induced him to join the "Winchester Boomerangs," a company incorporated into the 13th Virginia Infantry. He was promoted captain of Company H in March 1864 and survived the war with four bullet wounds in 35 engagements.

While all this was going on, we were much puzzled as to our destination. One hour we were on our way to Richmond and the next back to New Market and to further mystify us we were ordered into camp on top of the mountain and were impressed with the idea of a long rest. Men were paid off and there was every indication of a long stay and as suddenly all changed again and we were faced to New Market where we stood waiting for orders. When they came we were again faced about and started in the opposite direction and at full speed until at the foot of the mountain on the east side we came to forks of the road, one pike leading to Luray and the other to Madison Court House. Jackson seemed determined to take both of these roads, went a short distance on Luray route, then faced us about and started back to New Market and the next thing we knew was off in the direction of Richmond via. Madison Court House. We kept on to the river where we crossed and here again orders were changed and we started in the direction of Luray. At this juncture we ceased to speculate and every man seemed to think he was on a chessboard and Jackson played us to suit his purpose. The enemy was in the dark as much as we were, they surely could not tell at what point to expect Jackson and this is just what proved to be the case for they were surprised at every point.

MAJOR GENERAL NATHANIEL P. BANKS

COMMANDER, DEPARTMENT OF THE SHENANDOAH

Initially commanding two divisions with more than 20,000 men, Banks lost his only experienced troops on May 12 when Shields' division departed eastward to join McDowell near Fredericksburg. On the same day that Jackson's 17,000 troops advanced to within striking distance, an uninformed Banks, whose 10 infantry regiments were strung out over the northern Valley, wired a message to Washington.

Strasburg, Va., May 22, 1862.

Sir: The return of the rebel forces of General Jackson to the valley, after his forced march against Generals Milroy and Schenck, increases my anxiety for the safety of the position I occupy and that of the troops under my command. That he has returned there can be no doubt. We have information direct from the people of the neighborhood, from prisoners that we have captured from him, from deserters, and also from General Frémont, who telegraphs his march in this direction.

From all the information I can gather . . . I am compelled to believe that he meditates attack here. I regard it as certain that he will move north as far as New Market, a position which commands the mountain gap and the roads into the Department of the Rappahannock and enables him also to co-operate with General Ewell, who is still at Swift Run Gap. . . .

We are preparing defenses as rapidly as possible, but with the best aid of this character my force is insufficient to meet the enemy in such strength as he will certainly come, if he attacks us at all, and our situation certainly invites attack in the strongest manner. . . .

. . . At present our danger is imminent at both the line of the road and the position of Strasburg. Our line is greatly extended; the positions and property to be protected of vital importance, and the enemy is in our immediate neighborhood in very great superiority of numbers.

To these important considerations ought to be added the persistent adherence of Jackson to the defense of the valley and his well-known power. This may be assumed as certain. There is probably no one more fixed and determined purpose in the whole circle of the enemy's plans. Upon anything like equal ground his purposes will be defeated.

I have forborne until the last moment to make this representation, well knowing how injurious to the public service unfounded alarms become, but in this case the probabilities of danger are so great, that it should be assumed as positive and preparation made to meet it.

Front Royal and Winchester

Returning to the Valley after driving back Frémont, Jackson, by May 20, had established temporary headquarters just south of New Market. With Shields' division on its way to Fredericksburg, the Rebel commander was more determined than ever to bedevil the remainder of Nathaniel Banks' army, most of which was camped and digging in around Strasburg. About noon on May 21, Jackson got his foot cavalry moving again after a short rest. Most of Jackson's men probably expected to march north down the pike, in the direction of Banks' main force. But Jackson signaled a right turn at New Market and his troops headed east across Massanutten Mountain. By nightfall his lead elements had reached the village of Luray, with the army now headed toward Front Royal.

Behind the maneuvering lay a plan: At Front Royal was an unsuspecting contingent of Banks' army, a 1,100-man detachment under Colonel John R. Kenly. Jackson aimed to swallow this force whole and outflank Banks at Strasburg. This time the odds were well in his favor—in addition to Ewell's troops, Jackson had commandeered the two brigades of Johnson's Army of the Northwest. Stonewall outnumbered Kenly by more than 15 to 1.

At sunrise on May 23, Jackson sent Ashby and some of his troopers across the South Fork of the Shenandoah to cut the Manassas Gap Railroad at Buckton. Then, shortly after 2:00 p.m., he launched his infantry against the enemy garrison at Front Royal. Spearheaded by Rebel Marylanders and Louisiana Tigers, the Valley army swept through the town, brushing back Kenly's Union troops.

On Richardson's Hill outside Front Royal, however, the Federals stopped retreating and turned to fight. For more than an hour Kenly and his men stood firm. But when he noticed in the distance that Confederate cavalrymen were headed for the bridges across the South and North Forks—the only means of escape for his men—he gave orders to abandon the hill and race for the spans.

The Federals won the dash, but narrowly, and tried to make it difficult for the enemy pursuers. Yankee riflemen had the range of all three bridges, but their cannon could not be brought to bear on the South Fork railroad bridge. Colonel Henry B. Kelly and his men of the 8th Louisiana headed over that span, pick-

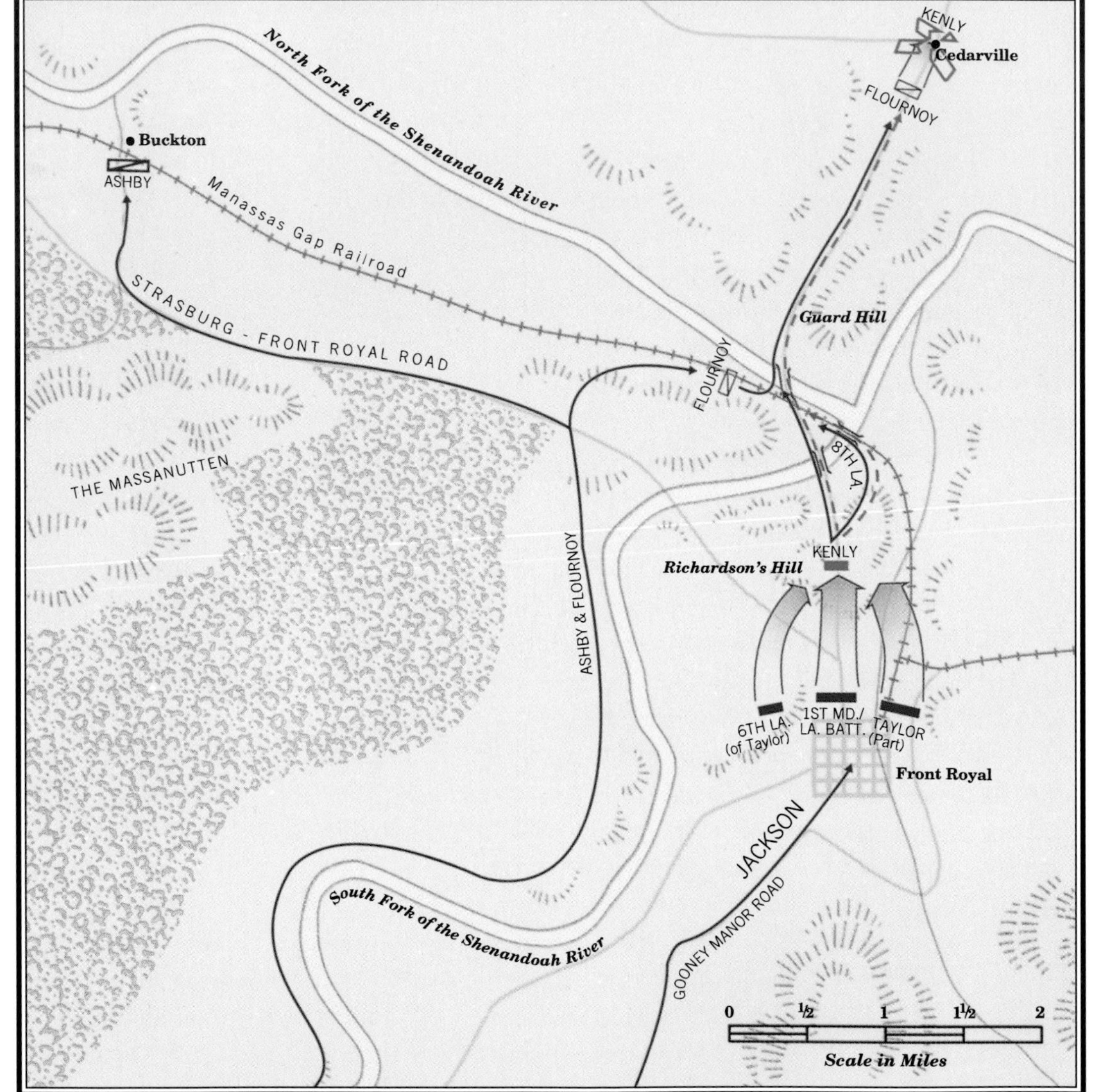

ing their way across the ties. The bridge over the North Fork, already set ablaze by Kenly's men, lay directly under the muzzles of Federal cannon and muskets on Guard Hill. Kelly decided to ford rather than face that deadly hail head-on. He plunged into the river, which was "wide, waist-deep and rapid," and his men followed. When they reached the far side, they found that the Yankees had already resumed their retreat, so Kelly's men turned to saving the vital span. Men braved the flames to throw blazing timbers into the river, some of them burning their hands and others falling through. Jackson rode across the bridge into their midst and kept going, urging on his men.

The fleeing Federals had outdistanced Jackson's infantry but were still within artillery range. The problem was that Jackson had no artillery. Because of faulty communications and crowded march routes, his longer range guns were only now making their way to the front. Just as the Confederate commander's hopes were sinking, he caught sight of the cavalry—about 250 troopers of the 6th Virginia Cavalry under the command of Lieutenant Colonel Thomas Flournoy. At Jackson's order, Flournoy's horsemen crossed the charred bridge and galloped off in headlong pursuit.

The Rebel cavalry caught up with Kenly's infantrymen and forced them to halt and deploy for a stand at Cedarville, about three miles north of Front Royal. Aligning themselves around an old stone house, the Federals awaited their pursuers. With the unflagging élan of early-war troopers, the Confederate horsemen formed up and galloped madly toward Kenly's Marylanders—and drove them away in wild

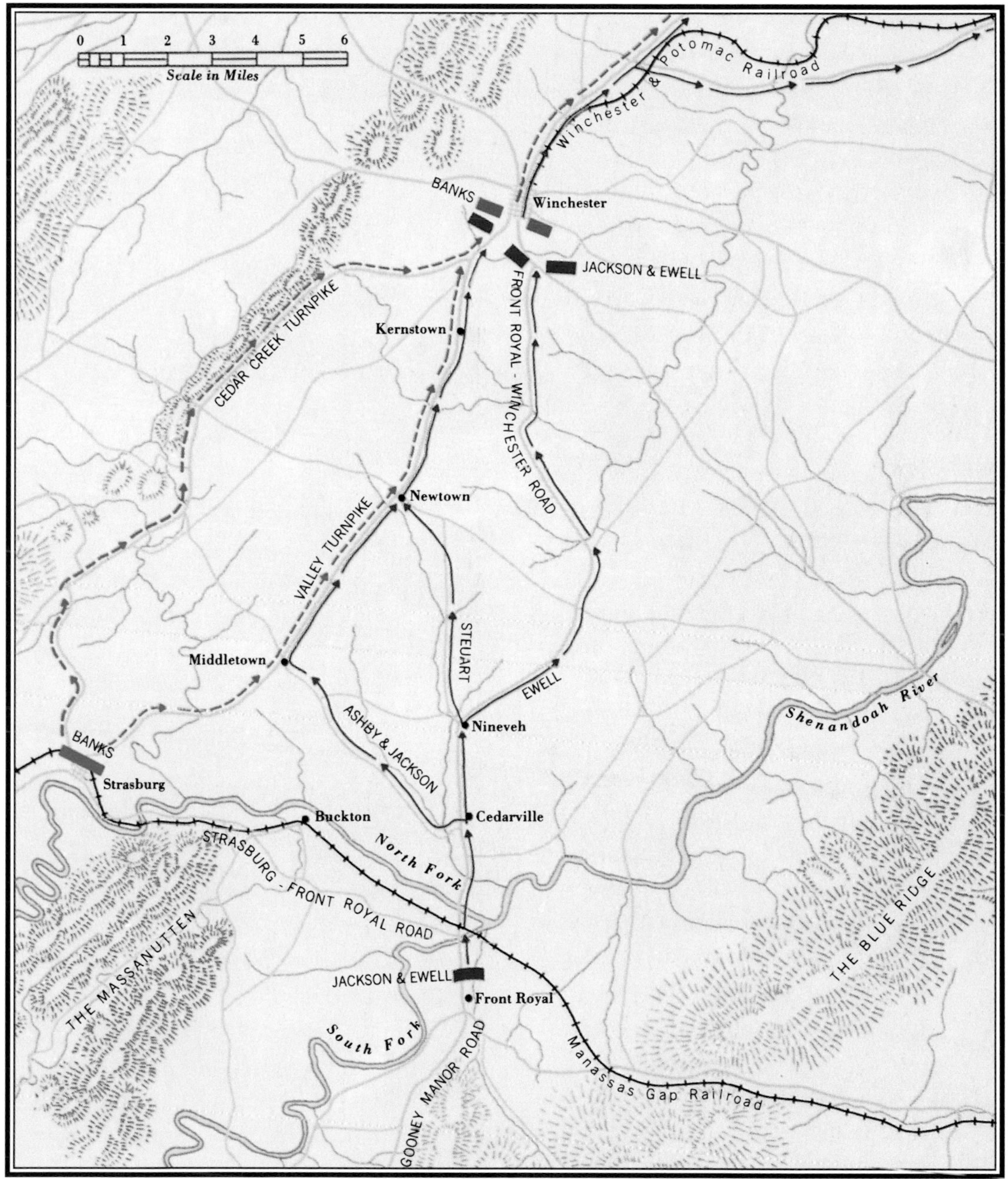

Outflanking Banks' main body at Strasburg, Jackson launched a surprise attack on the Federal garrison at Front Royal (left) on May 23. After a brief running battle, the Rebels routed the defenders and secured the bridges over both forks of the Shenandoah River.

The news from Front Royal spurred Banks into action. By the morning of the 24th, he had his army moving north toward Winchester. Jackson raced after the Federals, striking the retreating column at several points, but the bulk of Banks' front-line units escaped.

disorder. The leading company of the 6th lost 10 men killed, including the colorbearer, 18-year-old Dallas Brown, hit by some 20 bullets. But it was the Federals who took the beating at Front Royal and Cedarville. Kenly, who was badly wounded, lost 904 men, of whom 750 were captured. Jackson's casualties numbered only 35 men.

With Front Royal in hand, Jackson now pondered the options available to the enemy at Strasburg. Most likely Banks would try to escape, but how? Jackson guessed that Banks would either make a run for Winchester, or if Jackson abandoned Front Royal in his own dash for Winchester, Banks would slip behind him and pass through Front Royal on his way to refuge across the Blue Ridge.

As it happened, Banks ran for Winchester. Jackson found out on May 24 when he sent a cavalry detachment from Cedarville to Newtown on the Valley Turnpike, where the Confederates smashed into Banks' fleeing column with devastating impact. The Southerners captured hundreds of prisoners and scores of booty-laden wagons before they retired.

But that blow only struck the tail of Banks' column. Most of the Federal infantry and artillery was racing unimpeded up the Valley Turnpike toward Winchester. It was too late to trap Banks; now Jackson had to follow his enemy and bring him to bay. In pursuit, Jackson divided his forces, taking one column across to Middletown and then north toward Winchester, while Richard Ewell led his command up the Front Royal-Winchester road by way of Nineveh. The night of May 24-25 dragged endlessly for exhausted men following the inexhaustible Stonewall, driven by his iron determination. Despite the bounty snatched from the retreating Yankees, veterans of years of bitter warfare remembered this night as their worst. Sleepless for days, now asleep on their feet, soldiers tottered forward. Finally Samuel Fulkerson, Jackson's favorite colonel, prevailed on the general to halt briefly. While weary men collapsed, Jackson and Turner Ashby personally served as a two-man picket post on the turnpike.

After a short respite, the Confederates pressed forward again through a dawn shrouded in heavy mist. To the west, Jackson's column deployed for battle. Southeast of Winchester, Ewell groped blindly into the outskirts

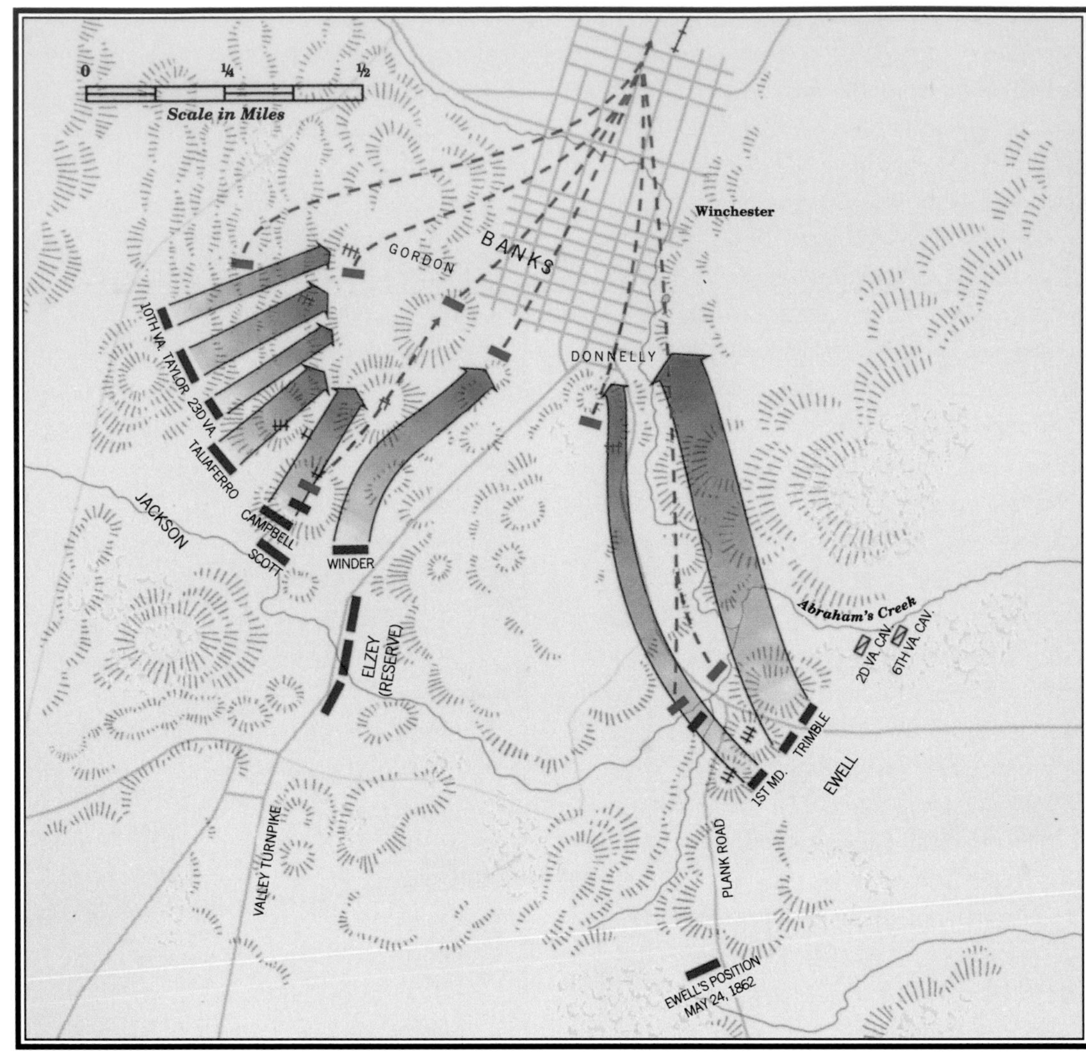

By dawn on May 25, Banks had his forces drawn up in a loose defensive line around the southern approaches to Winchester. After an ill-conceived attack by part of Trimble's brigade was repulsed, Jackson ordered Winder forward, supported by Campbell's brigade, but heavy Federal fire forced them to go to ground. The climax came when Taylor's Louisiana Brigade surged ahead to crumple the Union right. Within minutes Banks' entire line gave way, sending the Yankees in panic back through the streets of Winchester.

of town but received a nasty surprise when the 21st North Carolina was badly shot up by Colonel Dudley Donnelly's Federal brigade.

Banks' men had gone to ground in a series of ridges that loomed above Abraham's Creek south and southwest of Winchester. Confederate scouts reported that the nearest ridge seemed only lightly defended, which Stonewall confirmed himself by riding out to take a look. Jackson aligned three brigades of Virginians parallel to the enemy-held hills, then turned to Charles Winder, commander of the Stonewall Brigade. He pointed to a ridge commanding the turnpike and ordered Winder to take it.

Winder's troops moved up the hill quickly and against scant opposition. But when they reached the crest, they were almost immediately pinned down by a storm of artillery and musket fire pouring in from a second ridge that anchored Banks' line on the southwest corner of Winchester. When Winder asked for help, Jackson sent for General Richard Taylor's Louisiana Brigade. As the rowdy, hard-fighting men from the deepest South formed their lines, the brigade came under galling artillery fire, which prompted an outburst of cursing from Taylor. Jackson shot him a look of reproach for the intemperate language and said to him gently, "I am afraid you are a wicked fellow." Then he prudently rode away.

The Louisianans started across the field for the hill on the Federal right flank, slowly at first and then with a surge. Colonel Gordon saw a daunting sight over the top of the ridge : "Preceded by swarms of skirmishers, regiment after regiment of the enemy were moving in good order steadily but rapidly up the hill." General Alpheus S. Williams could see Southerners extending beyond his extreme right in "overwhelming force," preceded by so much lead that "the air seemed literally to be full of whizzing bullets."

Supported by the Rockbridge Artillery, and under heavy enemy fire, the Louisiana troops charged up the hill. Across the pike, Ewell's men were outflanking the extreme left of the Federal line. Everywhere Confederates moved forward. The Federal line bent under the weight of the attack, then broke.

A woman who lived on lower ground beyond the Union hilltop watched it happen: "I could see . . . the hill side covered with . . . a long line of blue forms lying down just behind its crest. . . . Suddenly I saw a long even line of grey caps above the crest of the hill, then appeared the grey forms that wore them, with the battle flag floating over their heads!" The Federal line, she wrote joyously, soon turned into "a confused mob of trembling, fainting objects."

The blue-clad soldiers fled, racing through the streets of Winchester. Southern cavalrymen gathered up many hundreds of prisoners as they chased the Federals northward. Banks himself tried to stem the rout, to no avail. The demoralized Union troops fled for 35 miles, not pausing until they crossed the Potomac into Williamsport, Maryland.

Stonewall Jackson had won Winchester, routed Banks, and threatened Washington. His casualties on this triumphant day totaled fewer than 400. Banks lost more than 3,000 at Front Royal and Winchester. For most of the residents of Winchester, May 25 was the brightest day of the long and dreary war. Cornelia Peake McDonald saw her neighbors "shouting for joy . . . and exultation at the discomfiture of the flying enemy. All were embracing the precious privilege of saying what they chose, singing or shouting what they chose," after weeks under enemy rule.

The impact of Jackson's victory reverberated far beyond the Valley. He had achieved a major strategic goal. When President Lincoln heard of the Confederate capture of Front Royal—even before the victory at Winchester—he sent a wire to General George McClellan near Richmond: "In consequence of General Banks' critical position I have been compelled to suspend General McDowell's movements to join you." The Valley army had kept the Federal forces divided and stymied the Union advance on the Confederate capital.

Despite this stunning success, however, Jackson's stay in the northern end of the Valley proved to be a short one. After taking a couple of days to rest, regroup, and sort out all the prisoners and booty, the Rebels pushed north to Harpers Ferry. There Jackson had not yet finished his deployment for an attack on the enemy garrison when reports started coming in of other Federal columns marching toward the Valley. Lincoln had not only suspended McDowell's reinforcement of McClellan, he had also ordered Shields' division and Frémont's command to converge on the Confederate force, coming at it from both east and west. Jackson dismissed the first reports of these movements that reached him early on May 29, but by the 30th there was little doubt that the Federals were closing in, Frémont heading for Strasburg and Shields for Front Royal. The trap was closing fast.

Jackson got his brigades moving south toward Winchester that afternoon—none too soon. Before the day was over word came that Shields had retaken Front Royal. For the next two days there was no rest for the foot cavalry as they pressed up the Valley Pike to escape the Yankee noose. Around midday on June 1 the last of the Valley army, except for a few hundred stragglers, passed through Strasburg, just hours ahead of Frémont. Jackson had thwarted his enemy's best chance to bag him, and within days he would give battle again.

BRIGADIER GENERAL RICHARD TAYLOR

Brigade Commander, Ewell's Division

A Kentucky native, Richard Taylor became a sugarcane planter and one of the wealthiest men in Louisiana after graduating from Yale in 1845. He began the war as colonel of the 9th Louisiana Infantry and was quickly promoted to command the celebrated Louisiana brigade. After distinguished service in the Valley campaign he returned home to command the District of West Louisiana and brilliantly defended his state from Federal invasion.

Off the next morning, my command still in advance, and Jackson riding with me. The road led north between the east bank of the river and the western base of the Blue Ridge. Rain had fallen and softened it, so as to delay the wagon trains in rear. Past midday we reached a wood extending from the mountain to the river, when a mounted officer from the rear called Jackson's attention, who rode back with him. A moment later, there rushed out of the wood to meet us a young, rather well-looking woman, afterward widely known as Belle Boyd. Breathless with speed and agitation, some time elapsed before she found her voice. Then, with much volubility, she said we were near Front Royal, beyond the wood; that the town was filled with Federals, whose camp was on the west side of the river, where they had guns in position to cover the wagon bridge, but none bearing on the railway bridge below the former; that they believed Jackson to be west of Massanutten, near Harrisonburg; that General Banks, the Federal commander, was at Winchester, twenty miles northwest of Front Royal, where he was slowly concentrating his widely scattered forces to meet Jackson's advance, which was expected some days later. All this she told with the precision of a staff officer making a report, and it was true to the letter. . . .

Convinced of the correctness of the woman's statements, I hurried forward at "a double," hoping to surprise the enemy's idlers in the town, or swarm over the wagon bridge with them and secure it. Doubtless this was rash, but I felt immensely "cocky" about my brigade, and believed that it would prove equal to any demand. Before we had cleared the wood Jackson came galloping from the rear, followed by

FRONT ROYAL, VIRGINIA, LOOKING SOUTH.—Sketched by C. L. B.—[See Page 411.]

This engraving from the June 28, 1862, edition of Harper's Weekly shows the town of Front Royal nestled at the foot of the Luray Valley near the confluence of the North and South Forks of the Shenandoah River. Visible just beyond the camp in the foreground is a train steaming eastward on the Manassas Gap Railroad. An unwary and badly outnumbered Federal force of 1,000 men was guarding Front Royal when Jackson attacked on May 23.

a company of horse. He ordered me to deploy my leading regiment as skirmishers on both sides of the road and continue the advance, then passed on. We speedily came in sight of Front Royal, but the enemy had taken the alarm, and his men were scurrying over the bridge to their camp, where troops could be seen forming. . . .

Under instructions, my brigade was drawn up in line, a little retired from the river, but overlooking it—the Federals and their guns in full view. So far, not a shot had been fired. I rode down to the river's brink to get a better look at the enemy through a field-glass, when my horse, heated by the march, stepped into the water to drink. Instantly a brisk fire was opened on me, bullets striking all around and raising a little shower-bath. Like many a foolish fellow, I found it easier to get into than out of a difficulty. I had not yet led my command into action, and, remembering that one must "strut" one's little part to the best advantage, sat my horse with all the composure I could muster. A provident camel, on the eve of a desert journey, would not have laid in a greater supply of water than did my thoughtless beast. At last he raised his head, looked placidly around, turned, and walked up the bank.

Having shot a Federal soldier dead in 1861 for insulting her mother, 18-year-old Belle Boyd gave further rein to her fierce patriotism by becoming a spy, charming information out of naive Yankees. On May 23 she braved skirmishers' bullets to reach Taylor's men with vital intelligence. She later was twice captured and escaped both times, finally fleeing to England.

COLONEL BRADLEY T. JOHNSON

1ST MARYLAND (C.S.) INFANTRY, STEUART'S BRIGADE

Johnson was forced to deal with insubordination in his regiment on May 23; scores of men refused to obey orders on the grounds that their terms of service had expired. With a speech that one of the men rated "the most effective eloquence to which it has been my fortune to listen," Johnson reinvigorated his ranks for the Front Royal fight.

The army was then within an easy march of Front Royal, where Banks had stationed a force to protect his flank. The next morning, the 23d, the march was begun, the First Maryland in the worst possible condition—one-half under arrest for mutiny, the rest disgusted with the service, and the colonel disgusted with them. A halt was made for rest about five miles from Front Royal, and during it an aide brought this order: "Colonel Johnson will move the First Maryland to the front and attack the enemy at Front Royal. The army will halt until you pass. JACKSON." The colonel turned on his regiment: "You have heard this personal order from General Jackson and you are in a pretty condition to obey it. You are the sole hope of Maryland. You carry with you her honor and her pride. Shame on you—shame on you. I shall return this order to General Jackson with the endorsement, 'The First Maryland refuses to face the enemy,' for I will not trust the honor of the glorious old State to discontented, dissatisfied men. I won't lead men who have no heart. Every man who is discontented must fall out of ranks—step to the rear and march with the guard. If I can get ten good men, I'll take the Maryland colors with them and will stand for home and honor; but never again call yourselves Marylanders! No Marylander ever threw down his arms and deserted his colors in the presence of the enemy—and those arms and those colors given you by a woman! Go!" This appeal settled it. The men in ranks cheered and yelled, "Forward, we'll show you!" The men under guard pleaded with tears to be allowed to

return to duty, ran back miles to the wagons, got their guns and rejoined their regiment by the time it attacked at Front Royal. The Marylanders marched forward, rejuvenated, reinvigorated, restored! The army halted. As they went by they could hear time and again, "There they go. Look at the 'game cocks.' " The Louisiana brigade, Gen. Dick Taylor, came to a front and presented arms. The Marylanders trod on air, for no men are so susceptible to praise or enjoy flattery more.

Clear of the column, they debouched from the wooded road into the open, where there was a long stretch of fields between them and the village of Front Royal. A squad of cavalry charged down the road. Captain Nicholas and Company G were deployed as skirmishers on each side of it. A mile distant, by the side of a fence was a blanket stretched from two fence rails as a shelter. A man got up, looked at the strange sight coming out of the woods, sheltered his eyes from the sun, then made a grab for his musket, but before he could fire, the cavalry was on him, and that picket was gobbled up. There were three men on post, but they did not have time to give the alarm. A cavalry man, with cocked carbine, trotted them to the rear. General Ewell, General Steuart and Colonel Johnson were riding at the head of the column.

Colonel John Kenly (inset) commanded the 1st Maryland (U.S.) at Front Royal. Caught unprepared, Kenly fell back fighting, but in the end he was severely wounded and his regiment overwhelmed, losing nearly 600 men—most of whom were captured. The Confederates climaxed their victory by seizing Kenly's flag (above).

"What regiment do you belong to?" was the colonel's eager inquiry. "First Maryland," was the response of the Dutchman. "There's the First Maryland," cried the Confederate, pointing behind. Great Heavens! was such good fortune ever given to a soldier? The Federal First Maryland had been recruited under the gallant Kenly, but it was largely composed of foreigners, and the Marylanders had always refused to recognize it as representing their State. They were the only simon-pure, genuine Marylanders, and if ever they got a chance they would show them! Here was the chance. As the news flew back through the ranks, shoulders were straightened, chests thrown out, and every man thanked God he was a Marylander and was there!

LUCY R. BUCK

RESIDENT OF FRONT ROYAL

The eldest daughter of a prominent Front Royal merchant, 19-year-old Lucy Buck (above, left, with her sister Nellie) kept a detailed diary beginning Christmas Day 1861 and continuing until her death in 1918. Watching from her family home of Bel Air, a stately house situated on high ground just outside of Front Royal, she and her sister bore witness to the action on May 23 and enjoyed a poignant reunion with a cousin serving in Ashby's cavalry.

Going to the door we saw the Yankees scampering over the meadow below our house and were at a loss how to account for such evident excitement on their part until presently Miss B. White rushed in with purple face and dishevelled hair crying—"Oh my God! The Southern army is upon them—the hill above town is black with our boys! Julia Ann, give me water or I shall die!" Of course, Ma and I did not wait to see the result of her case, but started for home in double quick time, all the time hearing the firing exchanged more and more rapidly. Found all excitement upon reaching the house—all the family upstairs at the windows. Nellie, spyglass in hand clapping her hands exclaiming—"Oh!—there they are! I see our dear brave fellows just in the edge of the woods on the hill over the town! There they are, bless them!" I looked in the same direction and saw surely enough some of our cavalry emerge from the little skirt of woods above the courthouse. As long as I live, I think I cannot forget that sight, the first glimpse caught of a grey figure upon horseback seemingly in command, until then I could not believe our deliverers had really come, but seeing was believing and I could only sink on my knees with my face in my hands and sob for joy. Presently someone called out "Only see!—The Yankees run!" Leaning out the back window we saw them, contrabands and Yankees together, tearing wildly by. One obese Dutchman as he ran through the yard sans arms heard cheering from the window likening his speed to the Bull Run race—he looked most malignantly at us over his shoulder, but had not time to give vent to his feelings in words. There had been quick random firing all this time, and now, those of the Yankees who did not run at the first alarm, rallied and formed into line, some climbing into the dome of the courthouse, some into the upper hospital windows, firing from these and making some feint of resistance.

By this time some scattered parties of Confederate infantry came up and charged their ranks, when firing one volley they wheeled about—every man for himself they scampered out of town like a flock of sheep—such an undignified exodus was never witnessed before. . . . However, when they reached the hill north of town—opposite to where our men were entering the place, they halted and drew up in line in support of a battery that had been planted there. We all stood on the upper porch and waved and cheered our dear Rebels, who were by this time pouring in eagerly from every direction. The larger body came down the Manor Grade, others down the Chester's Gap road, and others on the F. R. and Luray Turnpike, while there were yet others who eschewed all the regular roads and flocked through the fields and across the hills without regard to order or uniformity. Captain Alexander's company now dashed by the house, returning our salutations and cheering manfully. Two of them, who proved to be dear Walter and the captain himself, cantered up to the door to inquire which way the Yankees had gone. We had been all the afternoon vainly trying to obtain a glimpse of Walter and now that he was really among us, his own cheerful, confident self, we were almost beside ourselves with joy. The children caught and kissed his hand as if he had been a host of deliverers in himself. He turned to Nellie, who stood sobbing near him and exclaimed in his joyous way—"Why Nellie, child! Crying? Cheer up! Now is the time to be laughing. Jackson's army is coming and we're going to drive the Yankees away from you!"

Lieutenant William Walter Buck of the 7th Virginia Cavalry, whose home lay three miles south of Front Royal, scouted Union positions before the Rebel attack. A year later Buck joked that he wanted a wound so he could go home and see his family. Charging a stone fence at Upperville, Buck received his wound, but it was fatal.

PRIVATE WILLIAM A. MCCLENDON

15TH ALABAMA INFANTRY, TRIMBLE'S BRIGADE

A 17-year-old participating in his first battle at Front Royal, McClendon developed a bad case of nerves, recalled later in his memoirs, wryly subtitled How I Got In, and How I Got Out. In time he got over the worst of his jitters, rose to lieutenant, and surrendered at Appomattox. On one occasion McClendon tried to stop a wounded comrade's bleeding by placing his canteen stopper in the bullet hole.

A desultory skirmish was kept up for about one hour, when the Louisiana Tigers came to the front and was deployed as skirmishers and advanced to assist our Cavalry. Now look out boys, something is going to drop! the Tigers are in front and you will hear something directly. They had not advanced far before the firing became to be pretty heavy for the number of troops engaged. The Yankees offered a stubborn resistance in order that our strength might be developed. Our company was in line with the regiment standing in the road while the firing was going on. We were expecting every moment to be ordered to the front. While in this position Courtney's Battery of our brigade came dashing by and soon opened upon the Yankees with shot and shell. The firing increased to such an extent to cause us to believe that reinforcements were being pushed in by both sides, occasionally a wounded Tiger would pass, bloody and powder blackened, muttering something that I could not understand. All of these things created such suspense that it caused a chill to pervade my system to the extent of causing my knees and teeth to knock together as though I had an old fashioned shaking ague. The hair on my head seemed to rise and was sorter like the quills of a fretful porcupine, and I had some trouble in keeping my cap pressed down. I looked around to see if any one else was in my condition, and I soon found it to be a pretty general complaint among the boys. The complaint was not confined exclusively to the privates. Some of the officers were similarly affected. The countenance had undergone a change, the natural expression of the eye had banished and it looked to me as though each fellow was trying to conceal his condition and keep it unobserved by the other fellow. It was funny for me to think about afterward.

Major C. Roberdeau Wheat commanded the Louisiana Tigers, a battalion recruited from New Orleans' ex-convicts and wharf rats. Wheat controlled his men by standing up in his stirrups and shouting, "If you don't get to your places, and behave as soldiers should, I will cut your hands off with this sword."

PRIVATE JOHN GILL

1st Maryland (C.S.) Infantry, Steuart's Brigade

Gill confiscated a prized commodity from a dead Federal officer that would serve him well two months later when the 1st Maryland Infantry was disbanded and many of its soldiers, like Gill, joined the cavalry. Although the Confederate 1st Maryland had a short life, the regiment had secured its honor at Front Royal when "the real 1st Maryland whipped the bogus."

The last stand was made at the bridge over the Shenandoah River, and I distinctly recall one poor fellow who fell dead just as he turned to cross the bridge. He was in my immediate front. We were double-quicking and firing at the same time. I am not positive who killed him; I am glad I am not able to say; bullets were flying thick and fast. He was a well-dressed officer, and as I came up to his dead body I could not resist relieving him of a long pair of cavalry boots which he wore. The temptation was too great and I could not let some one else make this important capture. I stooped down and relieved him of them, and found them to be of great service for months and months after, and especially when I joined the cavalry a few weeks later.

This pair of boots belonged to Colonel Thomas T. Munford, who commanded the 2d Virginia Cavalry at Front Royal and all of Jackson's mounted forces after the death of Ashby. The extensive repairs made on the boots indicated the importance a cavalryman placed on this piece of his equipment.

LIEUTENANT JOHN M. GOULD

10th Maine Infantry, Donnelly's Brigade

A sergeant major in the 10th Maine, Gould became a commissioned officer in March 1862. He and his mates, entrenched at Strasburg with most of Banks' force on May 23, were oblivious of the rout occurring 12 miles to the east until survivors began appearing. After his enlistment expired, Gould continued his service with the 29th Maine.

May 23, 1862, *Friday*. Our pay rolls came back from the paymaster this evening, and we commenced signing them and hurrahing for the pay which we are told is coming to-morrow. We were nearly done when one of the men came into the church saying, "There's a *'Calvary'* man outside who says there's just been a fight in Front Royal and our boys are all cut up," &c. The rolls were folded in some haste, and the cavalryman hunted up. He said he was a pioneer of Gen. Banks, and had been re-building a bridge on the Manassas railroad, but the rebels had driven him off. A teamster just then came down hill on a mule and said "that's so! he's a bridge builder, I know him; all the matter with him is he stole a secesh hoss." Then came an infantry corporal belonging to the 1st Maryland Vols.; he was a boy and somewhat excited, but said he had been captured by the rebel cavalry after fighting and being "all cut up"; then waiting his chance he had slipped on one of the horses of the captors, and the "old mare came toward this town right smart!" Teamsters on mules or horses now came along singly and in squads, and told doleful stories. After these another group, wearing artillery jackets, came down mounted. One in the crowd recognized these, and shook hands with all of them with great earnestness, and inquired, "By —— Billy, how'd ye git out?" The aforesaid Billy held up two queerly shaped pieces of iron and brass, and remarked "all that's left of our No. 3 gun!" We learned that Knapp's Pennsylvania battery had two guns attached to Geary's 28th Pennsylvania regiment, and that one had been captured and the other abandoned on the road.

"The opposing Marylanders were equally anxious to kill each other, wanting no quarter and giving none."

Our boys were excited by all this news, and began to hurrah, but still the horses and mules came rattling past, some of them with harnesses on, but all steaming and out of breath, while the riders, especially if they were teamsters, said, "the rebels are right on us." A more intelligent Marylander came in, saying that the 1st Maryland Vol. infantry, Col. Kenly, was in the fight with a part of the 1st Maryland cavalry, together fighting the 1st Maryland rebels; and the opposing Marylanders were equally anxious to kill each other, wanting no quarter and giving none. Col. Kenly was killed he said, also their surgeon.

Massanutten Mountain, which for 55 miles forms the eastern flank of the Shenandoah Valley, rises on the eastern horizon in this 1885 photograph taken from the vicinity of Banks' Strasburg entrenchments. Signal Knob, the promontory at the northern end, served as an observation point and signal station for both armies. Banks was in Strasburg with 7,000 soldiers when he learned of the Front Royal attack. He retreated north to Winchester the next day.

CAPTAIN EDWARD H. MCDONALD

11TH VIRGINIA CAVALRY

With the majority of Jackson's army moving against the Federals at Front Royal, a smaller contingent of Rebel cavalry demonstrated against Banks' Strasburg defenses. McDonald was captured late in 1862 and escaped to return to his regiment, which he commanded with the rank of major in 1863. He was severely wounded five days before Appomattox.

My company was detached and went down the valley to Strasburg with Major Myers. We did not encounter any of the enemy or his pickets until within a few miles of Strasburg, which we reached just before dark. We drove in three pickets and then fortified ourselves on the hills overlooking the town, expecting to be attacked but night came on, and with our command of one hundred men we lay all night in sight of the enemy's camp fires, expecting in the morning to pay for our boldness, but Old Jackson never gave an order that his men could not execute if they would only obey orders and abide his time. We know that old Jackson was somewhere on their flank but what was to be the result we could not foretell. When morning came we found that Banks had abandoned his camp and was trying to flee from the coils of our army. We entered Strasburg early the next morning and found that Banks had gone in a great hurry, abandoning many of his stores and supplies, among other things we found 14 Sutlers Stores in which everything had been abandoned, filled with everything usually found in such stores. Our command was small and a single one of these stores furnished more supplies than they could consume or carry away. It was seldom that soldiers ever had such an opportunity for plunder and a great many ridiculous things occurred. I remember one soldier, Patrick McCarty, who first got drunk and then tried to carry away on his horse more than his horse could hold. He first rolled up things in new blankets and tied them on behind his saddle, then he tied bundles in front, afterwards he put new blankets and bags of things across the seat of his saddle, when this had been done, he found a handsome new saddle and put it on top of all his plunder, buckled it around his horse and then got on top of the last saddle with his arms full and pockets full of bottles of whiskey, wine and cigars, but the load was too much for both the horse and McCarty. He tried to follow us out of town but he and his horse both fell down and we pushed on and left him behind.

PRIVATE HENRY E. HANDERSON

9TH LOUISIANA INFANTRY, TAYLOR'S BRIGADE

Although raised in Ohio, Handerson sided with the Confederacy, influenced by a two-year stint as a tutor in Louisiana. The column he and his comrades helped put to rout had begun its withdrawal in good order, to the accompaniment of bands playing "Oh Dear, What Can the Matter Be," a question answered soon after by a Rebel cavalry charge.

The next day we left the main road to Winchester at Cedarville, and, taking a rather obscure wood-road to the left, advanced cautiously towards Middletown on the valley pike. We reached this point about 2 P.M., striking the rear of Gen. Banks's column in full retreat from Strasburg. The pike was filled with a column of cavalry, who, as we made our unwelcome appearance, rode madly along the road in the direction of Winchester in order to pass the point of danger. Hemmed in between two high stone fences, they could make but little resistance, and furnished an excellent target for our infantry, though in a few moments the dust hid all distinct forms from our sight. Quite a number were killed and wounded, though not nearly so many as one might reasonably expect. Banks's line, however, was cut in two, his rear guard being separated from the remainder of the column and driven back to Strasburg. As we jumped over the stone wall into the pike, however, a vicious volley of bullets whistled through our disordered ranks, splintering the rails of the neighboring fence and wounding several of my comrades, and, looking down the road towards Strasburg, I saw a company of Zouaves behind a stone wall firing vigorously upon our advance. Hastily leaving the open pike, we rushed forward under the protection of the houses and fences until, emerging from the southern end of the village, we found our enemies in rapid retreat. After a short halt to reform our ranks, we again advanced in skirmish line to find the enemy, but on reaching Cedar Creek were ordered to retrace our steps. The excitement of the battle had begun to wear off, and we soon felt the fatigue and hunger of men who had been marching all day with little or no food.

CAPTAIN DAVID H. STROTHER

STAFF, MAJOR GENERAL NATHANIEL P. BANKS

Strother was a Unionist Virginian whose home in Bath was vandalized by Jackson's men early in January. His father, imprisoned then released by the Confederates, died a week later. In Strother's account of the Yankees' escape from Strasburg, his characterization of fleeing ex-slaves reflected racial attitudes common in both armies.

At Cedar Creek bridge we were met by a wagon master at full speed and apparently terrified. The General questioned him and he informed us the head of the train was attacked and the enemy in force was formed across our road. Just ahead several field officers rode by confirming the tidings. This was a shock. I had to that moment been tenaciously incredulous of an enemy in our rear. This seemed proof positive; in fact, I saw a body of troops indicated as the enemy and waited to hear the opening cannon.

We rode forward at dead silence, each heart manning itself for the death struggle. We met wagons and mounted teamsters rushing furiously back while the main line of wagons stood in the road stopped and many of them deserted by their drivers. Still no firing was heard. I rode close to the General summing up our position. I had till this time stoutly denied the possibility of an enemy in our rear. I was mortified at the utter failure of my judgment. I saw little way for any of us but an honorable death, for with Ewell in our front, Jackson must of course be close in our rear. The desperate attempt to cut our way through was all that was left for us. . . . I saw the General's countenance betokening this resolution. He said gravely, but kindly, "It seems we were mistaken in our calculation." It seemed this sentence conveyed a rebuke for my positive incredulity. I merely bowed and replied, "It seems so."

Approaching Middletown, five miles from Strasburg, the master teamster rode by cursing furiously at his underlings for stampeding the trains, threatening and ordering the fugitives back to their places. As

Defending the Federal rear at Middletown on May 24, Charles H. T. Collis (seated at left in this 1864 image) posted his Zouaves D'Afrique behind a stone fence where they fired several volleys, checking the Confederates' momentum. Later that year, at Fredericksburg, Collis rallied his Zouaves, now the 114th Pennsylvania, by shouting, "Remember the stone wall at Middletown."

soon as I heard this, I took heart and resumed my first opinion. . . . We had started out of Strasburg with the intention of taking position at Middletown, but the march was still continued. I had strongly advised General Banks not to sacrifice anything at Strasburg. He said we would not, but at the same time precautionary orders were given to burn our stores there in case we retired still farther. With this information and the fact still potent that our communication with Winchester was open by road and telegraphy, the retrograde movement was continued. Captain Abert of the Topographical Engineers with Collis' Zouaves was left at the Cedar Creek bridge to burn it when the last of our troops passed over.

At Newtown there was a demonstration on our right flank by some seventy-five or a hundred cavalry, to repel which a battery and a brigade of infantry were ordered out. We also heard a considerable firing of artillery in our rear. The enemy had attacked it near Middletown with horse and artillery. They cut off about fifty wagons, and captured the infantry escort and also the Zouaves D'Afrique, Collis and all. Thus ends the bodyguard for the present, and Collis' pretty little Jewish wife will tear her ebony hair for a while. Abert got off. Our baggage line was interspersed with wagons loaded with Negro families fleeing with the army. From the greybeard sire to the apish pickaninny at the breast, they streamed along, in wagons, on horseback, and on foot.

After leaving Newtown I left the staff and rode forward to Winchester, feeling so exhausted that I must have rest and food at all hazards. Since an early and hasty breakfast I had only tasted a bit of bread and butter with some Bolognian sausage from the General's snack. I overtook Colonel Brodhead and we rode together into town. He laughingly said the people of Winchester had prepared dinner for Jackson.

Lieutenant George Kurtz of the 5th Virginia, leading two companies of Winchester boys, inched toward their hometown after midnight in the van of Jackson's exhausted army. "I rallied men from both Companies," Kurtz wrote, "and cleared the road by shooting a volley down the Pike through Kernstown."

LIEUTENANT HENRY DUTTON

5TH CONNECTICUT INFANTRY, DONNELLY'S BRIGADE

Banks' men awoke on Sunday, May 25, aware that the Confederates were nearby and battle imminent. Dutton and his regiment took the opening blows of the infantry fight on the Front Royal road when they were attacked by the 21st North Carolina and 21st Georgia of Trimble's brigade. Dutton was killed at the Battle of Cedar Mountain the following August.

Just as day broke, before we had recovered from the chill of the night air or eaten our frugal breakfasts the rebel batteries and ours opened fire, and in a few minutes Bang! came a shell right in our midst and buried itself in the ground. Then several shot and shell came pouring into the field where we were stationed making those unearthly sounds you have heard of so often. The men got into place remarkably well under the circumstances and formed companies and then the command was given to wheel into line. I had just shouted the order when whizz, whizz came a swarm of leaden hornets amongst us. We rushed forward and with a yell gave them a tremendous volley at very close quarters and through the wreaths of smoke I could see the grey scoundrels fairly piled up in heaps and giving signs of breaking. Just then down came their flag and our boys cheered lustily but another sergeant raised it aloft again. All the while the batteries on both sides were playing over our heads and shot and shell were falling in the field where we were stationed. At last we drove them over a stone fence and received orders ourselves to retreat in line behind another.

"Kirkland's fine bay mare, richly caparisoned, went dashing through the field, riderless and frantic."

CAPTAIN WILLIAM C. OATES

15TH ALABAMA INFANTRY, TRIMBLE'S BRIGADE

Positioned in the rear of the brigade, Oates witnessed the opening fight at Winchester, in which the 21st North Carolina was mauled by Donnelly's brigade. The 15th Alabama, on the Confederate right, was only lightly engaged on May 25. A year later at Gettysburg, Oates, now the regimental colonel, led the 15th Alabama up the side of Little Round Top and was driven off with heavy losses.

Just as day dawned Colonel Kirkland moved forward with the Twenty-first North Carolina down the pike, supported by the Sixteenth Mississippi and Twenty-first Georgia, and began the attack. The Fifteenth Alabama was held in reserve until the battle was fairly over. Kirkland, Posey and Mercer drove the enemy handsomely for a short distance; the firing then became heavy and their advance was temporarily checked. Kirkland's fine bay mare, richly caparisoned, went dashing through the field, riderless and frantic. A few moments later four men bore him past us on a litter, shot through both thighs. Now the firing opened heavily on the Strasburg Pike and in the southern suburbs of the town. Jackson's old division was there. Early closed the gap in our lines between Trimble's left and Jackson's right. A battery in the town was firing vigorously on Trimble's three regiments engaged, and a movement was made by a body of Federals to flank him on the right. This led the Fifteenth through a field of tall wheat, which wet us to the waist with cold dew, and in double-quick time we outflanked the flankers and formed line squarely in front of the battery, which was now paying its respects to us with both spherical case shell and solid shot. After a rectification of alignment a forward movement caused the battery to withdraw to a safer position. Our comrades were now in plain view, driving the Yankees.

Colonel William W. Kirkland (left) was leading his 21st North Carolina down the Front Royal road when it was ripped by volleys from two directions. He ordered a bayonet charge, only to see his second in command, Lieutenant Colonel Rufus K. Pepper (center), mortally wounded by a bullet that passed through his hips. Included among the wounded were Kirkland, shot in the thigh, and Private John H. Ferguson (right), a 20-year-old farmer who was captured two years later and held until the end of the war.

PRIVATE ROBERT T. BARTON

ROCKBRIDGE (VIRGINIA) ARTILLERY

Veering to the left of the Valley Pike to take position in an elevated clover field, the cannoneers were subjected to a fire that Captain William Poague called "an ugly predicament," one that cost him 18 men. Barton, a Winchester native, survived the maelstrom, but his older brother Marshall was mortally wounded.

Daylight had come, and with it the guns of the enemy from the hills back of what was then the Hollingsworth Mills, now the Hack place, were sending their screaming shells over our heads. When we reached the toll gate our column halted and the men were directed to find shelter behind a stone house that then stood just to the right of the road as we approached the town. . . .

. . . In our mess of 10 were Bob Lee, the General's son, and Bob McKim, a fine young fellow, full of fun, from the City of Baltimore. We were called "The Three Bobs." Feeling a little of the sense of safety which the stone house afforded, Bob McKim slapped me on the shoulder and said "I will breakfast with you this morning in Winchester" and I replied, "I will dine with you when we get to Baltimore."

. . . Soon the call to "fall in and mount caissons" came to us, and we ran out from behind the stone house to where the screaming shells seemed to come closer and closer down to the road, as if they were hunting for us and screaming in anger because they did not find us. All but I climbed quickly upon the caissons, I don't know why I did not do that also, unless it was because I thought we would move but a little before we should unlimber for action again. Here I made a mistake. The horses went off at once in a trot, and I had only time to catch hold of an iron seat-guard on a caisson, when the horses were lashed into a gallop. I hung on with both hands, swinging to and fro and only now and then touching the ground with my feet. The men on the seat could not pull me up, and to let go would mean that the plunging horses and the heavy pieces and caissons, which they drew, would crush me to death if I fell. But I did succeed in holding on, thanks perhaps to my light weight of about 115 pounds. I still had hold with both hands when the battery slowed up by the grave yard by the old mill wall just this side of the Hacks, then the Hollingworth house. When I let go there was hardly a patch of skin on the palms of my hands and the inside of my fingers. We did not stop, but hurried along the road leading up the hill, while the terrible noise of firing guns and bursting shells just above us drowned even the sound of voices close by. Behind us was a column of infantry, with two other batteries and their accompanying caissons intervening. As we mounted the hill the shells seemed to spit in our faces, as they threw all around us the ragged pieces which their explosions scattered right and left. . . .

All along the line voices sung out "Fall in men," and without hesitation every man sprang to his place and I wondered why I had ever feared that I or any other soldier would not rather go to death than show a lack of courage.

The battery and the column following it moved forward like clock work. . . .

. . . we passed the dead and wounded of our battery, and there lay Bob McKim dead, his fine and happy face stained with blood and his forehead crushed in by a bullet or fragment of a shell. By his side lay another man of the battery whose name was called on the roll just before mine, and he too had fallen dead at this post. . . .

Here we were directed to lie down for shelter while the guns of the three batteries were placed in line so that we could all advance together to the top of the hill again, the men of the first section taking their places on our left to go back with us and recover their guns. Lying in the grass awaiting this formation, an officer of the next battery, engaged in getting his guns in place, almost rode over me with his nearly frantic horse.

Marshall was tall (over six feet), with black curling hair and a black moustache, a very handsome man. I thought he looked splendid as he rode up on his grey mare, turning and giving commands to his gunners, under that awful fire, as cool as on dress parade.

Recognizing him as my oldest brother, some eight or ten years older than me, I called out "Don't ride over a fellow," and he, looking down almost pityingly, said "Are you here boy?" But before I could make any answer, we all ran to our places, and the fourteen guns moved up abreast and got in line with the two abandoned guns, and at once the sixteen opened their throats and sought the range of batteries opposite them. . . .

. . . we were working our guns as fast as we could load and fire them. About equi-distant between the enemy's batteries and ours was a heavy stone fence and behind it a line of Federal infantry had been located, whose good shooting was responsible mainly for the killing and wounding of some twenty-five men of our battery.

A skilled cartographer, Jedediah Hotchkiss (right) was a valuable addition to Stonewall Jackson's staff in the spring of 1862. The New York native was exhilarated by the Confederate victory at Winchester and the subsequent pursuit of what he called the "haughty and insolent foe." After the war he produced this detailed map of the May 25 battle.

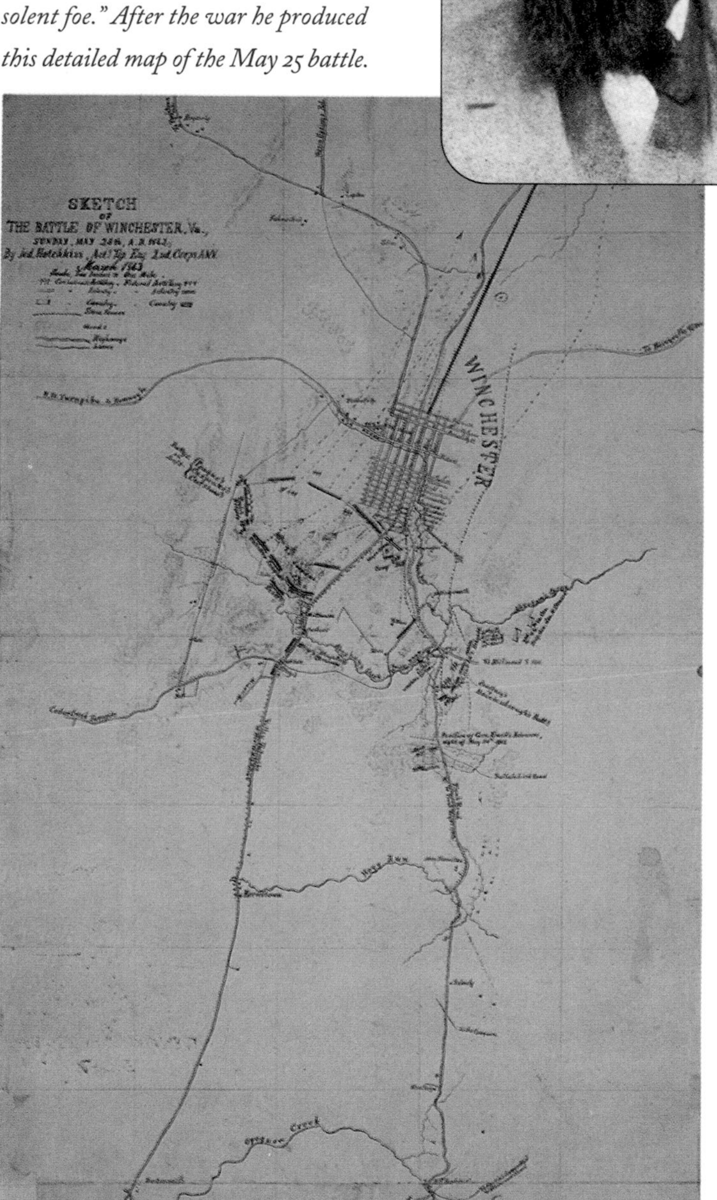

SERGEANT JOHN H. WORSHAM

21st Virginia Infantry, Campbell's Brigade

After a brief advance, Worsham's regiment and the rest of Jackson's division came under fire from four Union infantry regiments on Bower's Hill, the dominant ground at the southwest edge of Winchester. With Trimble's brigade stymied by the Federal left, Jackson sought to crush the enemy's right flank. Worsham witnessed the classic infantry assault by Taylor's Louisianans that swept across Bower's Hill.

About this time General Jackson made his appearance and rode to one of the hillocks in our front. Our brigade commander, Colonel John A. Campbell, accompanied him on horseback, while Colonel Patton of the 21st Virginia and Colonel Andrew J. Grigsby of the Stonewall Brigade followed on foot. They were met by a hail of grape and musket balls. Campbell was wounded; Grigsby had a hole shot through his sleeve and said some ugly words to the Yankees for doing it. General Jackson sat there, the enemy continuing to fire grape and musketry at him.

It was right here that Jackson issued his celebrated order to the commander of the Stonewall Brigade: "I expect the enemy to occupy the hill in your front with artillery. Keep your brigade in hand and a vigilant watch, and if such an attempt is made, it must not be done, sir! Clamp them on the spot!"

Colonel John A. Campbell, a VMI graduate and lawyer, commanded the 48th Virginia Infantry until Jackson selected him to head Jesse Burks' former brigade. Wounded at Winchester, Campbell needed four months to recuperate. He resigned from the army in protest after he was denied command of his former brigade because of the politically motivated appointment of another officer.

His left elbow shattered by a ball on Bower's Hill, Lieutenant Colonel Francis R. T. Nicholls of the 8th Louisiana was taken into Winchester, where the arm was amputated. Too weak to move, he fell into enemy hands when the Yankees reoccupied the town. He was later exchanged and promoted to brigadier general. Nicholls led a brigade at Chancellorsville, where a shell tore off his left foot. He later served two terms as governor of Louisiana.

After satisfying himself as to the location of the enemy, General Jackson quietly turned his horse and rode back in a walk. Arriving at the road in our rear he called for Taylor's brigade, led them in person to their position, and gave General Taylor his orders.

General Taylor acknowledged the orders, then added: "You had better go to the rear. If you go along the front in this way, some damned Yankee will shoot you!"

General Jackson rode back to him at once and said, "General, I am afraid you are a wicked fellow, but I know you will do your duty."

Taylor formed his brigade in the road about two or three hundred yards to our left. We were on his flank and could see nearly the whole of his advance. His march was in an open field, up a steep foothill or high bank, and then on a gentle rise to the top. Near the top stood the same stone wall that was in our front, with the enemy's line of battle extending beyond Taylor's left. As soon as General Jackson saw that Taylor had commenced the advance, he rode back to the hillock in our front to watch the effect of Taylor's attack.

The enemy poured grape and musketry into Taylor's line as soon as it came in sight. General Taylor rode in front of his brigade, drawn sword in hand, occasionally turning his horse and at other times merely turning in his saddle to see that his line was up. They marched up the hill in perfect order, not firing a shot! about halfway to the Yankees Taylor, in a loud and commanding voice that I am sure the Yankees heard, gave the order: "Charge!" up to and over the stone wall they went! This charge of Taylor's was the grandest I saw during the war. There was all the pomp and circumstance of war about it that was always lacking in our charges. Yet it was no more effective than ours which were inspired by the old Rebel Yell, in which most of the men raced to be foremost.

As Taylor's men went over the stone wall, General Jackson gave the command in that sharp and crisp way of his: "After the enemy, men!" Our whole line moved forward on a run. The enemy broke and ran in all directions.

LIEUTENANT JULIAN W. HINKLEY

3D WISCONSIN INFANTRY, GORDON'S BRIGADE

A descendant of a Plymouth Colony governor, Hinkley grew up on a farm in Wisconsin. He left in 1858 to teach school and try his hand at carpentry. Four years later Hinkley was a company officer on Bower's Hill facing an onslaught by the Louisiana Brigade. His regiment lost 101 men at Winchester—86 of them taken prisoner.

Our skirmishers were promptly advanced, and commenced firing on the enemy in their entrenchments. Supported by a battery in our rear, which fired over our heads into their position, we were maintaining a lively fire, when suddenly it was discovered that the enemy was passing around upon our right, with the evident intention of getting in our rear. The Twenty-Seventh Indiana and Twenty-Ninth Pennsylvania were hurriedly moved to the right, but had hardly reached their position when they were furiously assailed both in front and flank by the advancing Confederates. The Twenty-Ninth Pennsylvania received the first brunt of the attack, and soon was in full retreat. The

"I saw that the whole street behind us to the south was swarming with Confederate soldiers, not fifty feet away."

Twenty-Seventh Indiana came in for the next attack, and they also fell back about a quarter of a mile to some stone walls on the outskirts of the city. Our Regiment and the Second Massachusetts, which as yet had scarcely been engaged, were now faced about and marched to the rear, until we reached the fenced lots on the outskirts of the town. Here we were halted, and opened fire on the enemy, who had appeared in large numbers upon our front.

We had soon checked the Confederates immediately before us. I was looking around to see how things were going with the others, when I became aware that Company F and a portion of my Company were entirely alone. It appears that orders had been sent around by General Banks to fall back to the north side of the city; but we, being separated from the rest of the Regiment by an intervening street, had not heard them. There we were, fighting the whole Southern army by ourselves! I hastened to Captain Limbocker to call his attention to our position. He saw the situation at a glance, and left-facing the companies, marched double-quick through the back streets toward the main road of the city. By this time our men had discovered that they were in a close place, and moved rapidly. Just as we reached the main street and turned north, I stopped to speak to the Captain, who was in the rear. As I did so, I saw that the whole street behind us to the south was swarming with Confederate soldiers, not fifty feet away. They were in such confusion, however, that it was impossible for them to fire, and in fact they did not seem to try. From that point until we were clear of the street, it was simply a foot race, in which we were the winners. They evidently soon tired of the race, for before we were clear of the street they had some artillery in position, and shot and shell were flying harmlessly over our heads.

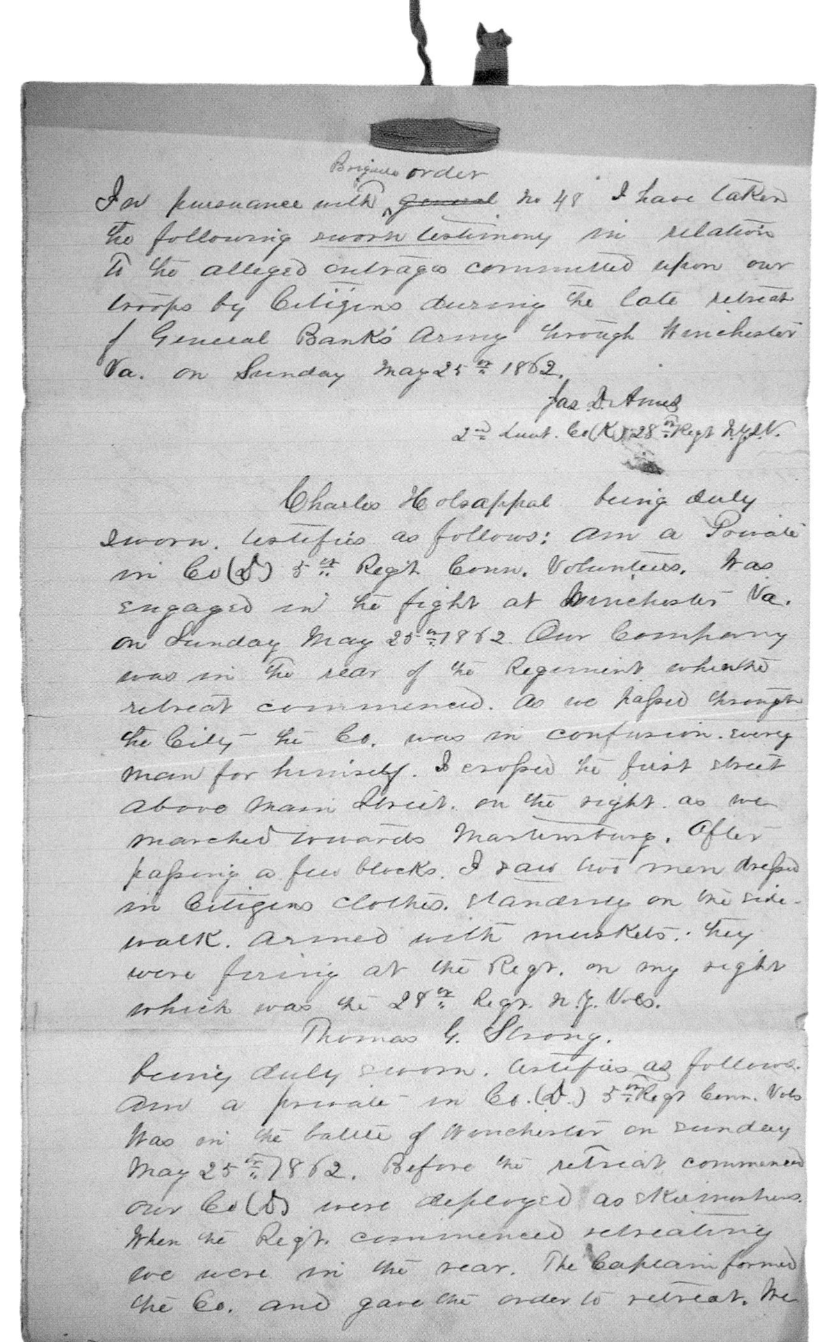

In pursuance with Brigade order No 48 I have taken the following sworn testimony in relation to the alleged outrages committed upon our troops by Citizens during the late retreat of General Banks' Army through Winchester Va. on Sunday May 25th 1862.

Jas. D. Ames
2nd Lieut. Co (K) 28th Regt N.Y.V.

Charles Holsappal being duly sworn, testifies as follows: Am a Private in Co (D) 5th Regt Conn. Volunteers. Was engaged in the fight at Winchester Va. on Sunday May 25th 1862. Our Company was in the rear of the Regiment when the retreat commenced. As we passed through the City the Co. was in confusion. every man for himself. I crossed the first street above Main Street. on the right. as we marched towards Martinsburg. After passing a few blocks. I saw two men dressed in Citizens clothes. standing on the side-walk. armed with muskets. they were firing at the Regt. on my right which was the 28th Regt. N.Y. Vols.

Thomas G. Strong.
being duly sworn, testifies as follows. Am a private in Co. (D.) 5th Regt Conn. Vols Was in the battle of Winchester on Sunday May 25th 1862. Before the retreat commenced our Co (D) were deployed as skirmishers. When the Regt. commenced retreating we were in the rear. The Captain formed the Co. and gave the order to retreat. We

This sheet is part of a U.S. War Department file documenting supposed outrages committed by Winchester citizens against Federal soldiers during their flight. Shown is the testimony of Charles Holsappal of the 5th Connecticut, who claims he "saw two men dressed in citizens clothes . . . firing at the Regt. on my right."

LIEUTENANT COLONEL WILDER DWIGHT

2D MASSACHUSETTS INFANTRY, GORDON'S BRIGADE

Caught up in the panic that engulfed the Federal ranks as they made their way through the town, Dwight was captured along with nearly 3,000 other Union prisoners. By most accounts the Yankee captives were well treated, and when Jackson was forced to give up Winchester a few days later he issued orders that all the Federal wounded should be left behind. Dwight was paroled and exchanged, returning to his regiment in time to be killed in action at Antietam.

I had dismounted to go down toward the wall, and was directing the officer in charge of the piece where his fire could be directed with most effect, when I heard a cry. I turned and saw that the Twenty-seventh Indiana, which had just opened its fire, had broken and was running. I saw that the enemy were pouring up the hillside and round on our right. I saw, also, that the Twenty-ninth Pennsylvania had broken and was following the Twenty-seventh Indiana. The enemy were coming on at a run, with yells, but not in any regular order. The officer commanding the piece said to me, "What shall I do? I have got no support for my gun." "Blaze away at 'em," said I. "I shall lose my gun," said he. "Well," said I, "you must do as you choose." I turned and found that our regiment was withdrawing. I could not see my horse anywhere, and so I followed on foot. As we passed off the hill the enemy rose on its crest. Their cracking and whistling fire followed us closely. I recollected an unmailed letter in my pocket, and preferring to have it unread, rather than read by hostile eyes, I tore it up as we went down the hill. A few of our men would turn and fire up the hill, reloading as they went on. I delayed a little to applaud their spunk. . . .

We passed down into the edge of the town. As I came along, a young soldier of Company C was wounded in the leg. I gave him my arm, but, finding that he was too much injured to go on, advised him to get into a house, and went on. The regiment was forming in line when I reached it. Before I had time to go to the left, where Colonel Andrews was, the regiment moved off again, and I followed. It now became a run. A fire began to assail us from the cross streets as well as from the rear. I turned in at the Union Hotel Hospital to get on to the next street, but found the same fire there. Just as I was near the edge of the town one of our soldiers called out to me, "Major, I'm shot." I turned to him, and took him along a few steps, and then took him into a house. I told the people they must take care of him, and laid him down on a bed, and opened his shirt. I then turned to go out, but the butternut soldiery were all around the house, and I quietly sat down. . . . A soldier soon came in and took me prisoner. I made friendly acquaintance with him.

On May 25, 1862, one year after joining a number of his Harvard classmates in the 2d Massachusetts, Captain Charles R. Mudge was wounded at Winchester. Six members of the regiment dragged him to safety and placed him in a wagon heading north. Promoted to major, Mudge was killed on July 3, 1863, at Gettysburg.

CORNELIA PEAKE MCDONALD

Resident of Winchester

The sight of fleeing Federals produced emotions in the Winchester populace in contrast to those they had experienced two and a half months earlier when Union troops first took the town. Mrs. McDonald, who was reduced to fits of weeping when Jackson's army was forced to evacuate on March 11, shed tears of joy when the Southern army returned to drive the Federals away in dramatic fashion.

I could see from the front door the hill side covered with Federal troops, a long line of blue forms lying down just behind its crest, on top of which just in their front a battery spouted flame at the lines which were slowly advancing to the top. Suddenly I saw a long even line of grey caps above the crest of the hill, then appeared the grey forms that wore them, with the battle flag floating over their heads! The cannon ceased suddenly, and as the crouching forms that had been lying behind the cannon rose to their feet they were greeted

by a volley of musketry from their assailants that scattered them. Some fell where they had stood but the greatest number fled down the hill side to swell the stream of humanity that flowed through every street and by way, through gardens and over fences, toward the Martinsburg turnpike, a confused mob of trembling, fainting objects that kept on their mad flight till they were lost in the clouds of dust their hurrying feet had raised. Nothing could be distinguished, nothing but a huge moving mass of blue, rolling along like a cloud in the distance.

At different points the battle continued, and through the streets the hurrying masses still rushed. Occasionally a few would pause to fire at their pursuers, but all were making frantically for the one point of egress that was left open to them. Arms, accoutrements, clothes, everything was thrown away as they sped along, closely followed by their victorious foes, who never paused except to give a word or smile to the friends who were there to greet them.

I put on my bonnet and went in town, and the scenes I there witnessed I could not describe to do them justice. Old men and women, ladies and children, high and low, rich and poor, lined the streets. Some weeping or wringing their hands over the bodies of those who had fallen before their eyes, or those who were being brought in by soldiers from the edge of the town where the battle had been thickest, and others shouting for joy at the entrance of the victorious Stonewall Brigade, and exultation at the discomfiture of the flying enemy. All were embracing the precious privilege of saying what they chose, singing or shouting what they chose.

People in different spheres of life, who perhaps never before had exchanged a word, were shaking hands and weeping together. All seemed as if possessed by one heart and one mind. Baskets of foods were brought from the houses and passed hastily among the thronging soldiers, who would snatch a mouthful and go on their way.

Winchester's citizens express their joy and gratitude to Stonewall Jackson upon the liberation of their town in this William D. Washington painting. The artist's view is facing north on Main Street, with the balconied Taylor Hotel directly behind Jackson. The euphoria expressed by the civilians was boundless. "I cannot describe the beaming countenances and the congratulations passed between citizens," wrote one resident in his diary. The town's deliverance would be undone a week later, however, when Jackson withdrew and the Yankees returned.

CORPORAL JOHN E. ANDERSON

2D MASSACHUSETTS INFANTRY, GORDON'S BRIGADE

Separated from his unit in the chaos of the retreat, Anderson was attempting to slip back toward the Potomac River when he was captured. The courthouse yard that held the Federal captives had been used two months earlier for Confederate prisoners taken at Kernstown.

I attempted to keep pace . . . and succeeded to do so until afternoon when extreme weariness overcame me and I laid down on that mountain top. Committing myself to the care of the maker of the universe I fell into a sweet and refreshing sleep. In two or three hours I awoke restored to my usual spirits. But how still everything was. Where was my companions. I went along on the ridge of the mountains to an opening and looking down the mountain side towards the Martinsburg pike could see moveing objects miles in the distance and had no doubt that the Rebels were still following and capturing our poor retreating army. And going to the other side of the ridge and looking down into the valley below I saw in the distance two or three members of Banks body guard straggling along they were to far away for me to make them hear me should I hallo. And so I seemed to be left alone. . . . My plan being to travell nights and rest in the mountains in the day time to avoid going through a small village called Pughtown I was compelled to travell in a dense growth of underbrush following a crooked path for three miles or more and after foarding a creek I came on to the pike some two miles beyond the town. Congratulating myself that there would be no further danger of capture my object being to get as far from Winchester as possible not for a moment thinking that there was any force of Rebels near all care and caution was for the time abandoned. Emerging from a piece of woods I came almost to a halt as just a few rods in front of me there was sounds of Cavelry scabards rattling on the ground in an instant the challenge came "Who comes there." At the same time three pieces were brought to bear upon me I could plainly see the barrells of the pieces as they rested over a fence I thought to run but calculated my chances and concluded to find out who was behind those pieces before allowing them to fire So I answered "A friend" the reply came "Advance friend with the countersign" my reply was "A friend without the countersign." The reply was "Advance friend." The challenge was done so perfectly that my hopes were that I had come on to the outpost of our own pickets. My surprise was complete when advancing to the guards who were dressed in grey they ordered me to surrender. My capture was made not far from twelve o'clk at night and about twenty two miles from Winchester by a squad of twelve Virginia Cavelry belonging to Ashby's command. They took me into the little house that was used for their H'd Quarters and presented me to their Lieutenant in those words "Here's another Yank." The Lieutenant was quite talkitative and informed me that they had captured all or quite all of Banks men. And in fact they had so many Prisinors on hand that they hardly knew what to do with them. I felt heartily sorry for him and said that if he would allow me to depart, there would be one less to care for. The offer was not accepted however and rolling myself up in my blanket I laid down, but not to rest, my mind was to active for sleep The chagrin at my capture and thoughts of how I should escape kept my mind freely occupied until daylight. At daylight we started for Winchester there was three of us to guard. The Lieutenant with one of his men went with us while the rest of his company took another road in hopes to capture more prisoners. The Lieutenant was accquainted with the inhabitants along the route and pointed out several houses in which he said lived Union familys. He claimed to be a native of the county and by the way those charming Southern girls greeted him I should judge that he was a general favorite. When about four or five miles from Winchester a Negro came along the road driving an old horse in a tip cart. Our Lieutenant ordered us to get into the cart and ride into town. . . . The Negro whipped up his horse into a trot and we soon drew up before the Court-house where I was greeted by familiar voices with the remark "Halo Em," is that you "Where did you come from." And looking over the fence into the yard, or inclosure, of the Court-house, I saw familiar faces representing nearly if not all the Companys of my Regiment of the six hundred in the yard about eighty were of the Second Mass and quite a number of them were from my own Company we were soon added to the number I had no sooner got into the yard then I was completely surrounded by our men all anxious to hear the story of my capture.

"Banks made an appeal to the soldiery to rally and make a stand. 'My God, men, don't you love your country?' "

LIEUTENANT EDWIN E. BRYANT

3D WISCONSIN INFANTRY, GORDON'S BRIGADE

Entering the war as a private, Bryant rose through the ranks to assume command of his company at Cedar Mountain. Positioned on the left flank of the Federal line on Bower's Hill, the 3d Wisconsin was forced back through the town with the rest of Gordon's brigade. Once on the far side of Winchester most of the panic in the ranks subsided as the troops concentrated on reaching safety across the Potomac.

When we were out some five miles, Banks made an appeal to the soldiery to rally and make a stand. "My God, men, don't you love your country?" he pleaded. "Yes," said one, near the writer, "and I am trying to get to it as fast as I can." Here a halt was made, quite a line was formed, the enemy checked, and the train was allowed to move further to the rear; and then the line, formed of volunteers without respect to organization, soon melted into the retreating mass.

At Martinsburg a brief halt was made. There was nothing to be had in the way of food; and the tired band soon moved on to the Potomac, thirteen miles further, arriving at from 10 till 11 o'clock. Those who were fortunate enough to have saved in the retreat their regimental wagons and to find them in the chaotic jumble on the banks had some supper. Those not so fortunate sat down to rest, too weary to heed the pangs of hunger. Gen. Banks took a cup of coffee offered him by a soldier and drank it with much relish. The Third Wisconsin pulled itself together in part and lay down until three o'clock when the men were roused up to take the ferry which had been plying all night. Two companies of the regiment and two of the Second Massachusetts were left on the Virginia side as rear guard. The other companies as soon as they had crossed were put in line of battle to cover the remnants still hovering on the Virginia side waiting their turn at the ferry.

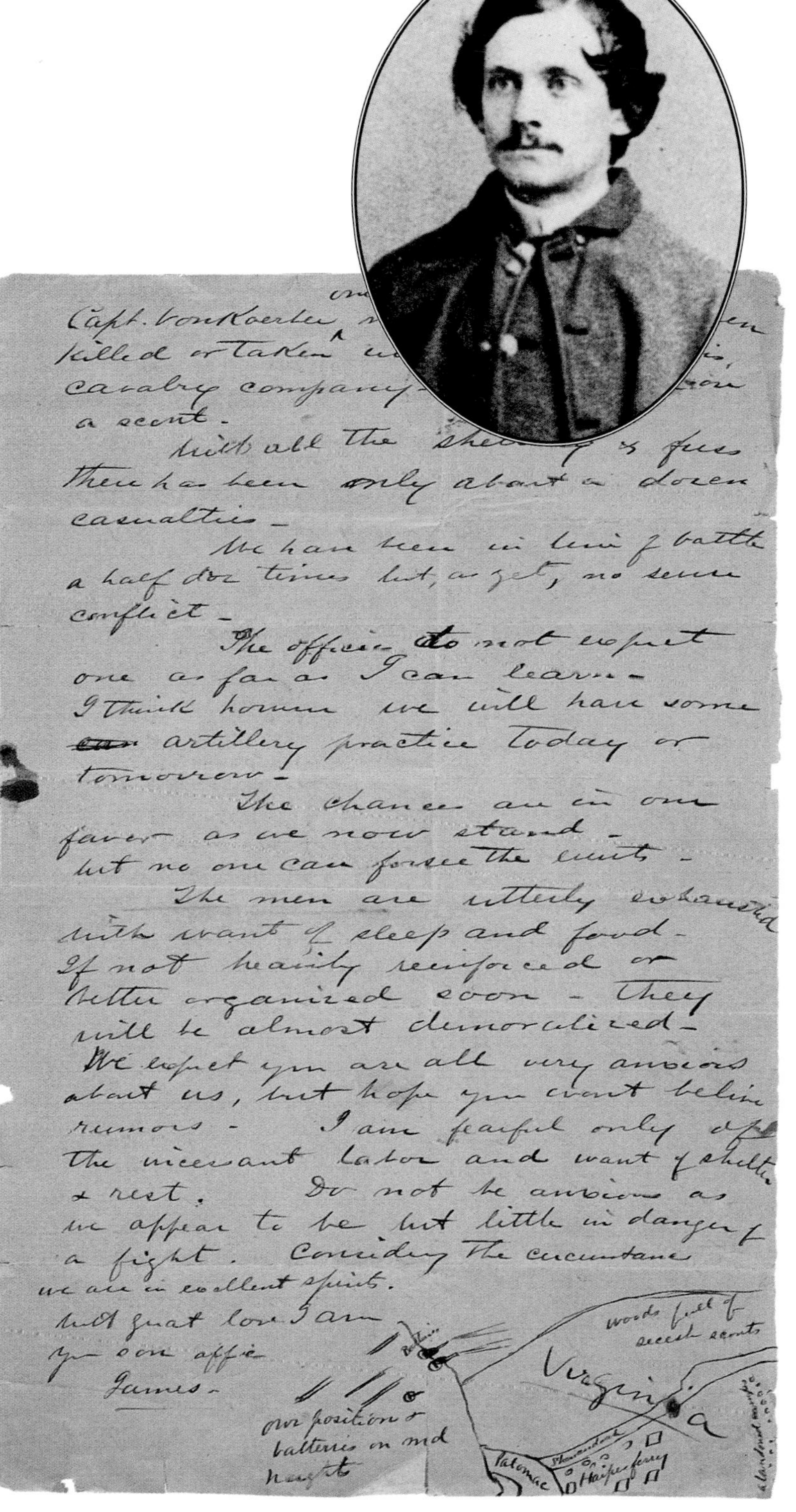

Capt. vonKoerber [illegible] [illegible] killed or taken [illegible] cavalry company [illegible] a scout.

With all the shelling & fuss there has been only about a dozen casualties.

We have been in line of battle a half doz times but, as yet, no severe conflict.

The officers do not expect one as far as I can learn. I think however we will have some artillery practice today or tomorrow.

The chances are in our favor as we now stand — but no one can foresee the events.

The men are utterly exhausted with want of sleep and food. If not heavily reinforced or better organized soon — they will be almost demoralized.

We expect you are all very anxious about us, but hope you won't believe rumors. I am fearful only of the incessant labor and want of shelter & rest. Do not be anxious as we appear to be but little in danger of a fight. Considering the circumstances we are in excellent spirits.

With great love I am
your son affec
James.

A member of the 3d Maryland (U.S.) Infantry, Lieutenant James Gillette (inset) fled Harpers Ferry to the safety of Maryland Heights on the opposite side of the Potomac River when Jackson's infantry appeared on May 30. "The men are entirely exhausted for want of sleep and food," wrote Gillette to his parents the next day, but he added, "We appear to be but little in danger of a fight." His letter (left) includes a hasty sketch of the opposing forces around Harpers Ferry.

LIEUTENANT MCHENRY HOWARD

STAFF, BRIGADIER GENERAL CHARLES S. WINDER

Approaching Harpers Ferry on May 30, Jackson was informed by General Elzey that the Federals had heavy guns on Maryland Heights. Jackson reddened the former artilleryman's face by chiding, "General Elzey, are you afraid of heavy guns?" But there was to be no attack. Concerned by reports of Federals closing in back up the Valley, Jackson ordered all but Winder's brigade back to Winchester. Then came news of Yankees in Front Royal and orders to Winder to make a hasty return.

Late that night I was roused by some one stumbling over the tent ropes and found it was a courier from General Jackson, who had lost his way and was several hours late in bringing his dispatch. This, when read, was alarming, and the more so for being thus belated. Jackson wrote that he was leaving Winchester and ordered General Winder to fall back immediately and that if he found Winchester in possession of the enemy, he must make his escape by the Back Road. This is a road which goes up the Valley some distance to the west of the great Valley Turnpike. The 2d Virginia was immediately recalled from Loudon Heights and early in the morning, May 31, the brigade and the 1st Maryland started back on a forced day's march. When, late in the evening we got to Winchester, we found it deserted by all except a few stragglers and we pushed on through to Newtown where at night we went into a cheerless, rainy bivouac. We had marched over twenty-eight miles and the 2d Virginia several miles more.

The next morning, June 1, we resumed the march. Before we had gone many miles we heard artillery firing in our front, towards Strasburg, which made us apprehensive that we might be too late and find ourselves cut off at that place. But soldiers take things of that sort philosophically. At or near Middletown I was riding about a hundred yards ahead, as I was very apt to do, when I saw a group of cavalry men in front, standing in the mouth of the road which forks off to Front Royal, the same road by which we had come into the Valley Turnpike from that place eight days before. When I approached, one of them rode out from the mouth of the road to meet me and I recognized the brown face of Ashby. "Is that General Winder coming up?" he asked. I said it was. "Thank God for that," he exclaimed. When the General came up, Ashby shook his hand warmly and said, "General, I was never so relieved in my life. I thought that you would be cut off and had made up my mind to join you and advise you to make your escape over the mountain to Gordonsville." . . . we could plainly see the smoke of the discharges of the guns we had heard, seeming to be almost in our front as the Turnpike was then running, and we knew that Jackson was holding back Fremont until we got by.

Looking west toward Strasburg (labeled 3), Edwin Forbes sketched Jackson's escape on June 1, 1862. Clearly visible is the long Confederate supply train making its way south "up" the Valley Pike (5). Frémont's army (2) approaches too late from the west, while Shields' column sits 10 miles eastward near Front Royal. The Union soldiers on the hill in the foreground are General George Bayard and his staff, who are reduced to watching yet another opportunity lost by Federal forces in the Valley.

"We could plainly see the smoke of the discharges of the guns we had heard, seeming to be almost in our front as the Turnpike was then running, and we knew that Jackson was holding back Fremont until we got by."

CAPTAIN JAMES F. HUNTINGTON

Battery H, 1st Ohio Light Artillery

Huntington, shown with his wife, Ellen, left the Valley on May 16 with Shields' division and marched into Falmouth six days and 100 miles later. On Friday, May 23, President Lincoln reviewed Shields' troops before their planned advance with McDowell to Richmond. Those plans were changed later that day after the debacle at Front Royal. Huntington wrote of Shields' return to the Valley, a trek that began on May 26 and averaged 20 miles a day for five days.

I trust that the Recording Angel was too much occupied to make a note of the language used in Shields' division when we learned, with mingled feelings of rage and incredulity, that we were to return to the Valley by forced marches. About noon on Monday, we turned our steps again towards the Shenandoah, proceeding *via* Manassas Junction.

The nearer we approached Washington, the more alarming were the reports. Jackson, with twenty, thirty, forty thousand men, was marching straight on that devoted city. We reached the Junction about noon on Tuesday, where we found the gallant band that under General Geary had retreated in hot haste from Thoroughfare Gap. According to their own account they had narrowly escaped being gobbled up bodily, whereas there had not been a Confederate soldier within twenty miles of them.

We took the road to Thoroughfare and pushed rapidly on. Soon we met squads and scattered men coming along, a lot of Geary's pickets whom in the hasty departure they had forgotten to call in, but who, after vainly waiting some twenty-four hours for their relief, relieved themselves. On reaching the scene of Geary's "last stand," we found fresh evidence of a cowardly and disgraceful panic, in the shape of commissary and quartermaster property burnt or abandoned, personal baggage of officers left in tents still standing; it was disgusting.

The advance of our division occupied Front Royal early on Friday, May 29. The 1st Vermont Cavalry made a gallant charge on a regiment of Jackson's infantry who were holding the town, taking many prisoners, but with heavy loss to themselves. Instead of pressing right on to join hands with Frémont, who was approaching Strasburg by the Franklin Road, the division halted at Front Royal.

This unfortunate delay was largely due to a rumor, that pressed heavily on Shields' mind, that Longstreet was advancing by the Luray Valley with a large force. In fact, had all the rumors of advances been true, Lee would hardly have had a corporal's guard left with which to hold Richmond.

CAPTAIN WILLIAM C. OATES

15th Alabama Infantry, Trimble's Brigade

Resting on Fisher's Hill after narrowly escaping the Federal pincers movement on May 31, Oates summed up why Jackson had thus far outperformed his adversaries: "So much in Generalship depends on celerity of movement." With Shields' troops set to advance from Front Royal and Frémont's army directly threatening from west of Strasburg, Jackson continued to push his weary troops—who had already marched nearly 300 miles in May—southward once again early on June 1.

That evening the rain poured in torrents. We remained on the hill until about one hour after dark. The hillside was muddy and almost as slick as glass. The files had to lock arms to steady each other, and many fell in the mud. One little fellow named Woodham, belonging to my company, fell several times; at last he sat down in a small pool of muddy water. The splash attracted attention, and he looked around with-

Pursuing Jackson, cavalry from Frémont's Mountain Department crosses the North Fork of the Shenandoah River near Mount Jackson. An incompetent on Frémont's staff had hampered their progress when he saw a putative enemy battery across the river and ordered an Ohio battery to put it out of action. Wrote one of the Yankee gunners, the Rebel battery "proved to be six innocent rail heaps, which his eye had clothed with the panoply of war."

out attempting to rise, and exclaimed, "Well, damn me if I don't wish that the war would come to an end before daylight!" That young man, later in the war deserted. Trimble's brigade was the rear-guard of the infantry that night and the next day. Fremont's cavalry was commanded by Sir Percy Wyndham, an Englishman, supported by the "Buck-Tail Rifles," a Pennsylvania regiment which carried no baggage and kept up with the cavalry. Wyndham was an enterprising officer, and made attacks upon our rear day and night. We would march a mile or two and form line of battle across the road, facing to the rear, when they would halt and open on us with artillery. We would then move on again. At night some other brigade would take the rear. It rained every day and night. The road was shoe-mouth deep in mud. My feet were blistered all over, on top as well as the bottom. I never was so tired and sleepy. Several times I went to sleep as I marched at the head of my company, and my orderly-sergeant, Joe Balkum, who was an iron man, would catch me by the arm and call me, "Captain, Captain!" to arouse me.

LIEUTENANT ROBERT G. SHAW

2D MASSACHUSETTS INFANTRY, GORDON'S BRIGADE

Shaw received temporary leave on May 17 to travel to Washington with two other officers to present President Lincoln with a plan to raise a black regiment. The plan was rejected—though it would be accepted eight months later—and Shaw finished his leave with a two-day visit home before returning to his regiment in time to fight in the Battle of Winchester. Reaching the safety of the northern side of the Potomac, a humbled Shaw explained the situation to his sister.

Williamsport, Md.
June 6, 1862
My Dear Susie, . . .

As you see from the date of this, I can hardly be said to write from the seat of war. There are only four regiments on this side now. General Banks is at Winchester, and we are only waiting for clothes. The late rains have swollen the Potomac so that we shall have a good deal of difficulty in getting over if we go this week.

We had the same frightful accounts . . . of the barbarity of the Rebels the first day after we arrived here, but since then it has turned out to be a mistake. No doubt, in the heat of passion, a good many cruel things are done, but it is probably the same on every battle-field. A good many of our men were taken and subsequently escaped, and they were all treated well. Major Dwight and Dr. Stone met with nothing but kindness. A sergeant of my company died from wounds in the hospital there. General Jackson released a dozen non-commissioned officers and privates of this regiment for escort; furnished a coffin and ambulance, and they buried him with honours. All our wounded were left in the hospital at Winchester, and the Major says Jackson was very angry with one of his officers for wishing to carry some of them off, as he said it was inhuman. From all they tell us of Jackson, I should think he was a good man. He is certainly an able commander, for he has escaped everything, when it seemed almost impossible. Dwight says all the officers he saw seemed tired to death of the war, and the men still more so. Colonel Kenley, who was said to have been killed in an ambulance, is here with a slight wound in his head. A man at Harper's Ferry showed me a coffin, which he said contained Colonel Kenley's body; so much for rumours.

The papers say, that, for some unaccountable reason, the picket of the First Maryland, at Front Royal, gave no notice of the approach of the enemy. It may seem unaccountable to some people, but it doesn't to me, for I was down there one day, and saw half of them asleep in the grass, and the rest fishing and bathing in the brook.

We have a beautiful camp here, and shall be sorry to leave it, though it looks bad to date our letters from Maryland.

July 5, 1862.] FRANK LESLIE'S ILLUSTRATED NEWSPAPER. 217

WAR IN THE SHENANDOAH VALLEY—DIVISION OF THE NATIONAL ARMY UNDER GEN. BANKS RECROSSING THE POTOMAC FROM WILLIAMSPORT, MARYLAND, TO ATTACK THE REBEL ARMY UNDER GEN. JACKSON—THE BAND OF THE 46TH PENNSYLVANIA VOLUNTEERS PLAYING THE NATIONAL AIRS ON THE VIRGINIA SHORE.—From a Sketch by our Special Artist, Edwin Forbes.—See Page 225.

This Forbes engraving shows Banks' army recrossing the Potomac "to attack the rebel army under Gen. Jackson"—an attack that never took place. "Whatever may be said of our recent movement," Banks wrote shamelessly to his wife concerning his flight from Virginia, "I can assure you that it is one of the most remarkable that has occurred or will occur during the war."

LIEUTENANT JAMES BUMGARDNER

52D VIRGINIA INFANTRY, STEUART'S BRIGADE

A teacher and lawyer, Bumgardner fought at Kernstown as a 5th Virginia company officer but was not reelected in mid-April. He was elected a lieutenant of Company F of the 52d Virginia on May 1 and participated in the rearguard action as Jackson pulled his force back through Harrisonburg early in June. Bumgardner was commissioned captain of his company three months later and commanded the regiment from May 1864 until his capture four months later.

The rear guard halted at the eastern foot of a wooded ridge about two and one-half miles from Harrisonburg, the cavalry in line of battle on both sides of the road to Cross Keys and the supporting infantry brigade in line of march in the same road. While in this position Sir Percy Wyndham, in command of a Federal regiment of cavalry, rode out of Harrisonburg, boasting that he was going to bag Ashby and his command. The regiment to which I belonged was lying in the road a short distance in the rear of the line of cavalry. My attention was aroused by a sharp command given by General Ashby to the cavalry in the field on the south side of the road, and immediately afterwards I saw General Ashby gallop up to the high stake-and-rider fence between the field and road. The splendid stallion on which Ashby was mounted leaped the fence and landed in the road a few feet in front of me, then leaped over the fence into the field on the north of the road. General Ashby galloped to the center and front of the cavalry there and gave the command to move forward. The cavalry started forward, first in a walk, then in a trot, then in a gallop, and then disappeared from my sight as they entered the woods on the slope of the hill, and next was heard his ringing voice as he commanded the charge. For a few minutes the supporting infantry in the road heard wild yells and shouts, the cracking of pistols, and the clanking of sabers, and then all was quiet. A few minutes afterwards Sir Percy Wyndham and a part of his command passed along the road occupied by the supporting infantry as prisoners of war. This was the last time I saw General Ashby alive.

Later in the evening the Federals attacked the rear guard of Jackson's army with cavalry and infantry. General Ashby called up the supporting infantry, part of which was placed on the front line and another part, including the 52d Virginia Infantry, was placed in the rear in reserve. There was a desperate fight, with heavy loss on both sides, but the Federal attack was repulsed.

Just after the close of the action four mounted cavalrymen, riding abreast and bearing a dead body covered with a gum blanket and resting on the necks of their horses in front of the riders, passed immediately by. Captain Garber, of Company A, 52d Virginia Infantry, to which company I belonged, asked them who it was they were taking to the rear. The reply was: "It is General Ashby." The bearers of the dead General were all in tears and so overcome with emotion that they could hardly respond intelligently to the question. . . .

After the encounter between Ashby's Cavalry and the regiment commanded by Sir Percy Wyndham, who rode out of Harrisonburg for the express purpose of bagging Ashby, the Federal prisoners and their guard

An Englishman who once fought with Garibaldi's Redshirts in Italy, Colonel Sir Percy Wyndham raised and commanded the 1st New Jersey Cavalry in Frémont's army. He boasted that he would vanquish Turner Ashby. After his regiment was routed by Ashby on June 6, Wyndham reportedly dismounted and surrendered, saying, "I will not command such cowards." He was exchanged in September.

passed along the road, which was full of infantry support, and as they were moving by my company a man named Sheets, who is still living, noticed Wyndham's very striking appearance, differing from any Federal prisoner that we Confederates had ever seen. He was very tall, elegantly dressed, wearing every ornament permissible under regulations. His low-topped boots had gold tassels hanging in front. As he passed by, Sheets, pointing to him, called out: "Look yonder boys; there is a Yankee colonel!" This was the straw that broke the camel's back. Instead of bagging Ashby, he was going to prison under guard along a line of ragged, shabby-looking Rebels, one of whom actually called him a Yankee. He, a titled Englishman, descended from a Crusader, to be called a Yankee by a stupid, ragged Rebel! He stopped and turned to poor Sheets and, with a withering look of scorn, said: "I am not a Yankee, you —— Rebel fool." Sheets did not drop on his knees and make a humble apology. Wyndham's indignant assertion that he was not a Yankee met with a roar of laughter. He swore, O how he swore! The louder he swore, the louder the —— Rebels laughed. His guards moved him along with their other prisoners, and he went on swearing and kept on swearing as long as his voice was audible to the Rebels who filled the road.

This flag was carried in the Valley by Company I of the 13th Pennsylvania Reserves, more familiarly known as the Bucktails because of the distinctive deer tails they wore draped from the sides of their kepis. A battalion of the regiment under Colonel Thomas L. Kane served with Frémont's cavalry during its pursuit of Jackson. The "Harrisonburg" honor, acknowledging participation in the June 6 fight, is probably unique to the Bucktails' color.

LIEUTENANT GEORGE W. BOOTH

1st Maryland (C.S.) Infantry, Steuart's Brigade

The rout of Wyndham's 1st New Jersey Cavalry did not end the rearguard action east of Harrisonburg. Frémont sent out fresh cavalry supported by Kane's Bucktails against Ashby's cavalry, the 58th Virginia, and Bradley Johnson's 1st Maryland. After the Maryland infantry disbanded, Booth joined Johnson as an aide, then transferred to the 1st Maryland Cavalry. Promoted to captain, Booth rejoined Johnson's staff in 1864 and finished the war as his assistant adjutant general.

We had reached a point some four or four and one-half miles from Harrisonburg, and the afternoon was well spent, when General Ewell directed our regiment and the 58th Virginia to retrace our steps and assist General Ashby. We had gone but a short distance when we were turned into a heavy body of oak wood and formed in line of battle. General Ashby reported the enemy were in position at the farther end of the timber, and gave it as his judgment they were but dismounted cavalry, and if we would move forward promptly we would be able to "take them in," as he expressed himself. Captain Nicholas and myself were detached, with a portion of our respective companies, and directed to deploy as skirmishers and advance until we developed the enemy. We had not moved forward but a few hundred yards before we found the object of our search, and, under the cover of the woods, I succeeded in getting down pretty close to their line, when, to my surprise, instead of cavalry I discovered a well-formed infantry line, sheltered behind a stout fence on the edge of the timber. Halting my line, I made my way back and so reported. Generals Ewell and Ashby were together, but the latter insisted I was mistaken. The 58th Virginia was directed to move forward to the point where my line was formed, when I was to advance and fire signal shots, and then they were to charge the enemy. It was a well laid plan, but it failed most woefully in execution. I returned to my skirmishers, Nicholas being somewhat to the right, moved my line forward and fired the signal shots, when the 58th, with a loud cheer, advanced, to be met with a staggering fire from the Bucktails, who poured volley after volley into us as our line hesitated and finally halted and began to return the fire. My position was decidedly uncomfortable; we were between the two lines and subjected to the fire from both. Fortunately for us, the 58th, in their confusion, were firing too high to do execution. If the Bucktails had been in the tree tops, I think it likely they mostly would have been killed. As it was, they remained on *terra firma,* and with great coolness and deliberation kept up a most effective fire. For some ten minutes or more it appeared almost certain we would be wiped out. . . . Taking private Ackler, of my company, I carried their colors forward and implored them to stop firing and charge with us, but they were immovable, and Ackler was shot down by my side. At this juncture General Ashby rode forward and urged them to advance, riding through their line, begging them to rally and follow him, but without avail. He then commenced firing his pistol at the federal line, which was such a short distance off. Under the withering fire of the enemy he soon fell. . . .

I had just determined to make an effort to extricate my men, when, with a familiar yell, our regiment, under Colonel Johnson, came charging forward on the flank of the enemy and broke their line, and as they retired over the open field, Nicholas moved down with his end of the skirmish line, and under the combined destructive fire the Bucktails fell as thick as leaves in Vallombrosa. Colonel Kane was left on the field badly wounded and fell into our hands. It was impossible to pursue the advantage, as the federal batteries and supports covered the field in our front, and it was not the intention to bring on a general engagement.

The loss of the regiment in this affair was quite heavy. Captain Robertson, of I company, was killed, also my dear friend, Lieutenant Snowden, and private Beatty, of my own company. The 58th Virginia also suffered severely and paid penalty for their indecision, while the death of Ashby was a misfortune which could not be repaired. Take the affair altogether, it was a sad incident, the only redeeming feature of which was the gallant example set by Colonel Johnson and his command, which was duly recognized by General Ewell in general orders authorizing the regiment to append to their color staff, as a trophy, one of the captured bucktails, the insignia of the command which so bravely and at such cost resisted our attack.

In the shades of the evening we gathered our dead and wounded and took up the march a mile or two further on, when we halted for the night. Early the next morning we buried our dead comrades and then took position at Cross-Keys.

This photograph of Turner Ashby's corpse—the only known picture of a Confederate general killed in action—was made at the Frank Kemper house in Port Republic, where Ashby was taken to be prepared for burial. Hearing of Ashby's death, Stonewall Jackson paced the floor "for some time, in deep sorrow."

General Ewell ordered this trophy, taken from a captured Bucktail, to be appended to the flag of the 1st Maryland to honor its performance in charging the Pennsylvanians and driving them from the field. Writing to one of the Bucktails 36 years after the war, Bradley Johnson stated that Harrisonburg was "a game fight for you, and I heartily congratulate you on it."

Cross Keys and Port Republic

In the first week of June, Stonewall Jackson was in full retreat up the Valley Pike hotly pursued by Frémont's army. Even before the sharp fight at Harrisonburg on June 6, Jackson knew a major action was in the offing, but his army desperately needed at least a brief rest. By June 7 he had pulled his men back to camps between the hamlet of Cross Keys and the town of Port Republic. Jackson established his headquarters just outside the latter, confident that he was beyond the immediate reach of his pursuers.

Stonewall Jackson hoped to enjoy religious services the next morning, but unexpected Northern raiders interrupted his Sabbath. Because of an inept Rebel cavalry screen covering the advance of Shields' division down Luray Valley, Jackson was unaware that this other Federal force was on his doorstep. Gunners of an Ohio battery, supported by Indiana infantry, both from Colonel Samuel S. Carroll's brigade, shattered the morning's calm with a roaring cannonade. Soon Federal cavalry dashed into the streets of Port Republic and came within a few yards of capturing the Confederate commander.

A handful of Virginians posted near Jackson's headquarters rallied against the raiders and delayed their advance long enough for Confederate reinforcements to rush to the scene and stifle the threat. During the furor Stonewall had galloped through a covered bridge as artillery shells crashed into its superstructure, then faced a Federal cannon at point-blank range across the booming waters of the North River.

By the time the crisis at Port Republic passed, cannon fire echoing through the Valley signaled the beginning of a battle at Cross Keys, four miles north. General Frémont had finally decided to fight and had advanced with uncharacteristic vigor. His opponent, Richard Ewell, commanding the rear division of the Confederate force, was well prepared to meet him. Ewell had spread his regiments and batteries across commanding heights that rose in a crescent above Mill Creek. As soon as the oncoming Yankees got within range, Rebel artillery opened up, soon followed by return fire from a half-dozen Union batteries.

On the Confederate right, General Isaac R. Trimble had no desire to stand idle and endure the bombardment. After receiving a report of enemy movements beyond his front, he got his brigade in motion, thrusting it north of Mill Creek and then positioning it to await the Federals. The 8th New York, leading the advance of General Julius Stahel's so-called German brigade, stumbled into Trimble's waiting muskets and was badly mauled. Excited Confederates chased the survivors back whence they came, then drove away several supporting Federal regiments.

Trimble's furious drive carried him a mile beyond Ewell's line, but Ewell was largely unaware of Trimble's success and more concerned with his own center and left. There the artillery duel had intensified and an enemy advance appeared imminent. After much indecision, Frémont finally gave the nod to General Milroy, who had been pressing for an assault. First Milroy's four regiments pushed out across Mill Creek, followed shortly by General Robert C. Schenck's brigade on the right. Despite some anxious moments, Ewell took full advantage of his superior position to maul the attackers, and with this repulse the fighting sputtered to a halt. The clash at Cross Keys had cost Frémont 800 casualties, with nearly a third of them from the 8th New York. Ewell lost fewer than 300 men, but Jackson had need of the battle-worn division.

Jackson still had to deal with Shields. Counting on continued inaction by Frémont, Stonewall would shift first his own division and then all but a rear guard from Ewell across to the east side of the Shenandoah River. Then, when the last troops were over, he would burn the bridge and keep Frémont from linking up with Shields.

Throughout the night of June 8, Port Republic hummed with urgent activity. Troops were able to cross the North River on a bridge, but the South River lacked a span—and it was roaring after an unusually wet spring. A detachment of black pioneer troops fashioned an ersatz crossing by winching wagon bodies into the stream, then laying boards across the tops. Very early on the 9th, Jackson sent Winder's Stonewall Brigade across the precarious span, then marched it downstream along the right bank of the Shenandoah.

Shields' division lay in wait for the oncoming Southerners near Lewiston, home place for the Lewis family's farm. General Erastus B. Tyler's brigade had only about 3,500 men with which to resist Jackson, but it occupied a good position. A farm lane, part of it sunken and all of it lined with fences, ran perpendicular to the Confederate advance. Tyler's sturdy infantrymen from Ohio and Pennsylvania and Indiana also had impeccable anchors for the flanks of the lane: the right on the raging Shenandoah, the left on a commanding knob known as the Coaling.

Lewiston's farm operations had long turned wood into charcoal atop the knoll. Now it served as a spectacular artillery vantage point. Union cannon on and around the Coaling swept the approaches to Tyler's position as thoroughly as any artillery concentration on any battlefield in Virginia. Jackson's only hope for a victory was to seize the Coaling; and he had to take it promptly, before Frémont's troops from Cross Keys arrived on the commanding heights across the Shenandoah. Another problem was that the makeshift and precarious bridge at Port Republic created a bottleneck that ensured the piecemeal arrival of Confederate troops to the battlefield.

Jackson divided Winder's regiments as they came up, sending two plowing into the dense thickets on the mountainside to attack the Coaling, while the others moved toward Lewiston through grain fields near the river. Both attacks were repulsed by the storm of metal unleashed from the guns on the Coaling and the rifles of the Federal infantrymen in the farm lane.

Next across the spans, Richard Taylor hurried his Louisiana regiments toward the front, and Jackson ordered them to swing wider to the right and flank the Coaling. Taylor's men plunged into the hills and reached the crest of a ravine opposite the Coaling just as the Virginia troops were about to be driven off the field below them. The Louisiana men boiled out of the woods, across a narrow valley, and up into the batteries at the Coaling. The Louisianans' charge surprised the Federals and drove them off. Incredibly, the Yankees managed to rally and retake the gun-covered knoll—then recapture it a second time after being driven off again. Finally a third Rebel surge secured the pivotal hilltop for good. Now the Coaling frowned down on the flank of a Federal position it had once protected. Tyler's men had no choice but to run. Confederates chased them for miles, capturing hundreds of prisoners. Federal captives swelled Shields' casualties to about 1,100. Jackson had lost more heavily in killed and wounded during the fighting; his casualties numbered nearly 1,000, but he had his revenge for Kernstown.

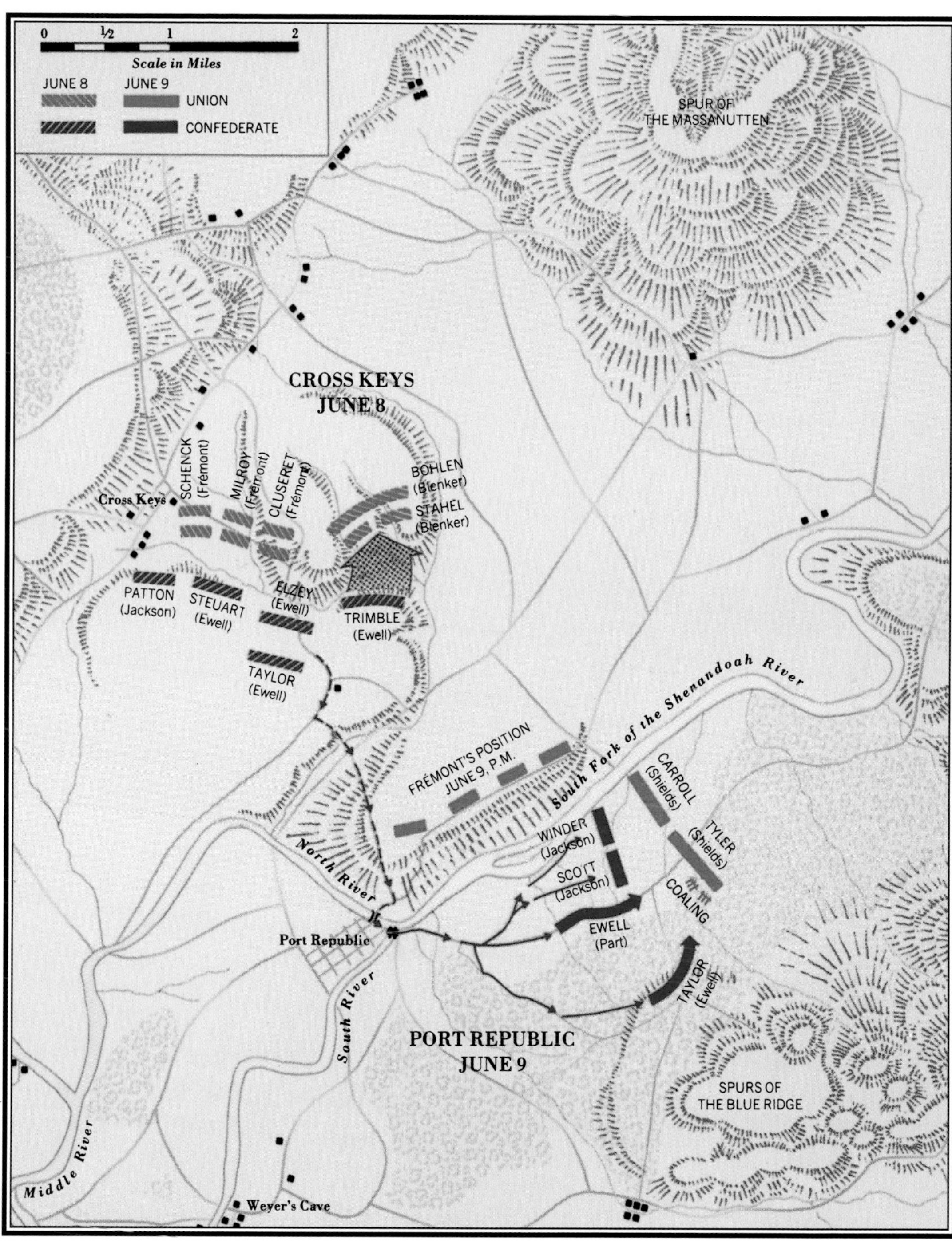

Seemingly caught in a Federal vise, the Confederates turned the tables in two days of battle. After Ewell's decisive repulse of Frémont at Cross Keys, Jackson brought his army across to the east side of the Shenandoah River's South Fork, burned the bridge to isolate the two Union forces, and then drove Shields back up Luray Valley.

On June 6 Stonewall Jackson established his headquarters at Madison Hall, the elegant residence of Dr. George Whitfield Kemper Sr., located on a hill just west of the village of Port Republic and named for the original builder, a cousin of President James Madison. Two of Dr. Kemper's sons, William and George, were serving in the 10th Virginia Infantry, Taliaferro's Brigade, and took part in the fighting near their family home. Both would die in action later in the war. When Colonel Samuel Carroll's Yankees hit the town on June 8, Jackson had near him only his staff, three understrength infantry companies, and an untested artillery battery.

LIEUTENANT HENRY K. DOUGLAS

STAFF, MAJOR GENERAL THOMAS J. JACKSON

Sunday, June 8, promised to be a peaceful interlude in Jackson's campaign. The pious commander planned to reconnoiter his lines, then observe the Sabbath by attending a religious service. But the morning stillness was shattered by artillery fire announcing the surprise arrival of Federal cavalry. Douglas was one of four staff officers who followed Jackson in a dash across the North River Bridge. The other seven were either captured or escaped to the rear.

Between seven and eight o'clock, while the General and a few of his staff were walking in front of the house, enjoying the morning away from the hum of camp and watching the horses grazing over the green lot, a courier rode up with a report that the enemy, cavalry, artillery, and infantry, were at the Lewis House, three miles distant. He was very indefinite and was sent back. He was not out of sight when a lieutenant of cavalry arrived and said the enemy were in sight of Port Republic. And just then a quick discharge of cannon indicated that the little town was being shelled. Then there was hustling for horses. My horse was saddled and fastened to the fence, for I intended to ride. The greatest anxiety was to get the General off, and I offered him my horse, running with an orderly to get his, farthest off, of course, in the field. But the General waited and was soon mounted. Pendleton, being ready, followed, and I was delayed a little getting my horse. Few of the staff got off in time. If any other crossed the bridge in that John Gilpin race with the General but Pendleton, I do not remember him. I was the last to get over, and I passed in front of Colonel S. Sprigg Carroll's cavalry as they rode up out of the water and made my rush for the bridge. I could see into their faces plainly and they greeted me with sundry pistol shots.

SURGEON HUNTER MCGUIRE

STAFF, MAJOR GENERAL THOMAS J. JACKSON

McGuire, Jackson's 27-year-old medical director, found himself caught in the chaos of the Yankee onslaught on Port Republic. Hastening to evacuate Confederate wounded, he was cut off and captured by troopers of the 1st Virginia (U.S.) Cavalry, the lead element of Carroll's Federal raiding force.

Early Sunday morning . . . I left Gen. Jackson and his staff at the old Kemper house, which is at the southern extremity of the village, and rode on down the main street to a little church where I had made a temporary hospital for a few men wounded when Ashby was killed. Ashby's body had been sent to Charlottesville to be buried the day before. When I reached the church, I found the ambulances I had ordered the evening before with several wagons backed up against the front steps of the church to receive the wounded. Just as I arrived at the church, the Yankees opened a piece of artillery from a little knoll of ground on the east side of the village and fired five or six shots at the steeple of the church. One or two of the shots hit the Steeple and sent down over the drivers and horses a shower of broken shingles. I had great difficulty to keep the drivers from running off, and was riding up and down the line of ambulances threatening to shoot the first man who left, and in order to enforce my commands was using some profane language. While engaged in this work, I felt somebody touch me on the shoulder, and looking around, found it was Gen. Jackson, who had left the Kemper house with his staff and ridden on down the main street of the village until he came to the church. He asked me: "Doctor, dont you think you can manage these men without swearing?" I told him I would try. Immediately after this he left me and went down to the bridge, which was at the northern end of the village. Just as he got to the bridge, a regiment of Yankee cavalry came across. Jackson was not half across the bridge when the Yankees reached the Port Republic end of it. The two staff officers captured were Col. Crutchfield and Capt. Edwin Willis. Crutchfield escaped that night and returned to us; Willis came in the next day with his guard. He waited for the fellow to go to sleep that night, pretending all the while to be asleep himself, then seized his gun and brought him in a prisoner.

The ambulances were soon loaded, and a train of about six ambulances and two wagons started on through the village to the Staunton road. After seeing them fairly on the way, I left them and went on down towards the bridge, expecting to meet Gen. Jackson. I heard a great commotion in the street about the bridge, but thought it was some of our cavalry who had been on picket, and were driven in. I rode on down to meet them, and could see them form in line to charge. Still thinking they were our men, I rode toward them, when I was surprised at their demanding my surrender. I told them that I surrendered, but had no arms to give up. They asked me if I would give them my parole not to attempt to escape, but I did not answer them. I went along with them in the charge, and was among the front line when Capt. Moore fired into them and emptied a good many saddles. When he fired, the Yankees went back for some distance, and the officers were trying to get them to re-form and charge again when the second volley from Capt. Moore was received, and then I left them. I ran off by a side street and escaped.

CAPTAIN SAMUEL J. C. MOORE

2D VIRGINIA INFANTRY, WINDER'S BRIGADE

Moore commanded one of three small companies of infantry that had been deployed in Port Republic the day before the fight. Alerted to the Federal presence, he hurried his two dozen soldiers to a position near Jackson's headquarters. Despite the odds against them, the Virginians waged a stalwart defense that bought time for Jackson to hurry reinforcements from the camps across the North River.

The next morning at daylight, I became aware of an unusual commotion in the village, which was quickly followed by two cannon shots, the shells exploding in the village. I at once ordered my men who were at the blacksmith shop to form, and while this was being done, a cavalry man rode up in great haste, with the information that Genl Shields' advance guard had driven in the videttes on the right or east bank of the river, and had forced a passage over the South branch. . . . The man who brought me this information had been a member of my company; had been at his request, transferred to the cavalry, and was one of the pickets on the road, who had been driven in by Shields' advance guard. His name is Henry D. Kerfoot. . . .

I directed him to gallop at once to Genl Jackson's Head Quarters at D Kemper's house, in rear of my position and in full view of it, and inform the General of the situation, and then to ride to a field where I had learned that a battery which had arrived the evening before, was encamped, and request the Captain to come to the front with his guns. Kerfoot volunteered to return to me after having carried out my directions, which he did, and when he reported to me, told me that Genl Jackson's reply to him when he delivered my message, was "go back and fight them," spoken without excitement or change of countenance. In the meantime I had withdrawn the guard from the bank of the river and put them in the line, except two of them who were recent conscripts and had never been under fire, who availed themselves of the opportunity to escape up the river bank, so that I had, including the sergeant, twenty muskets.

I then marched up the road about three hundred yards, and took a strong position on the road by which the enemy must advance to at-

Jackson's chief of artillery, Colonel Stapleton Crutchfield, was one of three staff officers captured by the Yankees before they could make their escape across the North River Bridge. Crutchfield's "heart went down to the bottom of his breeches pockets," but he soon managed to break free from his captors.

Federal gunners sighted their cannon on Port Republic using the steeple of the town's Methodist Episcopal Church—the small community's only house of worship—which was serving as an improvised hospital for Confederate wounded. Several shells struck the building as Dr. McGuire struggled to evacuate his patients.

tack our wagon train, and put the men in line to await their advance.

I told the men to keep cool; not to fire a shot until I gave the order; and when they did fire to take good aim; that the preservation of our army depended on us, and the time had come when we must drive back the enemy or die. In a few moments the head of their column of cavalry came in sight, moving with caution towards us, and as I glanced along the column, I estimated their number to be at least three hundred, moving in column of fours. I withheld my fire until they got within very short range, when at my command a volley was poured into them, which emptied many saddles, and hurled the head of the column back upon the men in their rear. My men then loaded quickly, and I led them forward about fifty paces, where we delivered a second volley which increased the confusion in the enemy's column.

About this time as they were forming to renew the attack the battery I had sent for came up, two guns first arriving and at once opening fire down the street, and in a few minutes they were followed by the other two guns, and the main street was soon cleared of the enemy's cavalry, who moved over to the back street next to the South branch.

SERGEANT JAMES GILDEA

Battery L, 1st Ohio Light Artillery, Carroll's Brigade

An Irish-born mechanic, James Gildea joined the artillery in October 1861 and was soon appointed his battery's quartermaster sergeant. Taking charge of a cannon that had been manhandled into position on the Port Republic side of the North River Bridge, the sergeant narrowly missed an opportunity to fell Stonewall Jackson, who once safely across the river apparently mistook Gildea's gun crew for Confederates.

The cavalry crossed the ford and we followed with two guns, leaving the center section under Lieut. Chas. H. Robinson, a brother of the Captain, on the east side of the ford. There being no Lieut. with the left section, Capt. Robinson led it and when we reached the street he turned the first piece, Capt. Phil. Housor in charge, to the south and ordered me to take Sargt. Lee T. Beatty with his piece up to the bridge and hold it. As we advanced to the bridge, I noticed a large circle of fire in front of a blacksmith shop at the south end of the bridge. They had been shrinking wagon tires. I saw that a good chance to fire the bridge if orders had not prohibited it. I could have had it in a blaze before jackson could have got his men up to charge it. We unlimbered and pointed the guns across the river to a crest at our left of the bridge and loaded just as we saw four or five mounted men come over the crest and ride down the slope. I commenced to adjust the elevating screw to fire when the Captain came up and shouted, "Jim dont fire there, those are our men." I replied they are not, they are Rebs. He said dont fire until I see Carrol. He rode down to where Carrol was talking to a captured Major and soon heard a shout of "give them hell." He was too late. If it was Jackson, he had discovered his mistake and was making fast time over the crest before I could lower the screw to get his range. If I had fired, I had 27 ounce balls in the gun I might have stopped the war sooner, but I could not disobey orders? In a few minutes after this we saw a column come up on the crest where he had appeared. They opened fire from the hip without sighting. This volley started our horses which were standing faced to the rear and they ran off with the limber chest just as Corpl. Wm. Garey had lifted a charge of canister out of it. The same volley struck No. 3, Frank Piles, in the forehead as he was inserting a friction primer in the gun. He fell back in my arms and I took the lanyard out of his hand. I then helped him up behind Sergt. Beatty and told the Sergt. to take him to the rear. As I looked around after this, I found that the entire gun squad had left, with the exception of Corpl. Patric Burns and Wm. Carey I took the trail handspike and they at the wheels, we ran the gun on to the bridge. I found we had only one friction primer left, so I had Carey ram his canister down on top of the charge already in. Then I told them to light out, that I would remain to fire it when the Rebs. started across. Just then the Captain came up with orders to take the gun away. I told him I had no horses to haul it and if I left there they would cross over and capture us all. He said if I would do so he would save the other piece. Burns and Carey both refused to leave, saying that I might get shot and then one of them could fire it. I passed the lanyard through the wheel and fixed the primer in the vent, then knelt on one knee with my arm on the tire, waiting for the charge which I saw forming in the other end of the bridge in column platoon. I heard the order given, "Forward, Rout step, march," and as they gained the center I raised with a steady pull on the lanyard, fired and ran for my life, as I had tied my horse by the blacksmith shop on first going into position and did not have time to get him. The gun was not pointed straight into the bridge but quartering, with the intention of weakening the timbers and to ricochet the shots. I had no time to see what execution it did.

PRIVATE WILLIAM A. MCCLENDON

15TH ALABAMA INFANTRY, TRIMBLE'S BRIGADE

Marching south from Harrisonburg at 9 a.m. on June 8, the vanguard of Frémont's army approached the left flank of Ewell's forces near Cross Keys. McClendon's 15th Alabama—positioned on the far left of Ewell's line—was destined to bear the brunt of the initial Yankee attack. Threatened with encirclement, the Alabamians made a hasty withdrawal from their exposed position near Union Church.

Early in the morning the 15th Alabama was formed in line of battle on the left of the turnpike at the end of a piece of woods that surrounded the church. . . . Desultory firing had been going on all the morning and from the way that the Couriers and staff officers were dashing around an attack was momentarily expected. We were not long in suspence, for all at once Co. A was attacked with such overwhelming numbers that they had to fire in retreat. They soon came in sight, passing through the cemetery, frequently taking shelter behind a tomb-stone long enough to fire and load. Well do I remember seeing Ben Ryans of Co. A when he took shelter behind a tomb-stone and fired back at the Yankees. The odds were so great against Co. A that they came in and took their place in line. It was on this move that Lieut. Berry of that company was captured. When the Yankees reached the opening near the cemetery, they halted for awhile; a deathly stillness prevailed in our ranks while we were waiting for the Yankees to come in reach, for we were anxious to get a shot. While we were waiting Colonel Cantey rode to the right up to the pike, when he saw just over the hill a brigade of Yankess in line of battle marching past our right flank. Had they known our position they could have changed front forward on tenth company and had us completely at their mercy, for an attack from that direction would have caused considerable confusion. The Colonel came back and called us to attention, and give the command to retire by the right of companies, which we did, moving in quick time through a wheat-field. The Yankees seeing this retrograde movement advanced through the cemetery, and began to fire into our rear, which caused us to change our time of march, from a quick to a double quick. Zip! Zip! Zip! came their bullets. Whap! and down went Bill Toney of Co. K, mortally wounded or dead. What! and down went Jim Trawick of Co. G. The ball cutting his hat band through to his head, it only stunned him and he rose to his feet and came on. There might have been others hit but I don't remember now. We broke into a run for a short distance until we crossed a fence. . . . We were moved off to the right, to meet a column of Yankees that were advancing to turn our flank.

In 1861 the 15th Alabama was among 120 Confederate units issued a new-pattern silk battle flag. The regiment carried this banner in the Valley campaign. Most Virginia units in the Valley still fought under the Stars and Bars or the state colors.

CHARLES H. WEBB

SPECIAL CORRESPONDENT, NEW YORK TIMES

Dodging Rebel shellfire as he rode along the deploying Federal formations near Union Church, newspaper reporter Charles Webb was frustrated by his inability to get a clear view of the escalating battle south of Cross Keys. He finally fell in with General Frémont's headquarters staff, only to find that the Union commander was equally uncertain of what was transpiring on the front lines.

Soon after the cannonading commenced. I pressed forward in advance of Gen. FREMONT and his Staff—the firing still distant—anxious to gain a position *in sight* of, and yet at a safe angle from the scene of conflict. Few people, I imagine, are aware, untried, how much or little nerve they may possess in near approach to the

> "The musketry was heard in volleys, telling of fearful havoc, slaughter and bloodshed."

horrible tearing screech of cannon balls that are meant to kill.

I turned aside to the left, from the main road, to gain a little eminence near one of our batteries that had just opened fire. They were aiming across a plain to a skirting of timber, three-fourths of a mile distant, where, it was said, a large number of the enemy had been seen. Very soon after, Gen. STAHL'S Brigade of infantry, being the First of the Blenker Division, filed into the edge of the woods near this battery.

After waiting some ten or fifteen minutes and no response from the enemy, I went on down the road, toward where the heavier cannonading was going on. It turned out that my "first position" was the left wing of our line; and on that field, at a later part of the day, with STAHL'S Brigade, was the most desperate fighting and heaviest losses on our side of the whole day's battle.

Arrived at the Brick Church, near where the roads converge, I halted a moment, uncertain which road to take, when a cannon-ball came bursting through the graveyard fence, a few feet to the left of where I stood. Of course I took the other road! But as I passed beyond the other corner of the church another ball came tearing through the limbs of the trees, nearly over my head. As this seemed near enough "under fire" for all practical purposes to a newspaper reporter, who was expected to furnish a list of killed and wounded, I continued on at right angles with the range of the balls to the public house known as the "Cross-Keys." Here I found three intelligent females, a baby and a timid army Chaplain, all about equally alarmed for their safety. I endeavored to quiet their fears, as there was a dense forest of timber between them and the guns, which were half a mile or more distant. But the Chaplain's alarm overcame my philosophy. They locked up the house and departed, Chaplain and all, by another road over a hill, screened by more timber, and off a mile or two out of the way. . . .

Presently the firing opened again, further to the right, by our guns, and I moved forward on the other road about half a mile, to the other side of the timber, passing one dead rebel on the way. An open field was now before me, over which our guns were firing, but still no enemy in sight. . . . This was near the centre of our line, and Gen. MILROY'S Brigade. I could see the flash and smoke of our guns to the right through the woods, but saw no results, nor what they were aimed at. I then returned to seek the headquarters. I found them on a gentle eminence, and open ground, a little to the left of the centre, and in the rear of our line. Here I found the reports coming in of how the fight was progressing; but no part of it was to be seen.

The musketry was heard in volleys, telling of fearful havoc, slaughter and bloodshed, and in the houses in our rear we could see the results upon the wounded brought in in ambulances. Many of them were slight wounds, and it was a relief to see the cheerful and uncomplaining aspect of the men, and the fortitude with which they bore their pain. Poor fellows, their greater trials were yet to come in the weary weeks of hospital life beyond.

A German immigrant like most of his comrades in the ill-fated 8th New York Infantry, Bavarian-born Karl Heinrich Brunner was only 13 years old when he marched in the ranks of Company K at Cross Keys. Brunner—seen here in a post-war photograph—somehow survived the slaughter of the regiment unscathed but was captured the following December during the Fredericksburg campaign.

The Battle of Cross Keys Sunday June 7th 1862 - E Forbes -
Genl Fremont - and Genl Jackson -

Edwin Forbes' panoramic eyewitness sketch depicts the opening phase of the Battle of Cross Keys from a position near the center of the Union line. In the foreground a cavalry detachment waits in reserve near a cluster of ambulance wagons (6), while a column of infantry from one of Frémont's brigades (5) marches toward the fight. The guns of three Federal batteries (4), positioned on a commanding elevation, exchange fire with Rebel guns positioned on the high ground (2) on the far side of Mill Creek.

CAPTAIN WILLIAM C. OATES

15th Alabama Infantry, Trimble's Brigade

Following its evacuation of Union Church, the 15th Alabama rejoined the rest of the brigade to meet the Yankee advance. Sheltered behind a rail fence on the right of Trimble's line, the Alabamians had a clear field of fire on Brigadier General Julius Stahel's brigade, led by the 8th New York. The New Yorkers moved forward unsupported and without skirmishers, marching into a murderous cross fire that cost the regiment more than 200 of its 600 men.

Colonel Canty had formed the regiment in line of battle along the crest of a little hill with a gradual slope and open field in our front about one hundred yards to the woods. A skirmish line of the enemy appeared at the edge of the woods; the men were anxious to fire, and I could hear the click, click, click of locks along the line; but just at that moment Colonel Canty gave the command, "By the right companies to the rear into column; double-quick, march!" and away we went for about a mile through wheat fields, crossing two or three rail fences, not firing a shot, and nothing that I could see but a line of skirmishers in hot pursuit, firing upon us and doing some execution, until Courtney's battery opened on them from a hill in our front and put a stop to their pursuit. . . . Colonel Canty gave his reason for ordering the retreat, that there was a regiment over in the field flanking us on the right. I did not see that regiment, but the colonel was mounted, and no doubt saw it. I think, however, that he made a mistake in retreating, and should have fought both regiments, the one on the flank as well as the one in front, and could have whipped both of them. The Fifteenth did on other fields afterwards do even better fighting than that would have been. But it was a new business with us then. . . . We were united with our Brigade and placed behind a fence, with a field of buckwheat 150 yards wide in our front between us and a body of woods. Blencker's division of Dutch people, of whose depredations and brutality there had been great complaint by the citizens of Virginia, now advanced upon us. Our men could not be restrained, and fired too soon—as soon as the enemy emerged from the woods. But the firing of the Fifteenth was immediately checked. A few moments elapsed and a column of the enemy, marching by the flank on the opposite side of a fence running at right angles from that behind which we lay and intending to flank us on the left, walked right up to the Twenty-first Georgia, which just mowed them down in piles at a single volley.

SERGEANT SAMUEL D. BUCK

13TH VIRGINIA INFANTRY, ELZEY'S BRIGADE

After the slaughter of the 8th New York, Trimble launched a counterattack that drove back Stahel's advance and nearly captured a Federal battery. Pressing his advantage, Trimble ordered the 13th and the 25th Virginia, temporarily under his command, to attack the left flank of Brigadier General Henry Bohlen's brigade. Buck recalled how the two small regiments found themselves facing an intimidatingly large Union force whose fire eventually forced the Rebels to seek shelter in some nearby woods.

As soon as we formed, Col. Walker ordered us forward and all went well. Our line was perfect as we moved through a piece of woods. We struck a high fence which we got over, forming as we did so and again we moved up the side of a hill through a wheat field on our left resting on a fence line leading to a barn. As we rose to the top of this hill, we came face to face with more of the enemy than I had ever seen in one position and with several pieces of artillery, which opened on us with grape, cannister, and small arms which were mowing the wheat about us like a hail storm, immediately in our front was a very strong post fence which could not be torn down; we could not go forward and would not fall back so our only alternative was to stand and take it and most nobly did the regiment do it, but most humbly do I now confess, nothing but pride and a sense of duty kept me from running. Fortunately, the enemy's infantry was not expecting us from that direction as this was on their flank, besides they thinking our force larger, fell back. . . .

. . . One of my company, McCopehaur, was badly wounded and fell almost on me begging me to take him off the field, but there was no time for favors then. . . . I have seen six men carrying one wounded man from the field, often four and always two; this in itself would render an army almost useless. The best way to protect our wounded friends was to do our duty in the line and drive the enemy from them.

Lieutenant Reuben Conway Macon, adjutant of the 13th Virginia, was shot in the right thigh during the attack on Bohlen's brigade but refused to leave his men until the fight was over. Macon took a bullet in his shoulder two years later at the battle of the Wilderness and was permanently disabled.

PRIVATE ELI S. COBLE

21ST NORTH CAROLINA INFANTRY, TRIMBLE'S BRIGADE

For six hours Federal artillery pounded Ewell's men, paving the way for a renewed attack on the embattled Rebel line. Hunkered down to avoid the heavy shelling, Coble and his comrades watched as Confederate batteries dueled with their Yankee counterparts. Coble, whose regiment supported the guns of Captain Alfred Courtney's Virginia Battery, was only one of many Rebel soldiers impressed with the good-humored gallantry of the young artillery officer Joseph Latimer.

The enemy battery of rifled guns was stationed about west of us and I think not far from the road. They used mainly cap shells, I think they were called shrapnell shells, and solid shot and I think they used three or four guns for the shots came in rapid succession. The conflict was terrific. . . . Three of our companies were [engaged to protect our guns and] the rest of the regiment were in a manner out of it. Under that fire we lost twenty five killed and I don't know how many wounded but perhaps as many. . . . Our artillery suffered the loss of several gallant men one of whom I think his name was Glascock & I believe he ranked as sergeant[.] He was hit near the top of the head, a glancing shot, knocking fragments of his skull away. After a few hours Captain Latimer had to call on our regiment for men to carry ammunition from the magazine near the foot of the hill to the guns. Captain Latimer stood two or three steps to the left side of the gun to the left hand and his cheeks wore a rosey tint and his face was that of a cheerful soul. There he stood giving [commands] to his gallant men, at every round. [Every] now & then came the order "Down" [and they would] fall flat to the ground, and in a few moments they were up at their guns again ready to fire. The guns were worked alternately, that is they fired in turn. Along about 2 p.m. Captain Latimer called our Colonel to have his men ready that the enemy was advancing[.] "Attention" was given & the boys sprang in line & was about to "forward." "Not yet, Colonel, I will give them a few more rounds" and then I think he used grape[.] At this juncture the cannonading ceased on their side. Whatever it was our gunners was giving them they give it like they had plenty of it and they were not the kind of fellows who shot just anywhere. After giving them several rounds the Captain called, "Colonel have your men ready the enemy is approaching." At this time the gunners [gave way] to the left to let us pass with guns at a "ready" and as [we passed] the sweaty powder black artill[ery men] pulled their caps and waving cheered us time and again and when we had come up in line with them the line of one accord bowed to them and returned the cheering heartily. After a few moments the line moved on to the top of the ridge but the Yankee like the dutchman's pig came up missing.

Eighteen-year-old Joseph Latimer left his studies at VMI to enlist in the Confederate army as an artillery officer. Trimble brevetted the teenager to captain's rank for his "heroic conduct" at Cross Keys, about which an admiring infantryman wrote, "I know we have worse generals by far than he wd. make." Latimer was fatally wounded at Gettysburg by a shell that severed his left arm.

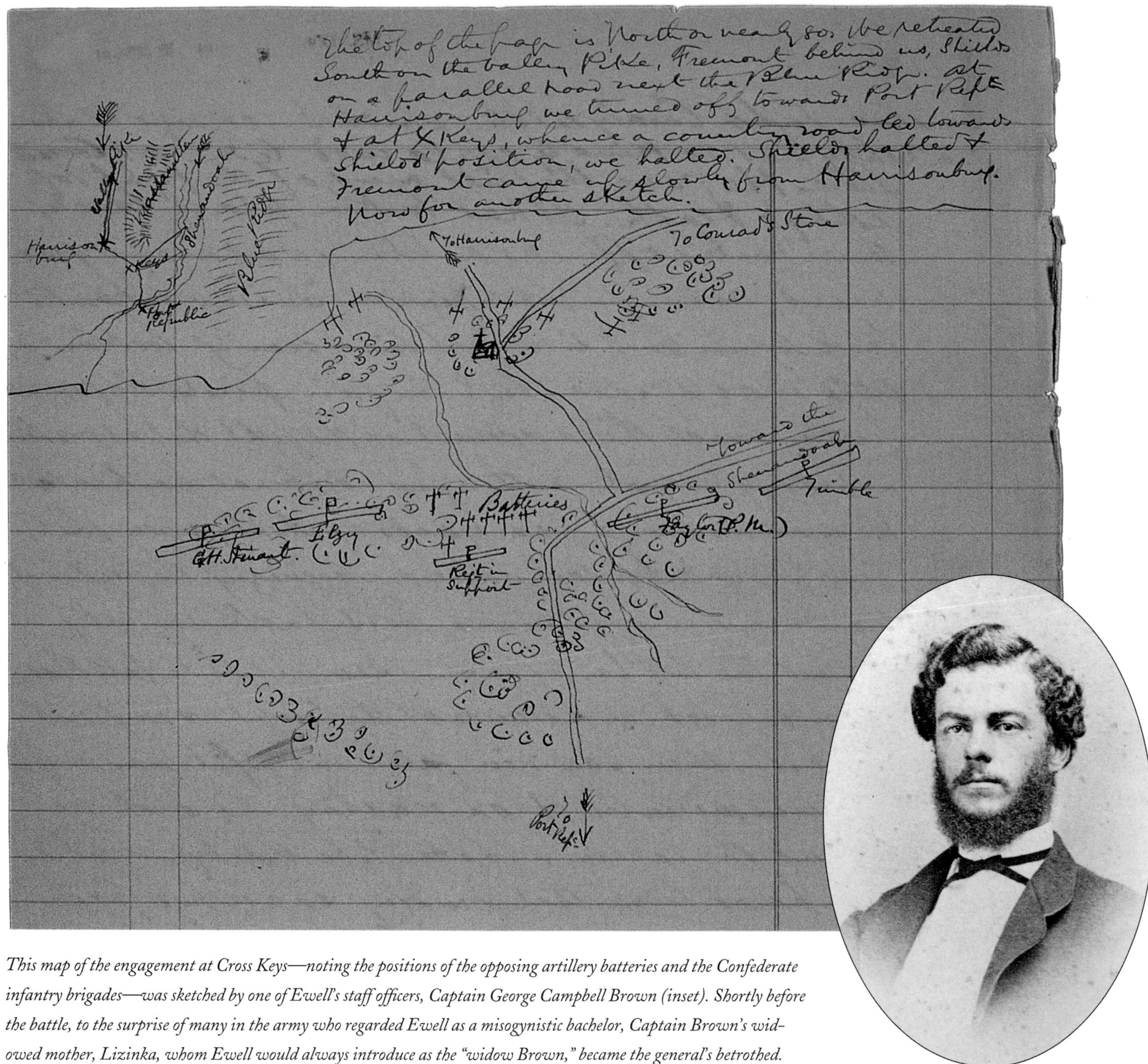

This map of the engagement at Cross Keys—noting the positions of the opposing artillery batteries and the Confederate infantry brigades—was sketched by one of Ewell's staff officers, Captain George Campbell Brown (inset). Shortly before the battle, to the surprise of many in the army who regarded Ewell as a misogynistic bachelor, Captain Brown's widowed mother, Lizinka, whom Ewell would always introduce as the "widow Brown," became the general's betrothed.

"I thought of all whom-ever I held dear—a mother and sister's tears will probably be poured out for my life."

PRIVATE THOMAS EVANS

25TH OHIO INFANTRY, MILROY'S BRIGADE

Lacking clear instructions from Frémont, fiery Brigadier General Robert Milroy decided to launch his four regiments in a charge on the left center of the Rebel position. Advancing in the ranks of Milroy's brigade, Canadian-born Evans was shaken by the carnage of the battlefield. The attack encountered stiff resistance, and the Federal lines became jumbled in the rolling, wooded terrain. The failed assault cost Milroy 182 men, 65 of them from Evans' 25th Ohio.

As soon as the enemy's true position was discovered we moved forward. The battle now became general. This was my first battle. Here I was rushing pell mell to probable destruction. I paused. I thought of all whom-ever I held dear—a mother and sister's tears will probably be poured out for my life. I may soon be in the eternal repose of death. I trembled with emotion. Then breathing a prayer to God for strength and protection, I commenced the work of Death. The deafening roar of musketry and the loud pealing of artillery. The bursting of shells, the whiz of grape and cannister. The crushing of timber by the dread missles mingled with the unearthly yells of opposing forces and the moaning of the dying and the screams of the wounded. Oh God, how terrible is war. How long must man thus strive with man? Here lies a dear comrade bleeding and dying at your side who can just breathe the name of Mother, sister or wife, and he is gone. Another in the prime of life is cut down without a second's warning.

BRIGADIER GENERAL ROBERT H. MILROY

BRIGADE COMMANDER, FRÉMONT'S COMMAND

An Indiana lawyer, Milroy was an aggressive, hot-tempered commander whose manner in combat prompted one soldier to liken him to "a crazy man." At Cross Keys Milroy displayed an initiative woefully lacking in most of the Federal high command, breaking off assaults only when ordered to do so by Frémont. In this account, written for his wife a week after the battle, he candidly describes how he twice led his men into the teeth of heavy enemy fire.

Seeing no enemy in sight I asked permission to advance which was granted and I advanced my four Regiments by heads of Regts. about half a mile when I found a fine position for my artillery in full view of 3 reble batteries—I threw my Regts. into a ravine under shelter from their batteries which had again opened on us and sent back by aids for my batteries. They soon come. I had them again thrown into position and they commenced preaching to the rebles in a most eloquent and striking manner. As soon as they got to work in fine style, I road forward myself to examine the ground and discover the best way of getting my Regiments up where they could use their Minnie Enfield rifles. After a few hundred yards I discovered a ravine, which could be reached without exposure, which led up into another ravine—that run along the foot of the hill on which the reble batteries were situated. I determined to bring my brigade up and deploy at the foot of the hill silence the batteries with my rifles and take them at the point of the bayonet. I brought them up caustiously along the ravine leading up to the 2nd but as soon as the head of my columns got within 60 or 70 yards of the 2nd ravine we discovered it was full of rebles laying behind a fence in the tall grass almost wholly concealed from view but they mowed down the head of my column by a deadly fire almost as fast as they appeared, and we could not return their fire with any effect as we could not see them. One of the best captains of the 25th Ohio fell mortally wounded here. I tried to dislodge or raise them by skirmishes but without effect. I then determined to throw my Bdg. across into a forest which I observed over the hill to my right. I sent skirmishes forward to feel the way—as soon as they rose the hill in the tall heavy wheat (we were in an open wheat field) they recd. a perfect storm of bullets from the woods which appeared to be full of rebles, but the folage was so thick we could not see them. I brought up my Regiments and opened a tremendous fire into the woods but a deadly fire come out of it and my

Lieutenant William J. Rannells of the 75th Ohio, in Schenck's brigade, saw more than his share of action in the war. Little of it occurred at Cross Keys, however, because Schenck failed to press forward against the Confederate left as Milroy had in the center. Two months later Rannells was captured at Second Bull Run. Paroled, he returned to his unit and was wounded at the Battle of Gettysburg. After his recovery Rannells again took the field, only to be captured in August 1864.

boys were droped by it rapidly—my noble horse Jasper recd. two shots in quick succession—the first across the hind leg the second in the left breast which ranged across and lodged in his right shoulder and totally disabled him. He rared and plunged and nearly fell with me—I sprung off and saw the blood spurting out of his breast and give him up for dead. I ordered my Regts. to push on and turn more to the right in order to turn to the left flank of the rebles. They did so and the 25th Ohio which was leading got half into the forest when one of Gen. Fremonts aids dashed up to me with an order for me to fall back with my whole Bgd. a mile to the position first occupied by me in the morning. I was never so astonished or thunderstruck in my life. I could not believe what the dutchman said and made him repeat it three times, the balls were whizzing around him like bees and he was dodging his head down behind the horse like a duck dodging thunder while he was repeating the order and as soon as he got through he dashed off at break neck speed. I was standing close behind the center of my Bgd. but felt ashamed to order them to cease firing and file to the rear. I called my aids to me and told them to order the Regts. to do so being careful to carry back all their dead and wounded . . . which they did with as much coolness as on a parade in peace all mad and cursing the order to retreat.

An 1859 graduate of VMI, Major John DeHart Ross of the 52d Virginia stood six feet three inches tall and was nicknamed Mad Boy for his combative disposition. During Milroy's assault Ross was shot in the leg and his right hand was mangled by a shell fragment, wounds that would eventually compel him to resign.

"The balls were whizzing around him like bees and he was dodging his head down behind the horse like a duck dodging thunder."

MAJOR JOSEPH H. CHENOWETH

31ST VIRGINIA INFANTRY, ELZEY'S BRIGADE

One of Jackson's best students at VMI, Chenoweth later taught at his alma mater. An inveterate diarist, he took advantage of lulls in the fighting to chronicle his experiences and vent his emotions in the pages of his journal. The day after he wrote this entry he was killed at Port Republic.

We have been firing in the fighting and poor Lt. Whitly has been killed, shot thro' the head. A cannon has been planted to our left, and several of our poor men have been wounded. I pity them from the bottom of my heart. We will be at it again soon I think, and Oh God I renew my earnest prayer for the forgiveness of my many sins, and for strength. In the name of Thy Son grant me mercy Amen. . . . All is now quiet. Our regiment (31st) is lying down in line of battle, in full view of the enemy's battery, which only an hour or two ago was pouring grape into the regiment. Noble soldiers! it tortures me to see them wounded. How many of them now, as they rest, looking quietly and dreamily up into the beautiful sky and thinking of the dear ones at home whom they have not, many of them, seen for twelve months. This is a hard life for us refugees, who fight and suffer without one smile from those we love dearest to cheer us up. But by the blessings of God, the fires of patriotism will keep our hearts warm, and a consciousness that we are trying to do our duty will always enable us to sleep sweetly when our day's work is done, and that we can wander over dreamland to the hearthstones of our kindred, and see again by imagination's rosy light the dear faces of the dear ones at home. Sometimes I fear, but always put aside the thought, that these very homes of which I have written will never be as happy, as peaceful, as they were before the war commenced. Can the convictive feelings of hatred which burn in the breasts of our Union neighbors be obliterated by a treaty of peace? Or will they be compelled to expatriate themselves, or be exiled deservedly, exiled from a land to which they have all proven themselves traitors in tho't if not in deed?

This primitive armored vest was abandoned during the Valley campaign by a Federal soldier who undoubtedly found the rigid, heavy covering cumbersome and impractical. Sutlers sometimes sold the vests to gullible volunteers, while others were supplied by well-meaning relatives. General Winder's aide McHenry Howard recalled that several breastplates were found along the roadside on the way to Port Republic, one of them pierced by a bullet.

PRIVATE HAMILTON SECHEVERELL

29TH OHIO INFANTRY, TYLER'S BRIGADE

Secheverell did not participate in the action at Port Republic, having been granted a medical discharge five days before. He reconstructed this account for a history of the 29th Ohio by interviewing survivors of the fight. His regiment helped repel the assault by Winder's brigade and the 7th Louisiana, the first Confederate units that Jackson rushed into battle against Shields' Federals east of Port Republic before Frémont could arrive with reinforcements.

On June 9th, in the dim light of early morning the enemy began to move, and soon our artillery opened a brisk fire on them. The Twenty-ninth regiment, under command of Colonel Buckley, was ordered to fall in, and at 6:45 o'clock marched out of the timber into the open field, and moved forward a short distance, when the men unslung knapsacks and other equipage and, reduced to light marching order, advanced by the right flank, and when near the rebel position came into line on the double quick. While doing so we were obliged to pass a board fence; and at this critical time the rebels opened a heavy fire of musketry, but the regiment moved steadily forward and took position in the open field. The rebels in front of our right wing were behind a strong post and rail fence. . . .

. . . The Twenty-ninth being about the right center regiment during the battle, and at this time in support of Huntington's battery, which was belching forth its shot and shell, doing deadly execution in the ranks of the advancing rebels. When in close range the rebels charged. Reserving our fire until they were almost upon us, the order was given, and with a yell the entire line poured its leaden hail into the gray clad columns of the chivalry, producing fearful slaughter, and following with a charge so impetuous that they were forced to retire from their secure position behind the fence, and here, for more than three hours and a half, our brave fellows, though outnumbered ten to one by the enemy and fighting against fate, kept them at bay and held the position. During this charge it is said that Allen Mason, of company C, Twenty-ninth regiment, captured the colors of the Seventh Louisiana Tigers, and Lieutenant Gregory and a part of company F made prisoners of twenty-five of the same regiment.

This early-20th-century aerial photograph provides a panoramic view of the battlefield at Port Republic, looking toward the southeast. The right flank of the Federal line was anchored on the South Fork of the Shenandoah River near the Lewis Mill, the large structure in the right center of the photo. The Union left occupied a strategic knoll—the clearing in the right background known as the Coaling—where the Lewis family burned wood for charcoal to use in stoves and blacksmithing.

"The sensation caused by the cutting of minie balls through the ripe grain was novel and not altogether pleasant."

Sergeant Samuel Hays left his Augusta County farm to enlist in Company E of the 5th Virginia Infantry, part of the famed Stonewall Brigade. After recovering from a wound he received at the Battle of Kernstown, Hays returned to the front and was wounded again at Port Republic, where the 5th Virginia lost 113 men in General Winder's unsuccessful charge on the Yankee line.

LIEUTENANT WILLIAM R. LYMAN

31st Virginia Infantry, Elzey's Brigade

Although the bloodied ranks of Winder's Stonewall Brigade were shored up by a regiment from Taylor's Louisiana Brigade, a Yankee counterattack had little trouble driving back the disordered Southern units. The timely arrival of reinforcements, including the 31st Virginia, restored the collapsing Confederate line—but only briefly. The charge by Lyman's regiment foundered in the same deadly cross fire that had savaged Winder's attack.

Just beyond the Baugher house and running from the river to the main road was a rail fence forming the Port Republic side of a large wheat field. . . . As [we] arrived on the field our left was hotly engaged. A piece of Artillery (Rockbridge) was drawing a severe fire in our immediate front and while getting into line several of our men were wounded. For a few minutes the 31st lay down in the ripening wheat and the sensation caused by the cutting of minie balls through the ripe grain was novel and not altogether pleasant. It was on this line of battle on the left of the field that Hays of the 7th La. was wounded. Col. De Choiseul was mortally pierced and many more gallant Louisiana boys fell to fight no more. Col. Skinner of the 52 Va. was badly wounded, Major Chenowith of the 31st Va. and many company officers including Capt. Bradshaw of my own company, were killed.

The 31st Va. took 240 men upon this field and lost over half. In my own company twenty one men out of forty were killed or wounded in the short period which elapsed from the time we were ordered up out of the wheat . . . and the order to fall back. . . .

A half witted little man was a member of Co. "B" and went with his company into the field. When the command was ordered up in the wheat field, this Billy Wright had become so thoroughly frightened by the whistling of the minie balls thro' the wheat, as not to obey the order. He laid still and when we were driven from the field and the enemy came on, Billy still held his position. He was a cadaverous looking little man at best, and, closing his eyes, Billy let the enemy roll him over and turn his pockets inside out, feigning death among the many actually warm dead bodies around him.

The enemy's possession of the field was as we have seen but of short duration and when Billy showed up he was boastful of the fact that he was the only member of the regiment who had actually *held the field*, and he was.

Lieutenant Colonel Charles DeChoiseul (above), a 43-year-old descendant of French immigrants, was one of 172 casualties suffered at Port Republic by the 7th Louisiana Infantry—the hardest hit of any Confederate regiment in the battle. DeChoiseul was struck in the lungs by a bullet and died 10 days later.

Sporting medals he received for valor in the service of Pope Pius IX, Irish-born Captain Daniel J. Keily (below) was photographed soon after he arrived in America to serve as a Union staff officer. Keily's valor at Port Republic won the praise of friend and foe alike. Grievously wounded by a bullet in the face, he kept in the saddle until his horse was killed beneath him.

SERGEANT WILLIAM F. GORDON

31st Virginia Infantry, Elzey's Brigade

Pinned down by musketry and raked with shells from the Federal batteries at the Coaling, Gordon's unit held its advanced position long enough for General Winder to rally his broken units. When the 31st finally fell back, it left 33 men dead and more than twice that number wounded. Gordon survived the battle, transferred to the cavalry, and in 1863 was captured and condemned to death as a spy. President Lincoln commuted his sentence to imprisonment at hard labor.

We crawled up through that oat-field on our bellies, rising to shoot, dropping again to load and advance. And every time we rose some comrades dropped to rise no more. We neared the crest until we could almost look down the black, sulphurous throats of those nine twelve-pounders that were belching grape and canister into our very mouths.

Five times had our colors fallen—one, two, three, four, five of our tallest brave fellows, one after another, rose with the regimental flag, and fell, shot through the forehead.

They had been picked off by the sharpshooters, one after another—those gallant Western Virginia mountaineers, as fast as a color-bearer fell, snatching up the flag and rising with it.

The fifth had fallen. A sergeant jumped from Company C to raise the standard.

"Better let the d——d thing alone, Bill!" growled Lieutenant Cooper. "Use both hands with your bayonet next rise."

Bill Cooper was a Pennsylvanian—as brave a man as crawled back with our little remnant of 114 that day. After we had reached safe quarters, and were lying down to rest in the woods, he turned to me to ask:

"What were you looking up and down the line *in there* for, Bill?"

"Lieutenant," was the answer, "I was looking for a chance to run."

"By G–d, so was I!" gruffly retorted the quondam man of valor; "but d——d if every fellow in the regiment wasn't looking right at me."

CLARA STRAYER

Resident near Port Republic

The daughter of a prosperous farmer, 19-year-old Clara Strayer witnessed the engagement at Port Republic from the upper porch of her family's home, which stood on a hill just west of the South Fork. The house was crowded with refugees who had fled their homes and were trying to discern the outcome of the battle through the low-lying smoke. The German immigrant "Dutchmen" in Frémont's army were widely held by Valley residents to be notorious scavengers and vandals.

On the 9th at six o'clock a.m. I noticed a party of horsemen grouped opposite this house on the rise below the Lewiston house where the road goes up the mountain—and immediately a stream of fire issued from the cannons' mouth, followed by a report that seemed to shake the very earth.

This Battery continued for a quarter of an hour without any response. It was perhaps an hour before we heard any response of small arms—in another hour the fight became general. . . . Our line was at one time so hotly pressed that it fell back some 200 yards above the Lewiston house and you may be sure it was an anxious moment for us though the suspense was of short duration as we soon saw the glitter of bayonets of reinforcement and heard the shout of *victory* which none knew how to give better than our own brave Confederates. . . . At first we saw every movement of the enemy, but as the battle progressed the view was somewhat obscured by the smoke. . . . Fremont who soon thereafter showed himself on the hill above us, saw only the smoking bridge at Port Republic and the hearse-like ambulances as they bore off the *dead* and *wounded* upon which he *fired* altho' *the yellow was displayed* from what was then the Fletcher house *now* the Lynwood house.

A rifle shell passed about 15 feet from the southwest corner of this house, another fell through the roof of a cabin on the upper edge of the orchard, within two feet of old Uncle Daniel who had been on the retired list. He yelled lustily, being more scared than hurt as the shell did not explode. Very soon after we saw a part of cavalry who kept on to the stable where the riding horses were kept, coming out leading old "Billy," Father's riding horse, but upon his telling them that it was too old for service they gave him up. It may be they spied other horses in the field below the house, seven of which they captured all young except Mother's old "Belle."

They next came to the house in search of Rebels and were reinforced by a detachment from Blenker's Division—who poured in every door, and such clanking of sabers, ransacking of presses; trying to break open doors, I never saw. They came into our chamber, when I remarked, "This is a lady's chamber and as such will be respected by *gentlemen.*" The leader, a big bluffy Dutchman, replied, "Yah, yah! if dere be any Dutch gentlemen! Come boys, let's go to town!"

Some of them were insolent to Father who was sick at the time, and upon my appealing to Capt. Conger of Fremont's Staff he drove them from the house. They had already stripped it of all edibles and next the smokehouse, dairy, and lastly, the Bee House where they were met not by hundreds but by thousands and were completely routed for the time, tho' they afterward came back with Hunter and drowning them in the Big Pond, took the honey. . . . Later in the day the servants fled to the woods where most of them remained until evening. Those were indeed stirring times. May we never see the like again!

The two-story porch of Bogota, the Strayer family mansion, provided outstanding vantage points from which to observe the battle. The estate's owner, 69-year-old Jacob Strayer, was one of the area's wealthiest citizens.

"The air trembled with a continual roll of musketry and the thunder of the artillery shook the ground."

CORPORAL GEORGE M. NEESE

CHEW'S (VIRGINIA) BATTERY

On the receiving end of the heavy Yankee fire cannonading down from the Coaling, Neese was in an uncomfortably good position to observe the Confederate rally. With Winder's units in disarray and Tyler's Federals surging forward, the Rebels averted disaster when Ewell lashed out at the exposed Yankee left flank with two Virginia regiments. Confederate artillery, including a portion of Chew's Battery, helped buy time, as Neese noted, for Taylor's brigade to move against the enemy guns.

When we left camp old Stonewall's cannon were thundering on the east side of the river below Port Republic, in front of General Shields. Shields had his forces strongly posted about one mile below Port Republic, his right on the river and his left butted up against a spur of the Blue Ridge that jutted boldly out into the plain. A little way up the side of the spur was a coaling which commanded the whole front of his line from the mountain to the river. General Shields quickly availed himself of the utility of this vantage ground on the extreme left of his line, by placing an eight-gun battery on the apparently invulnerable shelf up the mountain side, from which his batteries could sweep the whole field.

As we drew near and hastened toward the field the roar of battle grew fiercer and louder, the musketry being fearfully terrific. Just before we reached the field a goodly number of our wounded were returning to the rear, limping, bleeding, and groaning. Some of them greeted us to the field with the unpleasing and discouraging expression of "Hurry up; they are cutting us all to pieces."

When we arrived in sight of the field and smelled the battle smoke one of Jackson's aids came dashing from the front with a ready and prompt inquiry, "Whose battery is this?" "Chew's," was the quick response. "Have you plenty of ammunition?" The last question was answered in the affirmative, and the fleeting courier said, "Hurry to the front, captain." "Forward, double quick!" was the ringing command of our calm but gallant captain, and in a very few moments after we wheeled in battery on the battle-field, under a raking fire from the eight-gun battery strongly posted on the coaling against the mountain side, and with perfect command of the field we were in.

The fire of that battery was terrible for a while. However, we held our ground and opened on the coaling with all our guns, with the utmost endeavor to give the enemy the best work we had in the shop. Some of Jackson's batteries were in the same field with us, and were firing on the coaling battery. The air trembled with a continual roll of musketry and the thunder of the artillery shook the ground. The musketry right in front of us raged fearfully, far, far beyond the powers of description that my poor pencil can delineate. The shell from the battery on the coaling was ripping the ground open all around us, and the air was full of screaming fragments of exploding shell, and I thought I was a goner.

After we had been under this dreadful fire about thirty minutes I heard a mighty shout on the mountain side in close proximity to the coaling, and in a few minutes after I saw General Dick Taylor's Louisianians debouching from the undergrowth, and like a wave crested with shining steel rush toward the fatal coaling and deadly battery with fixed bayonets, giving the Rebel yell like mad demons. The crest of the coaling was one sheet of fire as the Federal batteries poured round after round of grape and canister into the faces of the charging Louisianians. Yet the undaunted Southerners refused to be checked by the death and carnage in their ranks which the Federal batteries were so lavishly handing around, but rushed up the steep slope of the coaling like a mighty billow of glittering steel and closed in on the belching batteries and their infantry supports with the bayonet.

BRIGADIER GENERAL RICHARD TAYLOR

BRIGADE COMMANDER, EWELL'S DIVISION

Some two hours into the battle, the fate of Jackson's army rested with the 1,700 soldiers of Taylor's Louisiana Brigade. Taylor maneuvered his command, unobserved by the enemy, upslope through heavy undergrowth southwest of the Coaling and prepared to flank the enemy batteries and their infantry support. But when couriers arrived with desperate pleas for help from commanders of the embattled units on the plain below, Taylor decided to charge the Yankee guns head-on.

From the mountain, clothed to its base with undergrowth and timber, a level—clear, open, and smooth—extended to the river. This plain was some thousand yards in width. Half a mile north, a gorge, through which flowed a small stream, cut the mountain at a right angle. The northern shoulder of this gorge projected farther into the plain than the southern, and on an elevated plateau of the shoulder were placed six guns, sweeping every inch of the plain to the south. Federal lines, their right touching the river, were advancing steadily, with banners flying and arms gleaming in the sun. A gallant show, they came on. Winder's and another brigade, with a battery, opposed them. This small force was suffering cruelly, and its skirmishers were driven in on their thin supporting line. As my Irishmen predicted, "Shields's boys were after fighting." Below, Ewell was hurrying his men over the bridge, but it looked as if we should be doubled up on him ere he could cross and develop much strength. Jackson was on the road, a little in advance of his line, where the fire was hottest, with reins on his horse's neck, seemingly in prayer. Attracted by my approach, he said, in his usual voice, "Delightful excitement." I replied that it was pleasant to learn he was enjoying himself, but thought he might have an indigestion of such fun if the six-gun battery was not silenced. He summoned a young officer from his staff, and pointed up the mountain. The head of my approaching column was turned short up the slope, and speedily came to a path running parallel with the river. We took this path, the guide leading the way. From him I learned that the plateau occupied by the battery had been used for a charcoal kiln, and the path we were following, made by the burners in hauling wood, came upon the gorge opposite the battery. Moving briskly, we reached the hither side a few yards from the guns. Infantry was posted near, and riflemen were in the undergrowth on the slope above. Our approach, masked by timber, was unexpected. The battery was firing rapidly, enabled from elevation to fire over the advancing lines. The head of my column began to deploy under cover

A wealthy planter and veteran of the Mexican War, hot-tempered Colonel Leroy Stafford led the 9th Louisiana Infantry in Taylor's charge on the Coaling. Spurring his horse over a wall that had stymied other mounted officers, the colonel was among the first to reach the enemy guns. Promoted to general in 1863, Stafford was mortally wounded at the Battle of the Wilderness the following year.

for attack, when the sounds of battle to our rear appeared to recede, and a loud Federal cheer was heard, proving Jackson to be hard pressed. It was rather an anxious moment, demanding instant action. Leaving a staff officer to direct my rear regiment—the 7th, Colonel Hays—to form in the wood as a reserve, I ordered the attack, though the deployment was not completed, and our rapid march by a narrow path had occasioned some disorder. With a rush and shout the gorge was passed and we were in the battery. Surprise had aided us, but the enemy's infantry rallied in a moment and drove us out. We returned, to be driven a second time. The riflemen on the slope worried us no little, and two companies of the 9th regiment were sent up the gorge to gain ground above and dislodge them, which was accomplished. The fighting in and around the battery was hand to hand, and many fell from bayonet wounds. Even the artillerymen used their rammers in a way not laid down in the Manual, and died at their guns. . . . I called for Hays, but he, the promptest of men, and his splendid regiment, could not be found. Something unexpected had occurred, but there was no time for speculation. With a desperate rally, in which I believe the drummer-boys shared, we carried the battery for the third time, and held it. Infantry and riflemen had been driven off, and we began to feel a little comfortable, when the enemy, arrested in his advance by our attack, appeared. He had countermarched, and, with left near the river, came into full view of our situation. Wheeling to the right, with colors advanced, like a solid wall he marched straight upon us. There seemed nothing left but to set our backs to the mountain and die hard. At the instant, crashing through the underwood, came Ewell, outriding staff and escort. He produced the effect of a reënforcement, and was welcomed with cheers. The line before us halted and threw forward skirmishers. A moment later, a shell came shrieking along it, loud Confederate cheers reached our delighted ears, and Jackson, freed from his toils, rushed up like a whirlwind, the enemy in rapid retreat. We turned the captured guns on them as they passed, Ewell serving as a gunner.

This war-torn national color was carried at Kernstown and Port Republic by the 5th Ohio Infantry, which sustained the heaviest regimental losses of either side at Port Republic: 269 men, of whom 197 were captured or missing. The flag saw no further service after the Valley campaign, but its fate immediately after the battle remains a mystery. Lieutenent Colonel John H. S. Funk of the 5th Virginia claimed in his official report that his regiment picked up a color of the 5th Ohio on the battlefield, but two members of the Ohioans' color guard maintained that they saved both of their regiment's flags by wrapping them around their bodies and then swimming the South Fork of the Shenandoah River to reach the safety of Frémont's command.

CAPTAIN JAMES F. HUNTINGTON

Battery H, 1st Ohio Light Artillery, Tyler's Brigade

The Federal cannon posted at the Coaling were drawn from three different batteries, with Huntington directing the three guns closest to the base of the hill. When Taylor's Rebel brigade stormed out of the woods near the crest, they first encountered two Parrott rifles commanded by Captain Joseph Clark of Battery E, 4th U.S. Artillery. While Clark's gunners grappled with the Louisianans, Huntington hastily evacuated his exposed position.

Soon we observed and shelled a column of infantry marching towards our left that, crossing the road, disappeared behind the trees. This was Taylor's brigade moving to the attack. In a short time, from the woods in front of our left was poured a tremendous volley of musketry at close range. In return we gave them canister in allopathic doses, and repulsed the attack without the aid of a musket. . . .

The situation of our left flank was awkward in the extreme, particularly in regard to Clark's guns, jammed into the coalpit so that it would be impossible to extricate them if the left was turned by the enemy's infantry and our line taken in reverse. . . .

Meanwhile the infantry on the right seemed to be gaining ground, keeping up a heavy fire and a vociferous cheering, though the prostrate forms behind them and the stream of wounded hobbling to the rear showed they were suffering some loss. In anticipation of another charge, I had our remaining supply of canister placed on the ground near the muzzles of the pieces ready for instant use, and searched the woods in our front with shrapnel.

My attention had been called to a fresh battery the enemy were establishing at some distance to our right, and I was watching it through a glass when from the woods on our left rushed forth the Tigers, taking the line in reverse and swarming among Clark's guns. His cannoneers made a stout but short resistance, as pistols and sponge staffs do not count for much against muskets and bayonets. His guns were taken, so was the howitzer, and if ours were to be saved they must instantly be withdrawn. The right piece was limbered to the rear and started. As the team of the next came up, two of the drivers fell, badly wounded, from their saddles. The remaining driver could not control the frightened animals, they broke away and dashed off with the limber, and the piece was abandoned. The gun in the road was in imminent peril. Hastening thither, I told the chief of that piece, a splendid soldier, to get up his team and limber to the rear. Cool as if on parade, the sergeant turned to

Sergeant Charles E. Butts was among the 205 casualties the 66th Ohio suffered in the desperate attempt to protect the Federal artillery against the charge of Taylor's Louisianans at the Coaling. Captured and taken to Richmond, the 25-year-old carpenter was eventually exchanged and returned to his unit. Severely wounded at Gettysburg and hit again during the Atlanta campaign, Butts finished his wartime service as a captain and acting quartermaster with the XIV Corps.

obey when he fell almost at my feet, shot through the heart, and died without uttering a sound. I ran myself to get the team up. It was under cover and the drivers were loth to leave it. By that time a force had broken out of the woods in our front, and yelling like demons came pouring up the road, straight for our remaining gun. No. 1, the loader, stood firmly at his post, but No. 2, who inserts the charge, went down just as he had put a cartridge in the gun. No. 1 picked up two of our big canisters and rammed them down. The man whose duty it was to fire actually got the primer in the vent when his heart failed him and he dropped the lanyard and ran. The gunner, who stood by the trail ready to help limber, seized it and fired. This opened a lane and checked the onset of that particular lot of Tigers for an instant, in which we limbered up the piece, the cannoneers jumped on, and the drivers lost no time in getting away with it to the rear. The gun saved, I felt rather at a loss what course to adopt. My first impulse was to lie down and surrender, as there seemed to be a very poor prospect of reaching cover with a whole skin. But having a wholesome dread of Southern hospitality as dispensed at that period, I concluded to take the chances and was lucky enough to slip out between the bullets.

SERGEANT SAMUEL D. BUCK

13TH VIRGINIA INFANTRY, ELZEY'S BRIGADE

Scrambling uphill to reinforce the Louisiana Brigade's attack at the Coaling, the 13th Virginia was among several Confederate units that lost their way in the tangled underbrush and rugged terrain. Arriving just as Taylor's second charge swept through the Yankee guns, Buck watched as Major Roberdeau Wheat slaughtered the artillery horses to prevent the enemy from removing the captured guns. The Federals briefly regained the Coaling but were routed by a third and final charge.

After crossing the river we were soon in range of a battery stationed two miles below the town and shelling our advance. Our regiment was ordered to the right of the line so as to flank the enemy's battery referred to and to accomplish this we had to march up the side of the mountain. Owing to our guide having lost the way we were much delayed. Our duty was to flank the enemy while Taylor's brigade charged the battery which was playing with terrible effect upon our troops in front of it. Owing to this delay we did not get into position until Taylor was making his second charge and succeeded in capturing but not holding it. So Major Wheat of the Louisiana Tigers cut horses throats or shot them so as to keep the enemy from carrying guns off before we could make another attack. This saved the guns for us as an effort was made to move the pieces but want of horses prevented. We came in sight and on flank just as Taylor made his second and successful charge. It was a sickening sight; men in grey and those in blue piled up in front of and around the guns and with the horses dying and the blood of men and beasts flowing almost in a stream. Major Wheat was as bloody as a butcher, having cut some of the horses throats with his knife.

A Federal officer's belt buckle and the brass hilt of an infantryman's saber bayonet were among the remnants of battle left upon the field of Port Republic. Civil War battle sites were usually still covered with all manner of debris after the armies had buried their dead and moved on, especially those like Port Republic in which the losers were lightening their load while fleeing from the field.

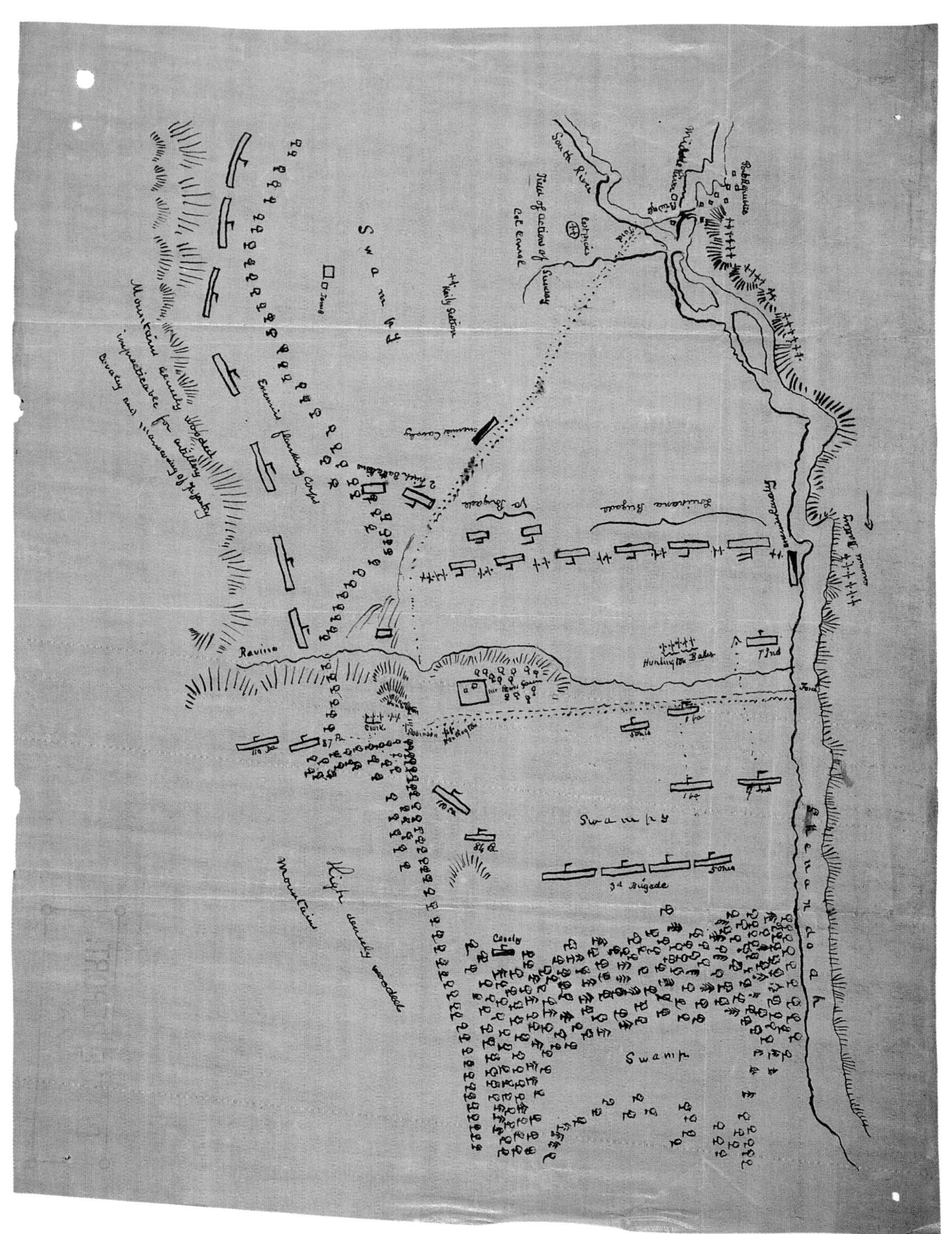

Though its maker is unknown, this map of the Port Republic battlefield was most likely drawn by a Federal participant from Tyler's brigade, as the units of that command are far more accurately depicted than the opposing Rebel formations. The Union artillery position at the Coaling is shown at left center, while the elongated blocks above are clearly meant to indicate the approach of Taylor's Louisianans. The clash with the 7th Louisiana down in the fields near the river probably led the artist to mistakenly place the entire Louisiana Brigade in that position.

CAPTAIN EDWARD H. MCDONALD

11TH VIRGINIA CAVALRY

The last of Jackson's troops to be committed to battle at Port Republic were the horsemen of Ashby's old brigade, now under the command of Colonel Thomas T. Munford of the 2d Virginia Cavalry. The Rebel troopers arrived as the Federal lines were collapsing and eagerly pursued the routed Yankees. Munford reported capturing six wagons, 800 muskets, and 150 prisoners, some of whom were grievously wounded, as McDonald describes.

We followed Jackson and soon were charging and capturing Shield's retreating column. When thus engaged I met my brother, C. W. McDonald, who had been in the fight and had been slightly wounded by a ball through his ear. Noticing the blood on his clothes I asked if he was much wounded—he said "No, not even a furlough." I had a few minutes conversation with him when we parted never to meet again, he being killed in a few days leading one of Jackson's regiments in an action near Gains Mills in front of Richmond. . . .

We followed Shields retreating column many miles capturing many prisoners. I remember a number of Federal wounded in a house who I was directed to parole and to bring back in an ambulance such as refused to be paroled. In passing from one to another I saw a young Federal soldier with a bullet just buried in his forehead. I asked him if he was willing to be paroled—he said No that he had taken arms to put down the rebellion and he would never agree not to do it. I explained to him the nature of the parole and his certain death if on account of his refusal I should be obliged to haul him several miles over a rough road, but he said he could die but not take the oath. He won my estimation for his zeal and bravery and I refused to bring him away. I never heard if he lived or died but he showed more pluck and genuine bravery than any Federal prisoner I ever met.

PRIVATE JOHN H. BURTON

7TH OHIO INFANTRY, TYLER'S BRIGADE

Burton was wounded four days after his 19th birthday as his regiment prepared to charge the disputed guns at the Coaling. Fortunate to make his way from the field, the Ohioan recounted his adventures in a letter to his mother, unfairly blaming the Union defeat on Colonel Carroll's failure to burn the Port Republic Bridge. Burton survived his wound and on July 25 was on his way home to Cleveland with a medical discharge.

Luray Page Co. June 11, 1862

Dear Mother,

I suppose before this letter can reach you news will have got to Cleveland that Shield Division has been fighting and that the 7th Ohio was in the hottest of the battle. I knew you would feel much anxiety about your boy and so I have hastened to let you hear from me. Last Sat part of our division started up the south branch of the Shenandoah on the east side to burn some bridges and thus cut off the retreat of Jacksons army. After marching between thirty and forty miles we came to a fork in the river. There was a bridge over each branch across both of which Jackson had to pass. The fourth brigade under command of Col Carroll of the 8th Ohio took possession of the east bridge and, as it is generally understood, had orders to burn it. Fremont in the mean while had attacked the enemy on the west side and after a severe engagement had forced him to fall back towards the river. Their army crossed the west branch and immediately burned the bridge which prevented Fremont from following him farther. Col Carroll, if he had obeyed orders and destroyed the bridge which he was holding would have pinned them in on the neck of land between the two branches. But he has won for himself the execration of the whole army by ordering the flames to be extinguished three times after it had been set on fire as often.

The fourth brigade was driven from its position and the enemy crossed the bridge in force estimated at from fifteen to twenty thousand while they were crossing. Robinsons battery played on the solid body of men in the bridge with fearful effect, but crossing they drove the battery from position and took some pieces which had been sent up into a town there. Having crossed the enemy had only the third and fourth brigades of our division to oppose them. Our regt is in the third brigade. we were stationed in the right centre behind one of Col Daums batteries. Col Daum cried out this way boys this way, here they come, dont let them flank us. Our right wing was then ordered to charge bayonet which they did in gallant style driving back the enemy. But we were driving them back where they were outflanking us on the left and thus they gained an advantage which decided the battle in their favor for that time. I was standing near Col Daum and just before the order was given to charge I was struck by a ball in the mouth injuring my jaw slightly and loosening several teeth. I was not going to give up at that and having loaded my gun sank down on my knees to fire once more when a piece of a shell which burst by my side, hit me in the shoulder disabling me so I could fight no longer. I walked up into a piece of woods where there was a doctor with other wounded. He got frightened and left promising however to send an ambulance for us. Four soldiers put me on to a blanket and were carrying me down toward the ambulance when a shell burst near at which they dropped me and took to their heels. I got up and walked nine miles when our own ambulance came along. Our Captain Crane compelled the driver to halt and he put me in and thus I got to Luray. . . .

. . . I have been attended to and feel quite comfortable today. As soon as I am able to I will try to come home . . . right arm was injured by the shell so I have got one of my regt to write for me. Write to me as soon as possible. . . . I want you to pray for me. Good bye. From your loving son

J. H. Burton

A poignant reminder of the human cost of war, this ambrotype of a young girl was found between two bodies—one a Union soldier, the other a Confederate—on the battlefield of Port Republic. Her identity has never been discovered.

Stonewall Jackson's Way

Following his victory at Port Republic, Jackson marched his men to Brown's Gap in the Blue Ridge and awaited his enemy's next move. But when Shields, at Luray, and Frémont, at Harrisonburg, showed no signs of advancing, Jackson descended again into the Valley, headquartering near Weyer's Cave between Port Republic and Staunton. It was there that Jackson spent his last days in the Valley as his campaign came to a close.

The Federals remained in the Valley. Jackson's forces were far too meager to expel the Yankees from the Shenandoah. It was not until the following September, when the Army of Northern Virginia marched through on its way north to fight at Antietam, that the Union troops finally abandoned the Valley.

Jackson had more than fulfilled his mission, however. His superb strategic diversion had crippled the Union's campaign to capture Richmond. It was an achievement that had already been recognized by his opposites in the enemy camp. Soon after Irvin McDowell's advance on Richmond had been suspended because of Jackson, he remarked to a comrade, "If the enemy can succeed so readily in disconcerting all our plans by alarming us first at one point, then at another, he will paralyze a large force with a very small one."

Ordered to join General John Pope's newly formed Army of Virginia, Banks' command snakes out of the Valley through Chester Gap in the first week of July. A month later his troops would clash once more with Stonewall Jackson at Cedar Mountain.

The tenacious Jackson was determined to keep plaguing the Yankees. Within days of his victory at Port Republic, he floated an ambitious idea in a message to Robert E. Lee. Give him reinforcements enough to bring his army to 40,000 men, Stonewall urged, and he would march north again to chase the last Federals from the Shenandoah. Then he would head for the Potomac, ford the river at Williamsport, and invade the North, charging into Maryland and Pennsylvania and threatening Washington.

The invasion, Jackson said, would send shock waves through the Union capital and force Lincoln to shift huge forces to meet it. Even McClellan's army outside Richmond would have to be withdrawn and shipped north. It would change the entire course of the war—and perhaps win it for the South.

Lee was tempted. But he was now in active field command of the Confederate army facing McClellan following the wounding of General Joseph Johnston. And now Lee felt the full weight of the 100,000 Federals pressing so close on Richmond they could hear the city's church bells ringing the hours at night.

Finally Lee decided. With the Federals in the Valley no longer seeming to pose a threat, Confederate priorities lay elsewhere, and as Lee wrote, "The first object now is to defeat McClellan." He needed Jackson's army.

On June 14, from his camp near Weyer's Cave, Jackson wrote to his wife, who was staying in Richmond. The letter ended wistfully: "Wouldn't you like to get home again?"

That would not happen. On June 17 Jackson left the Shenandoah Valley forever. He was bound for Richmond, where Lee, granted time by the Valley campaign, was preparing to attack McClellan.

The reputation that Jackson had earned in the Valley would only be enhanced by his skill and daring in battles to come, most notably at Second Manassas in September 1862 and at Chancellorsville in May 1863. It was at Chancellorsville that Jackson's illustrious career ended. Mortally wounded, he died eight days later. His body was taken to Lexington, in his beloved Valley, for burial.

In tribute, General Richard Taylor, a fellow officer, said of Jackson: "Praying and fighting appeared to be his idea of the 'whole duty of man.' What limit to set on his ability I know not, for his was ever superior to occasion."

"Our men curse him for the hard marching he makes them do, but still the privates of the whole army have the most unbounded confidence in him."

CORPORAL SIDNEY J. RICHARDSON

21ST GEORGIA INFANTRY, TRIMBLE'S BRIGADE

Having survived some of the hottest action at Cross Keys, Richardson wrote home about the fighting. At the time of this battle the 22-year-old farmer's son from Stewart County, Georgia, had been in the service for almost a year. Eleven months later he was slightly wounded at Chancellorsville. Richardson was killed in action during the Confederate attack on Union-held Plymouth, North Carolina, in April 1864.

Valley in the mountians June the 14th 1862
Dear Father and Mother, sisters and brother
I now take the pleasure of writing you all a few lines to let you know I was in a hard fight the eight of this mounth, which was last sunday, and I had the good luck to come out with out geting hurt. I have been in three fightes. We was in two last sunday, it was the hardest fight, every one has been fought in Virginia. We had to gain the victory, we lost a great number of men, there was only one in my company wouned, but I do not know how many men we lost out of our regiment, but there was a good many men, but in our army, ther was a large number of men killed and wouned; and the dead and wouned yankees was lying on the field as thick as black birds, the yankees lost was much larger then ours but it was the heardest fighting our army every had. Jackson is our commanding genral he commands twenty six thousand men at this time, and he had to fight two large yankey armys last sunday, he was one time cut off intilery, but he cut his way out by his wise movements, and bravery, he prayed to his lord to save him and his army, and it rally looks to me his prays was answered, . . . We are determed to drive the yankees off of our field, the yankees are now burning the towns and disstorying all the property they can, but we will kill the last one of them if they dont leave this state, I wish I could see you all and tell you all about it, I trust in God that he may spare my life to the end of the war so I may come home and see you and tell you all about my ups and downs in Virginia. Write soon nothing more at present I remain your effectionate son, Sidney J. Richardson

COLONEL SAMUEL FULKERSON

37TH VIRGINIA INFANTRY, TALIAFERRO'S BRIGADE

Even though Fulkerson joined other officers in filing a complaint against Jackson following the army's brutal Romney winter campaign, Jackson and the colonel from Estellville, Virginia, held each other in the highest regard. In the letter below, dated two days after the fighting at Port Republic, Fulkerson, a lawyer and judge, wrote admiringly of his commander. A few weeks later, Jackson wept at the news of Fulkerson's death at the Battle of Gaines' Mill.

We are now five or six miles from the battle fields. After the route of Shields' column on the 9th General Fremont became alarmed and retreated down the valley, and the last I heard of him he was at New Market. Jackson could have put him to total route on the 9th if he had not been attending to Shields. This is the second day we have been at this place, but I think it is more than probable that we will be on the march again tomorrow. We think that two days of quiet at one place is a wonderful resting spell. Our general will certainly not give us much time while there is an enemy to meet. He is a singular man and has some most striking military traits of character and some that are not so good. A more fearless man never lived and he is remarkable for his industry and energy. He is strictly temporate in his habits and sleeps very little. Often while near the enemy, and while everybody except the guards are asleep, he is on his horse and gone, nobody knows where. I often fear that he will be killed or taken. Our men curse him for the hard marching he makes them do, but still the privates of the whole army have the most unbounded confidence in him. They say he can take them into harder places and get them out better than any other living man and that he cannot be caught asleep or taken when awake. . . .

He is an ardent christian. On the 8th when he ordered me to charge through the bridge and take the enemy's guns at the other end, he turned his horse around, raised both hands, closed his eyes and prayed till the guns were taken and the enemy put to flight. All this has at least a good moral influence over the men.

John Palmer, a poet, playwright, physician, and newspaper correspondent, wrote "Stonewall Jackson's Way" during the Antietam campaign in September 1862. Set to music, the poem bears references to the hard marching performed by Stonewall's men in the Valley: "What matter if our shoes are worn? What matter if our feet are torn? Quick step! We're with him ere the dawn! That's Stonewall Jackson's way!"

CHAPLAIN J. WILLIAM JONES

25TH VIRGINIA INFANTRY, ELZEY'S BRIGADE

An eyewitness to the relationship between Jackson and Ewell in the Valley, Jones spent much of the next two years in hospitals before he was forced to resign because of illness. Jones' most noteworthy contribution to the South occurred after the war when he became an originator of the Southern Historical Society, which published a periodical dedicated to the memory of the Confederacy. Jones served as secretary of the society and contributed a piece in 1881 regarding Jackson's penchant for secrecy.

After the battles of Cross Keys and Port Republic we were resting for a season near the last battlefield, when I procured a furlough for forty-eight hours to go to my wife's home, in Nelson County. My uncle, Col. John M. Jones . . . was at that time chief of staff of Gen. Ewell, who was Jackson's second in command. As Col. Jones had told me that he was going up to Staunton at that time, I rode by Ewell's headquarters to get his company. Just as we were leaving, Gen. Ewell came out and said to us: "If you gentlemen desire to stay a little over your leave, it will make no difference. We are being largely reenforced, and will rest here for some days, when we will again beat up Banks's quarters down about Strasburg." I determined, however, to return to my command on time; and, arriving at Charlottesville two days afterwards, I found the head of Jackson's column passing through that town on its famous march to Richmond. Meeting my uncle a day or two afterwards, I asked him what made Gen. Ewell deceive us so grossly that morning in reference to the movement of the army. He at once replied: "Ewell did not deceive us. He was deceived himself. I am his confidential staff officer and receive all communications that come to our headquarters, and I know, absolutely, that everything that Ewell had received went to show that it was our purpose to move down the Valley again. The truth is, Ewell never knows anything about Jackson's plans until they are fully developed."

I remember, on that same march, that the whole army was completely deceived (as also were the citizens generally) as to Jackson's plans. When we reached Charlottesville it was currently believed that we would move on Madison C. H. to check a movement of Banks's across the Blue Ridge. When we camped at Gordonsville it was supposed that we would move toward Washington. I recall that the pastor of the Presbyterian Church there, the Rev. Dr. Ewing, with whom Jackson spent the night, told me, as a profound secret not to be breathed to mortal man, that we would move at daybreak the next morning on Culpeper C. H. He said there could be no mistake about this, because he had gotten it from Gen. Jackson himself. We did move at daybreak. The boys used to say that "Old Jack" always moved at daybreak except when he started the night before; but instead of moving on Culpeper C. H., he moved in the opposite direction, on Louisa C. H. and toward Richmond. . . .

Upon another occasion orders came for Ewell's command to be ready to move at daybreak the next morning. We broke camp, as ordered, and lay all day in the near-by turnpike ready to move. About noon Ewell rode up to the house of Dr. James L. Jones, near Gordonsville, and saluted him with: "Doctor, can you tell me where we are going to?" "That is a question," replied the Doctor, "which I should like to ask of you, General, if it were a proper one." "A very proper question," said Ewell, "but I should like to see you get an answer. Jackson ordered me to be ready to move at daylight this morning. I was ready, as you see, and my people have been lying there in the road all morning. I do not know whether we are going to march north, south, east, or west; or whether we are going to march at all; and that is about all I ever know about Gen. Jackson's plans." His higher officers sometimes complained that Jackson kept them in such profound ignorance as to his designs; but "Old Stonewall" used to have the ready answer: "If I can deceive my own people, I shall have no trouble in deceiving the enemy."

This page is from General Richard B. Garnett's copy of a transcript of a court-martial action brought against him by Jackson for Garnett's conduct as commander of the Stonewall Brigade at Kernstown. The hearing was suspended on the second day, when Jackson left to confront the Federals at Cedar Mountain. In the margin of this page, opposite a pair of Jackson's statements, Garnett wrote "lie."

CATHERINE V. BRAND

RESIDENT OF CHARLOTTESVILLE

Brand was a good Samaritan to Private Casper W. Boyd of the 15th Alabama Infantry, who took a bullet in the side during the advance of Trimble's brigade at Cross Keys. Boyd recovered enough by June 21 to write home from a Charlottesville hospital with Brand's help, saying, "I feel that I am with friends who care for me. We have things very comfortable here." But five days later the Alabamian took a turn for the worse, and Brand was soon faced with the sad task of writing the letter below.

Charlottesville
June 26, 1862
Mrs. Boyd
Dear Madam

This evening at 3 Oclock your son fell asleep as I trust in Christ. his last moments were peaceful I believ, on yesterday the Dr performed an opperation took a bullet from his side, the opperation he was not able to stand, when I called on him early this morning I found him sinking fast, he said to me should I die take the ring I send enclose in to mother & tell her to give it to my sister Mary. I do deeply sympathize with you, for your son won the respect of many. He had every kind attention shown him. I found him a gentleman This eve he asked for Icie I want to direct some but ere I got back his spirit was gone to him—who gave it, his nurse & Dr were beside his bed he will be decently buried, The only request he was able to make was to send the ring, he was not aware he was so near his end. I had a lock of hair also taken from his head which I will send you. The Dr has his purse. I know not how much money he has.

Last Sunday I wrote to you for him, he was fearful I would make you uneasy & said I must add next morning that he was better, He spoke of his Pious mother & is now I trust in Heaven, so weep not as those without hope. Please write immediately as I will feel anxious to know if you get this letter, ring & hair. May God bless the Father Mother Sisters & Brothers, is the wish of you & your sons friend.

LIEUTENANT BENJAMIN F. PERRY

29th Ohio Infantry, Tyler's Brigade

After a grueling two-week march back into the Valley, the 29th Ohio fought well at Port Republic. Positioned on the Federal right, the Buckeyes beat back the 7th Louisiana and captured its flag, retreating only after they were outflanked and shelled by Rebels in the Coaling. Some days after the contest, Perry took stock of his beleaguered regiment and wrote the letter below to Ohio senator Benjamin F. Wade. Perry resigned six days later.

Camp in the field near Luray V.A. June 14th 1862

Hon' B. F. Wade

Dear sir. I take the liberty of writing to you to ask you to do something for our Regt (29 O.V.I.). We went into the field in January last, with an organization of one thousand. We have now but, 331 enlisted men & 18 Officers. From the time we entered the field to the Present we have been constantly on duty of the severest kind & have been in

After serving briefly with the 52d Virginia Infantry at the start of the war, John Timothy Dwight Gisiner enrolled at VMI and marched to McDowell with the VMI Cadet Corps in support of Jackson. Shown here in his cadet uniform, Gisiner contracted an illness on the march that took his life a month later.

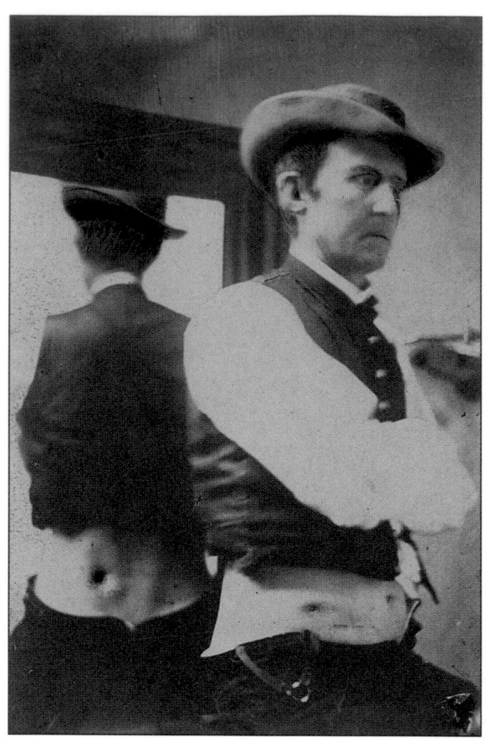

Captain James F. Charlesworth of the 25th Ohio Infantry took a musket ball in the midsection at Cross Keys, the shot passing through his abdomen and fracturing the top of his hipbone. Charlesworth barely survived this typically fatal injury, and he later had his wound photographed for inclusion in a volume on the medical history of the war.

two hotly contested battles, Winchester & Port Republic. Our loss in the last named Battle was terrible. Out of 29 Officers & 350 men that were in line when we went forward to meet the traitors, One officer was killed, four wounded & nine are missing. 14 Enlisted men were killed 40 wounded and 131 missing. We had several details on guard, With the wagon trains, &c that accounts for our not having more men on the battle field. The battle was fought Monday June the 9th. Our Regt Marched from camp near New Market V.A. May 12 & had been in constant motion from that time Having gone from New Market to Fredricksburgh by way of Front Royal, & then made our way back to Luray by way of Manassas and Front Royal, besides diversions and countermarches, that makes the distance in round numbers 500 miles. Much of the time it was raining & the roads bad so that it not only made it hard marching for the men, but compelled us to cut down our bagage & supplies to the least possible amount. This compelled us to live on [what was on] hand, on Pilot Bread & coffee & Bacon. Being compelled to dispense with vegitables for the most part. True we have with us Beef that could be killed But on a forced march that requires us to be moving from sun rise to sun down & frequently till much later, Fresh Beef is of no use. The men cannot use it to any advantage.

Now in Gods name, if you can do any thing to give us a chance to rest & recuperate I beseach of you to do so. The hand full that is left of us are worn out & absolutely unfit for duty. Besides our losses have been so great that we are in fact disorganized, & can be of no further use in the field at Present. If we are retained our Colonel will feel compelled to resign, which would result in nearly every officer following him. Our men would never serve in any other Regt. & the result would be a once noble Regt. would be disgraced after having nobly done its duty & after having been used up in the service of its country. What is to be done, must be done speedily for we are again under marching orders, & will soon be in motion. We have Men scattered here & there in hospitle, that if we had one chance could be got together & I doubt not but that we could get into working shape again within a reasonable time.

I am sir with much Esteem your Obedient Servant
Lieut Benj. F. Perry
To Hon B. F. Wade

LIEUTENANT WILLIAM WHEELER

13th Battery, New York Light Artillery, Koltes' Brigade

The campaign over, Wheeler reflected on fighting in Virginia against a force made up largely of Virginians. Wheeler felt some tempering of his patriotic sentiments at the thought of being an interloper. Two years later he was killed in action near Marietta, Georgia.

If I could succeed in looking upon this whole campaign as a sort of summer excursion or jaunt, nothing could be more pleasant and enjoyable. I have seen some of the finest scenery in the country, and that in sunshine and storm, at midnight and at sunrise, have lived always in the open air and in perfect health, spite of privations and exposure to rain and dew; have had the additional spice of a little danger occasionally, and the sensation of a bold, free life, and yet there has always been something which came in to spoil my enjoyment; it may have been the rough and reckless men we have under us, but more than this was the feeling that we were invaders, laying waste a fair and blooming country, and that our opponents were men fighting to save their firesides and their homesteads. It is by no means agreeable to deprive farmers of their grain and hay, and to carry off favorite horses amid the tears and supplications of the women folk; and you can yourself imagine how hard it was when we came back from Cross Keys, to see in Harrisonburg and New Market the women dressed in black and weeping as if their hearts would break. I cannot help mentally transferring the whole trouble to the Northern country, and thinking how I should feel if the "Louisiana Tigers," or some such notorious corps, should have a chance to march through Connecticut. Indeed I am sometimes in danger of forgetting the real reason and object of the war, because my mind is constantly occupied with the superficial losses and miseries which are daily before my eyes, but which "endure but for a moment," and which, when we succeed, will bring for us "a more exceeding weight of glory," in a preserved Constitution and established laws.

With Jackson on his way to Richmond, the defense of the Valley was left largely to cavalry. These Rebel horsemen taken prisoner in June near Woodstock fed some false information to their captors: The 3d Virginia Cavalry never served in the Shenandoah in 1862.

GLOSSARY

battery—The basic unit of artillery, comprising four to six guns. Or, an emplacement where artillery is mounted for attack or defense. A battery is generally open or lightly defended in the rear.
bivouac—A temporary encampment, or to camp out for the night.
brevet—An honorary rank given for exceptional bravery or merit in time of war. It granted none of the authority or pay of the official rank.
buck and ball—A round of ammunition consisting of a bullet and three buckshot.
Bucktails—Nickname for the 13th Pennsylvania Reserves. Recruits were required to bring in a deer's tail as proof of their prowess with a rifle. The men then wore the tails in their hats.
caisson—A cart with large chests for carrying artillery ammunition. It was connected to a horse-drawn limber when moved.
canister—A tin can containing lead or iron balls that scattered when fired from a cannon.
carbine—A lightweight, short-barreled shoulder arm used especially by cavalry.
cascabel—A knob or ring projecting from the breech end of a cannon, used with a rope or chain to secure the weapon or shift its position.
case shot—Properly refers to shrapnel or spherical case. The term was often used mistakenly to refer to any artillery projectile in which numerous metal balls or pieces were bound or encased together. See also *shrapnel.*
contraband—A slave who sought the protection of Union forces.
double-quick—A trotting pace.
Dutchmen—A term, often pejorative, for Union soldiers of German descent.
echelon—A staggered or stairsteplike formation of parallel units of troops.
elevating screw—A mechanism located under the breech of an artillery piece and used to raise or lower the angle of fire.
Enfield rifle—The Enfield rifle musket was adopted by the British in 1853, and the North and South imported nearly one million to augment their own production. Firing a .577-caliber projectile similar to the Minié ball, it was fairly accurate at 1,100 yards.
enfilade—Gunfire that rakes an enemy line lengthwise, or the position allowing such firing.
flank—The right or left end of a military formation. To flank is to attack or go around the enemy's position on one end or the other.
forage—To search for and acquire provisions from nonmilitary sources. To soldiers of the Civil War it often meant, simply, stealing.
garrison—A military post, especially a permanent one. Also, the act of manning such a post and the soldiers who serve there.
glacis—The outer rim of the defensive ditch protecting a fort's rampart. It usually sloped down toward the enemy.
grapeshot—Iron balls (usually nine) bound together and fired from a cannon. Resembling a cluster of grapes, the balls broke apart and scattered on impact. Although references to grape or grapeshot are numerous in the literature, some experts claim that it was not used on Civil War battlefields.
gum blanket—A waterproof blanket, treated with rubber and often in poncho form.
haversack—A shoulder bag, usually strapped over the right shoulder to rest on the left hip, for carrying personal items and rations.
howitzer—A short-barreled artillery piece that fired its projectile in a relatively high trajectory.
lanyard—An artillerist's cord with a handle on one end and a clip connector for a friction primer on the other. The friction primer was inserted into the touchhole on an artillery piece. When the gunner jerked the lanyard, friction in the touchhole ignited powder in the breech, firing the weapon.
limber—A two-wheeled, horse-drawn vehicle to which a gun carriage or a caisson was attached.
mess—A group of soldiers who prepare and eat meals together, or to eat such a meal; the place where such a meal is prepared and eaten.
Minié ball—The standard bullet-shaped projectile fired from the rifled muskets of the time. Designed by French army officers Henri-Gustave Delvigne and Claude-Étienne Minié, the bullet's hollow base expanded, forcing its sides into the grooves, or rifling, of the barrel. This caused the bullet to spiral in flight, giving it greater range and accuracy. Appears as minie, minnie, and minni.
musket—A smoothbore, muzzleloading shoulder arm.
parole—The pledge of a soldier released after being captured by the enemy that he would not take up arms again until he had been properly exchanged.
Parrott guns—Muzzleloading, rifled artillery pieces of various calibers made of cast iron, with a unique wrought-iron reinforcing band around the breech. Patented in 1861 by Union officer Robert Parker Parrott, these guns were more accurate at longer range than their smoothbore predecessors.
picket—One or more soldiers on guard to protect the larger unit from surprise attack.
prime—To pour gunpowder into the touchhole or vent of a cannon or musket.
provost guard—A detail of soldiers acting as

police under the supervision of an officer called a provost marshal.

rammer—An artillerist's tool used to force the powder charge and projectile down the barrel of a gun and seat them firmly in the breech.

ration—A specified allotment of food for one person (or animal) per day. The amounts and nature of rations varied by time and place throughout the war. *Rations* may also refer simply to any food provided by the army.

rifle—Any weapon with spiral grooves cut into the bore, which give spin to the projectile, adding range and accuracy. Usually applied to cannon or shoulder-fired weapons.

rifle pits—Holes or shallow trenches dug in the ground from which soldiers could fire weapons and avoid enemy fire. Also called foxholes.

secesh—A slang term for secessionist.

shrapnel—An artillery projectile in the form of a hollow sphere filled with metal balls packed around an explosive charge. Developed by British general Henry Shrapnel during the Napoleonic Wars, it was used as an antipersonnel weapon. Also called spherical case.

skirmisher—A soldier sent in advance of the main body of troops to scout out and probe the enemy's position. Also, one who participated in a skirmish, a small fight usually incidental to the main action.

solid shot—A solid artillery projectile, oblong for rifled pieces and spherical for smoothbores.

spherical case—See *shrapnel.*

sponge—An artillerist's tool that was used to clear a cannon barrel of grime, smoldering cloth, and other detritus between rounds.

sutler—A peddler with a permit to remain with troops in camp or in the field and sell food, drink, and other supplies.

vedette—A sentry on horseback.

vent—A small hole in the breech of a weapon through which a spark travels to ignite the powder charge and fire the piece.

Zouaves—Regiments, both Union and Confederate, that modeled themselves after the original Zouaves of French colonial Algeria. Known for spectacular uniforms featuring bright colors—usually reds and blues—baggy trousers, gaiters, short and open jackets, and a turban or fez, they specialized in precision drill and loading and firing muskets from the prone position.

PICTURE CREDITS

The sources for the illustrations are listed below. Credits from left to right are separated by semicolons, from top to bottom by dashes.

Dust jacket: front, Fredericksburg and Spotsylvania National Military Park, Fredericksburg, Va.; rear, Alabama Department of Archives and History, Montgomery.

All calligraphy by Mary Lou O'Brian/Inkwell, Inc.

6, 7: Map by Paul Salmon. 8: Courtesy R. W. Norton Art Gallery, Shreveport, La. 16: Valentine Museum, Richmond. 17: Frank and Marie-Thérèse Wood Print Collections, Alexandria, Va. 18: Virginia Military Institute Museum, Lexington, photographed by Larry Sherer. 19: Virginia Military Institute Museum, Lexington—courtesy Sally McCullough Futch, Galveston, Tex. 20: From *Stonewall Jackson's Way,* by John W. Wayland, McClure, Staunton, Va., 1940. 21: Frank and Marie-Thérèse Wood Print Collections, Alexandria, Va. 22: Courtesy Doug Bast/Boonsboro Museum of History, photographed by Larry Sherer; Library of Congress. 23: Library of Congress, Manuscripts Division. 24: Massachusetts Commandery of the Loyal Legion of the United States and U.S. Army Military History Institute (MASS-MOLLUS/USAMHI), copied by A. Pierce Bounds. 25: Library of Congress, Neg. No. LC-B-8184-10117; Museum of the Confederacy, Richmond. 26: Courtesy Doug Bast/Boonsboro Museum of History, photographed by Larry Sherer. 27: Courtesy Special Collections, James Graham Leyburn Library, Washington and Lee University, Lexington, Va; Valentine Museum, Richmond. 28: Frank and Marie-Thérèse Wood Print Collections, Alexandria,Va. 29: From *The Twenty-Seventh Indiana Volunteer Infantry in the War of the Rebellion,* by A Member of Company C., private printing, Monticello, Ind., 1899; MASS-MOLLUS/USAMHI, copied by A. Pierce Bounds. 30: Library of Congress, Neg. No. LC-B 8184-10117. 31: Antietam National Battlefield Park, photographed by Larry Sherer. 32: David Wynn Vaughan Collection, Atlanta. 33: From *Wearing of the Gray: Being Personal Portraits, Scenes and Adventures of the War,* by John Esten Cooke, E. B. Treat, New York, 1867—MASS-MOLLUS/USAMHI, copied by A. Pierce Bounds. 34: From *Letters from Two Brothers Serving in the War for the Union,* by Warren Hapgood Freeman, published by H. O. Houghton, Cambridge, Mass., 1871; courtesy Handley Library Archives, Winchester, Va. 35: From *Life and Letters of Wilder Dwight,* Ticknor and Fields, Boston, 1868. 36, 37: Courtesy Winchester-Frederick County Historical Society Archives, Winchester, Va.; Library of Congress, Forbes #020. 38: Courtesy Marilyn J. Clark-Snyder. 39: From *The Life and Work of George William Peterkin,* by Robert Edward Lee Strider, George W. Jacobs, Philadelphia, 1929. 41: Map by Walter W. Roberts. 42: National Archives, Neg. No. 111-BA-1568—Lee A. Wallace Jr., Falls Church, Va. 43: National Archives. 44: Jerry Wright Collection, photographed by Henry Mintz. 45: From *Itinerary of the Seventh Ohio Volunteer Infantry, 1861-1864,* edited and compiled by Lawrence Wilson, Neale, New York, 1907; L. M. Strayer Collection, Dayton. 46, 47: Library of Congress, Forbes #021. 48, 49: Pennsylvania Capitol Preservation Committee, Harrisburg (2); Blair County Historical Society, Altoona, Pa., photographed by Dick Heiler—Western Reserve Historical Society, Cleveland—courtesy Roderick Gainer, Arlington, Va. 50: From *The Wyatt Family Records,* by Lucile Rebecca Douglas Wyatt, Dietz Press, Richmond, 1957. 51: Frank and Marie-Thérèse Wood Print Collections, Alexandria, Va. 52: L. M. Strayer Collection, Dayton. 54: Southern Historical Collection, University of North Carolina, Chapel Hill. 55: MASS-MOLLUS/USAMHI, copied by A. Pierce Bounds. 56:

Courtesy Winchester-Frederick County Historical Society Archives, Winchester, Va.—courtesy Colin J. S. Thomas Jr. 57: Courtesy Doris Johnson Williams. 58: MASS-MOLLUS/USAMHI, copied by A. Pierce Bounds. 61: Map by R. R. Donnelley & Sons Co., Cartographic Services. 62: MASS-MOLLUS/USAMHI, copied by Robert Walch. 63: Frank and Marie-Thérèse Wood Print Collections, Alexandria, Va. 64: Hargrett Rare Book and Manuscript Library, University of Georgia, Athens; from *A Brief History of the Twenty-eighth Regiment, New York State Volunteers,* by C. W. Boyce, printed by the Matthews-Northrup Co., Buffalo, 1896. 65: Jerry Wright Collection, photographed by Henry Mintz; from *Recollections of a Maryland Confederate Soldier and Staff Officer under Johnston, Jackson and Lee,* by McHenry Howard, Williams & Wilkins, Baltimore, 1914. 67: New York State Division of Military and Naval Affairs, Military History Collection, photographed by Larry Sherer. 68: National Archives, Neg. No. 111-BA-1251. 69: Library of Congress; Library of Congress, Forbes #013. 70: From *The War between the Union and the Confederacy and Its Lost Opportunities,* by William C. Oates, Neale, New York, 1905. 71: Greenville County Museum of Art, Greenville, S.C., Museum purchase with funds donated by the John I. Smith Charities. 72: Private collection, photographed by Evan H. Sheppard. 73: Museum of the Confederacy, Richmond. 75: Map by Walter W. Roberts. 76: Lee-Fendall House, Alexandria, Va., copied by Michael Latil. 77: Virginia Military Institute Museum, Lexington, photographed by Larry Sherer. 78: Special Collections and Archives, Paul Laurence Dunbar Library, Wright State University, Dayton—from *Hearth and Knapsack: The Ladley Letters, 1857-1880,* edited by Carl M. Becker and Ritchie Thomas, Ohio University Press, Athens, 1988. 79: Courtesy Gregory A. Coco Collection, photographed by Mike Brouse. 80: From *History of the Doles-Cook Brigade, Army of Northern Virginia, C.S.A.,* by Henry W. Thomas, Atlanta, 1903, copied by Philip Brandt George. 81: Courtesy Richard L. Armstrong. 82: L. M. Strayer Collection, Dayton. 83: Museum of the Confederacy, Richmond, photographed by Katherine Wetzel—MASS-MOLLUS/USAMHI, copied by A. Pierce Bounds. 84: Georgia Department of Archives and History, Atlanta; Virginia Military Institute Museum, Lexington, photographed by Larry Sherer. 86: New Market Battlefield Park, Hall of Valor Museum, photographed by Larry Sherer; courtesy of the George and Katherine Davis Collection, Manuscripts Department, Howard-Tilton Library, Tulane University, New Orleans. 87: Western Reserve Historical Society, Cleveland. 88: Alabama Department of Archives and History, Montgomery—courtesy of the George and Katherine Davis Collection, Manuscripts Department, Howard-Tilton Library, Tulane University, New Orleans. 89: From *With the Old Confeds: Actual Experiences of a Captain in the Line,* by Samuel D. Buck, H. E. Houck, Baltimore, 1925, copied by Philip Brandt George. 90: Map by R. R. Donnelley & Sons, Cartographic Services, overlay by Time-Life Books. 91: Map by Walter W. Roberts. 92: Map by R. R. Donnelley & Sons, Cartographic Services, overlay by Time-Life Books. 94: Frank and Marie-Thérèse Wood Print Collections, Alexandria, Va. 95, 96: Warren Rifles Confederate Museum, Front Royal, Va., photographed by Larry Sherer. 97: From *Sad Earth, Sweet Heaven: The Diary of Lucy Rebecca Buck,* second edition, edited by William P. Buck, Buck Publishing Co., Birmingham, Ala., 1992. 98: From *Sad Earth, Sweet Heaven: The Diary of Lucy Rebecca Buck,* second edition, edited by William P. Buck, Buck Publishing Co., Birmingham, Ala., 1992; from *Gentle Tiger: The Gallant Life of Roberdeau Wheat,* by Charles L. Dufour, Louisiana State University Press, Baton Rouge, 1957. 99: Virginia Military Institute Museum, Lexington, photographed by Larry Sherer; MASS-MOLLUS/USAMHI, copied by A. Pierce Bounds. 100: MASS-MOLLUS/USAMHI, copied by A. Pierce Bounds. 101: Courtesy collection of William A. Turner; from *Yankee in Gray: The Civil War Memoirs of Henry Ebenezer Handerson,* biographical introduction by Clyde Lottridge Cummer, Press of Western Reserve University, 1962, courtesy Cleveland Health Sciences Library, copied by Philip Brandt George. 102: MASS-MOLLUS/USAMHI, copied by A. Pierce Bounds. 103: Courtesy collection of William A. Turner. 104: Virginia Historical Society, Richmond; courtesy Ellen Pepper Tilley, photographed by Henry Mintz; courtesy Peggy V. Ferguson, photographed by Henry Mintz. 105: From *The Story of a Cannoneer under Stonewall Jackson,* by Edward A. Moore, New York, Neale, 1907. 106: From *Stonewall Jackson's Way,* by John W. Wayland, McClure, Staunton, Va., 1940—Winchester-Frederick County Historical Society, Winchester, Va., photographed by Larry Sherer; courtesy Herb Peck Jr., Nashville. 107: *Civil War Times Illustrated,* Harrisburg, Pa.; from *A Narrative of Service with the Third Wisconsin Infantry,* by Julian Wisner Hinkley, Wisconsin History Commission, 1912, copied by Philip Brandt George. 108: National Archives. 109: MASS-MOLLUS/USAMHI, copied by A. Pierce Bounds. 110: Valentine Museum, Richmond, photographed by Larry Sherer. 111, 113: Library of Congress, Manuscripts Division. 114, 115: Library of Congress, Forbes #027a. 116: Edward C. Browne Jr. 117: Library of Congress, Forbes #028b. 118: Frank and Marie-Thérèse Wood Print Collections, Alexandria, Va. 119: MASS-MOLLUS/USAMHI, copied by A. Pierce Bounds. 120: Pennsylvania Capitol Preservation Committee, Harrisburg. 121: Museum of the Confederacy, Richmond, photographed by Katherine Wetzel; Stonewall Jackson Headquarters Museum, Winchester, Va., photographed by Larry Sherer. 123: Map by Walter W. Roberts. 124: Society of Port Republic Preservationists, Port Republic, Va., copied by Larry Sherer. 125: Courtesy Mary Stewart Gilliam, photographed by Thomas C. Bradshaw. 126: Virginia Military Institute Museum, Lexington, photographed by Larry Sherer—Society of Port Republic Preservationists, Port Republic, Va., copied by Larry Sherer. 128: Alabama Department of Archives and History, Montgomery. 129: David W. Patenge Collection at the U.S. Army Military History Institute (USAMHI), copied by A. Pierce Bounds. 130: Library of Congress, Forbes #026a. 132: From *Reminiscences of the Civil War,* by Emma Cassandra Reily Macon and Reuben Conway Macon, private printing, 1911. 133: Virginia Military Institute Museum, Lexington, photographed by Larry Sherer. 134: Courtesy Tennessee State Library and Archives, Nashville. 136: L. M. Strayer Collection, Dayton; Virginia Military Institute Museum, Lexington. 137: Virginia Military Institute Museum, Lexington, photographed by Larry Sherer; courtesy Edith Hosey. 138, 139: Society of Port Republic Preservationists, Port Republic, Va., copied by Larry Sherer. 140: Edward Franks Collection at USAMHI, copied by A. Pierce Bounds. 141: Historic New Orleans Collection; courtesy Brian Pohanka. 143: Society of Port Republic Preservationists, Port Republic, Va., copied by Larry Sherer. 145: From *General Leroy Augustus Stafford,* by George Mason Graham Stafford, ©1943, used by permission of the publisher, Pelican, New Orleans. 146: Robert Needham. 147: L. M. Strayer Collection, Dayton. 148: Society of Port Republic Preservationists, Port Republic, Va., photographed by Larry Sherer. 149: National Archives. 151: Eleanor S. Brockenbrough Library, Museum of the Confederacy, Richmond, photographed by Katherine Wetzel. 152: Library of Congress, Forbes #027. 155: Hargrett Rare Book and Manuscript Library, University of Georgia, Athens. 156: Eleanor S. Brockenbrough Library, Museum of the Confederacy, Richmond, photographed by Katherine Wetzel. 157: Virginia Military Institute Museum, Lexington, photographed by Larry Sherer. 158: National Museum of Health and Medicine, Armed Forces Institute of Pathology, Washington, D.C., No. CP 1247; USAMHI, copied by A. Pierce Bounds. 159: Library of Congress, Forbes #028.

ACKNOWLEDGMENTS

The editors wish to thank the following for their valuable assistance in the preparation of this volume:
Eva-Maria Ahladas, Museum of the Confederacy, Richmond; Clare Balawajder, Wright State University, Dayton; Barbara Blakey, Virginia Military Institute Museum, Lexington; Jerry Bloomer, R. W. Norton Art Gallery, Shreveport, La.; Keith Bohannon, East Ridge, Tenn.; Robert Bradley, Alabama Department of Archives and History, Montgomery; Mark Cave, The Historic New Orleans Collection, New Orleans; Robert Cayson, Alabama Department of Archives and History, Montgomery; Anita Cummins, Society of Port Republic Preservationists, Port Republic, Va.; Rebecca Ebert, Handley Library Archives, Winchester, Va.; Sue Farr, Lee-Fendall House, Alexandria, Va.; Keith Gibson, Virginia Military Institute Museum, Lexington; Douglas Gutshall, Monterey, Va.; Randy W. Hackenburg, U.S. Army Military History Institute, Carlisle Barracks, Pa.; Dick Heiler, Altoona, Pa.; Marilyn Hughes, Tennessee State Library and Archives, Nashville; Mary Ison and Staff, Library of Congress, Washington, D.C.; Jeff Jackson, Virginia Military Institute Museum, Lexington; Diane Jacob, Virginia Military Institute Archives, Lexington; Dr. Wilbur Meneray, Tulane University, New Orleans; Cynthia Middleton, National Archives, Washington, D.C.; Sue Miller, *Civil War Times Illustrated,* Harrisburg, Pa.; Barbara Moore, Society of Port Republic Preservationists, Port Republic, Va.; Lynda Moreau, Pelican Publishing, Gretna, La.; Nelson Morgan, University of Georgia Libraries, Athens; Richard Murray, Americus, Ga.; Robert Needham, Columbus, Ohio; RoseAnn O'Canas, High Impact Photography, Baltimore; Harva Owings, Pennsylvania Capitol Preservation Committee, Harrisburg; Courtney Page, Tulane University, New Orleans; Lisa Rasco, Pelican Publishing, Gretna, La.; Joan Redding, Armed Forces Medical Museum, Washington, D.C.; Susan A. Riggs, College of William and Mary, Williamsburg, Va.; Ben Ritter, Winchester, Va.; Teresa Roane, Valentine Museum, Richmond; Martha Severens, Greenville County Historical Society, Greenville, S.C.; Ann Sindelar, Western Reserve Historical Society, Cleveland; Timothy Van Scoyoc, Blair County Historical Society, Altoona, Pa.; Sandy White, Georgia Department of Archives and History, Atlanta; Michael J. Winey, U.S. Army Military History Institute, Carlisle Barracks, Pa.

BIBLIOGRAPHY

BOOKS

Armstrong, Richard L. *The Battle of McDowell: Jackson's Valley Campaign, March 11–May 18, 1862.* Lynchburg, Va.: H. E. Howard, 1990.

Barclay, Ted. *Letters from the Stonewall Brigade (1861–1864).* Ed. by Charles W. Turner. Berryville, Va.: Rockbridge, 1992.

Bean, W. G. *Stonewall's Man Sandie Pendleton.* Chapel Hill: University of North Carolina Press, 1959.

Brown, Edmund R. *The Twenty-Seventh Indiana Volunteer Infantry in the War of the Rebellion: 1861–1865, First Division 12th and 20th Corps.* Monticello, Ind.: private printing, 1899.

Buck, Lucy Rebecca. *Sad Earth, Sweet Heaven: The Diary of Lucy Rebecca Buck.* Ed. by William P. Buck. Birmingham, Ala.: Cornerstone, 1973.

Buck, Samuel D. *With the Old Confeds: Actual Experiences of a Captain in the Line.* Baltimore: H. E. Houck, 1925.

Clark, Charles M. *Yates Phalanx: The History of the Thirty Ninth Regiment, Illinois Volunteer Veteran Infantry, in the War of the Rebellion, 1861–1865.* Ed. by Francis Charles Decker. Bowie, Md.: Heritage Books, 1994.

Colt, Margaretta Barton. *Defend the Valley: A Shenandoah Family in the Civil War.* New York: Crown Publishers, Inc., copyright © 1994. Reprinted by permission of Crown Publishers, Inc.

Confederate Military History. (Vol. 2.) Ed. by Clement A. Evans. New York: Thomas Yoseloff, 1962.

Douglas, Henry Kyd. *I Rode with Stonewall.* Chapel Hill: University of North Carolina Press, 1968.

Dwight, Wilder. *Life and Letters of Wilder Dwight, Lieut-Col., Second Mass. Inf. Vols.* Boston: Ticknor and Fields, 1868.

Freeman, Warren Hapgood. *Letters from Two Brothers Serving in the War for the Union.* Cambridge, Mass.: H. O. Houghton, 1871.

Gill, John. *Reminiscences of Four Years as a Private Soldier in the Confederate Army, 1861–1865.* Baltimore: Sun Printing Office, 1904.

Gilmor, Harry. *Four Years in the Saddle.* New York: Harper & Brothers, 1866.

Glass, Paul, comp. *Singing Soldiers (The Spirit of the Sixties).* New York: Da Capo Press, 1968.

Gorden, W. E. "Under Sentence of Death: An Episode of the War." In *Camp Fires of the Confederacy.* Ed. by Ben LaBree. Louisville, Ky.: Courier-Journal Printing, 1898.

Gould, John M. *History of the First-Tenth-Twenty-ninth Maine Regiment.* Portland, Maine: Stephen Berry, 1871.

Haas, Ralph. *Dear Esther.* Apollo, Pa.: Closson Press, 1991.

Hall, James E. *The Diary of a Confederate Soldier.* Ed. by Ruth Woods Dayton. Philippi, W.Va.: private printing, 1961.

Handerson, Henry E. *Yankee in Gray: The Civil War Memoirs of Henry E. Handerson.* Cleveland: Press of Western Reserve University, 1962.

Howard, McHenry. *Recollections of a Maryland Confederate Soldier and Staff Officer under Johnston, Jackson and Lee.* Baltimore: Williams & Wilkins, 1914.

Huntington, James F. "Operations in the Shenandoah Valley, from Winchester to Port Republic, 1862." In *Papers of the Military Historical Society of Massachusetts.* (Vol. 6.) Wilmington, N.C.: Broadfoot, 1989.

Johnson, Geo. K. "The Battle of Kernstown, March 23, 1862." In *War Papers: Being Papers Read before the Commandery of the State of Michigan.* (Vol. 1.) Wilmington, N.C.: Broadfoot, 1993.

Jones, William. "Reminiscences of the Army of Northern Virginia." In *Southern Historical Society Papers: January to December, 1881.* (Vol. 9.) Wilmington, N.C.: Broadfoot, 1990.

Krick, Robert K.:
Conquering the Valley: Stonewall Jackson at Port Republic. New York: William Morrow, 1996.
Stonewall Jackson at Cedar Mountain. Chapel Hill: University of North Carolina Press, 1990.

Lang, Theodore F. *Loyal West Virginia from 1861 to 1865.* Baltimore: Deutsch, 1895.

McClendon, W. A. *Recollections of War Times.* Montgomery, Ala.: Paragon Press, 1909.

McDonald, Cornelia Peake. *A Woman's Civil War.* Ed. by Minrose C. Gwin. Madison: University of Wisconsin Press, 1992.

Neese, George M. *Three Years in the Confederate Horse Artillery.* Dayton: Press of Morningside Bookshop, 1983.

Opie, John N. *A Rebel Cavalryman with Lee Stuart and Jackson.* Dayton: Press of Morningside Bookshop, 1972 (reprint of 1899 edition).

Paulus, Margaret B., ed. and comp. *Milroy Family Letters: 1862–1863.* Vol. 1 of *Papers of General Robert Huston Milroy.* N.p., 1965.

Pryor, S. G., and Penelope Tyson Pryor. *A Post of Honor: The Pryor Letters, 1861–1863.* Ed. by Charles R. Adams Jr. Fort Valley, Ga.: Garret, 1989.

Quarles, Garland R. *Occupied Winchester, 1861–1865.*

Winchester, Va.: Winchester-Frederick County Historical Society, 1991.
SeCheverell, J. Hamp. *Journal History of the Twenty-Ninth Ohio Veteran Volunteers, 1861–1865.* Cleveland: private printing, 1883.
Shaw, Robert Gould. *Blue-Eyed Child of Fortune: The Civil War Letters of Colonel Robert Gould Shaw.* Ed. by Russell Duncan. New York: Avon Books, 1992.
Strider, Robert Edward Lee. *The Life and Work of George William Peterkin.* Philadelphia: George W. Jacobs, 1929.
Strother, David Hunter. *A Virginia Yankee in the Civil War: The Diaries of David Hunter Strother.* Ed. by Cecil D. Eby Jr. Chapel Hill: University of North Carolina Press, 1961.
Tanner, Robert G. *Stonewall in the Valley.* Mechanicsburg, Pa.: Stackpole Books, 1996.
Taylor, Richard. *Destruction and Reconstruction: Personal Experiences of the Late War.* New York: D. Appleton, 1879.
Trueheart, Charles, and Mary Trueheart. *Rebel Brothers: The Civil War Letters of the Truehearts.* Ed. by Edward B. Williams. College Station: Texas A&M University Press, 1995.
Wheeler, William. *In Memoriam: Letters of William Wheeler.* Cambridge, Mass.: H. O. Houghton, 1875.
Wilson, Lawrence, ed. and comp. *Itinerary of the Seventh Ohio Volunteer Infantry, 1861–1864.* New York: Neale, 1907.
Wise, Jennings C. *The Military History of the Virginia Military Institute from 1839 to 1865.* Lynchburg, Va.: J. P. Bell, 1915.
Worsham, John H. *One of Jackson's Foot Cavalry.* Ed. by James I. Robertson Jr. Jackson, Tenn.: McCowat-Mercer Press, 1964.

PERIODICALS

Boyd, Casper W. Letter dated June 26, 1862. *The Alabama Historical Quarterly,* Fall-Winter 1961.
Gillespie, Samuel. "Our Camp Correspondence." *Fayette County Herald,* April 17, 1862.
Grabill, John H. "Diary of a Soldier of the Stonewall Brigade." *Shenandoah Herald* (Woodstock, Va.), January 8, 15, 22, 1909.
Hutchison, Ephraim. "The Battle of McDowell: Our Little Band of Heroes." *Civil War Times Illustrated,* September 1982.
Lee, Alfred E. "Our First Battle: Bull Pasture Mountain." *Magazine of American History,* January-June 1886.
Pendleton, Alexander. "The Valley Campaign of 1862 as Revealed in Letters of Sandie Pendleton." Ed. by W. G. Bean. *The Virginia Magazine of History and Biography,* July 1970.
Ritter, Levi. "Letter from Dr. Ritter." *Hendrick County* (Ind.) *Ledger,* April 11, 1862.
Rodgers, James. "The 12th at McDowell." *Macon Telegraph,* n.d.
Simpson, James H. "Battle of Kernstown." *National Tribune* (Washington, D.C.), February 4, 1882.
Sponaugle, George W. "Recollections of George W. Sponaugle." *The Highland Recorder* (Monterey, Va.), February 25, 1927.
Webb, Charles H. "The Battle of Cross Keys." *New York Times,* June 17, 1862.
Wells, Harvey S. "A Volunteer." *Muncy* (Pa.) *Luminary,* January 8, 1862.

OTHER SOURCES

Allan, William. Family papers, 1802-1937. Chapel Hill: University of North Carolina Library, Southern Historical Collection.
Apperson, John. Diaries. Richmond: Virginia State Library.
Boyce, Charles H. Unpublished manuscript, n.d. Washington, D.C.: Library of Congress, Manuscript Division.
Brett, Martin W. Unpublished memoir, n.d. Atlanta: Emory University, Robert W. Woodruff Library, Special Collections.
Burton, John Howes. Letters. Carlisle Barracks, Pa.: U.S. Army Military History Institute.
Clark, Thomas. Letters, April 1862-May 1863. Annandale, Va.: Collection of Marilyn Clark-Snyder.
Coble, Eli. Civil War reminiscences, papers, and letters. Raleigh: North Carolina Department of Archives and History.
Colston, W. B. "The Personal Experiences of Captain W. B. Colston in the Civil War." Unpublished memoir, n.d. Private collection.
Dutton, Henry M. Letters. Winchester, Va.: Handley Library.
Evans, Thomas. Civil War diary and memoirs, n.d. Washington, D.C.: Library of Congress, Manuscript Division.
Fulkerson, Sam. Letters, n.d. Lexington, Va.: Virginia Military Institute.
Gallagher, William. Pension file and letters. Washington, D.C.: National Archives and Records.
Gillette, James J. Papers and letters. Washington, D.C.: Library of Congress, Manuscript Division.
Kauffman, Joseph Franklin. Diary. Chapel Hill: University of North Carolina, Southern Historical Collection.
Langhorne, James. Letters. Richmond: Virginia Historical Society.
Lee, Mary Charlton. Diary. Winchester, Va.: Handley Library.
Lyman, William R. Memoirs. New Orleans: Tulane University Library.
McDonald, Edward Hitchcock. Memoirs. Chapel Hill: University of North Carolina Library, Southern Historical Collection.
Mead, Rufus, Jr. Papers and letters. Washington D.C.: Library of Congress, Manuscript Division.
Moore, Samuel J. C. Papers. Chapel Hill: University of North Carolina Library, Southern Historical Collection.
Oates, William C. Unpublished manuscript, n.d. Montgomery: Alabama Department of Archives and History.
Richardson, Sidney J. Letters. Atlanta: Georgia Department of Archives and History.
Sperry, Kate S., Jr. " 'Surrender! Never Surrender!': The Diary of a Confederate Girl." Unpublished diary, n.d. Winchester, Va.: Handley Library.
Waldrop, Richard Woolfolk. Papers, 1850-1867. Chapel Hill: University of North Carolina Library, Southern Historical Collection.

INDEX

Numerals in italics indicate an illustration of the subject mentioned.

H

J

K

L

M

N

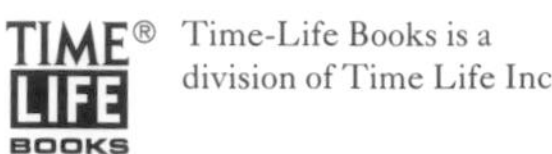

Time-Life Books is a division of Time Life Inc.

TIME LIFE INC.
PRESIDENT and CEO: George Artandi

TIME-LIFE BOOKS
PRESIDENT: John D. Hall
PUBLISHER/MANAGING EDITOR: Neil Kagan

VOICES OF THE CIVIL WAR

DIRECTOR, NEW PRODUCT DEVELOPMENT: Curtis Kopf
MARKETING DIRECTOR: Pamela R. Farrell

SHENANDOAH 1862

EDITORS: Henry Woodhead, Paul Mathless
Deputy Editors: Kirk Denkler (principal), Harris J. Andrews, Philip Brandt George
Art Directors: Ellen L. Pattisall, Ray Ripper, Barbara M. Sheppard
Associate Editor/Research and Writing: Gemma Slack
Senior Copyeditor: Judith Klein
Picture Coordinator: Lisa Groseclose
Picture Associate: Connie Contreras
Editorial Assistant: Christine Higgins

Initial Series Design: Studio A

Special Contributors: Gary L. Ecelbarger, Robert K. Krick, Brian Pohanka, David S. Thomson (text); Paul Birkhead, Charles F. Cooney, Robert Lee Hodge, Susan V. Kelly, Michael McAfee, Henry Mintz (research); Roy Nanovic (index).

Correspondents: Christina Lieberman (New York).

Vice President, Director of Finance: Christopher Hearing
Vice President, Book Production: Marjann Caldwell
Director of Publishing Technology: Betsi McGrath
Director of Photography and Research: John Conrad Weiser
Director of Editorial Administration: Barbara Levitt
Production Manager: Marlene Zack
Quality Assurance Manager: James King
Chief Librarian: Louise D. Forstall

Consultants
Richard L. Armstrong, a Civil War historian and author, has written nine books concerning the war. Since 1989 he has contributed to the Virginia Regimental History Series and the Virginia Battles and Leaders Series. *The Battle of McDowell* remains his most popular volume. Apart from continuing his research on McDowell, he is working on a book about the Virginia militia system.

Gary L. Ecelbarger, formerly president of the Bull Run Civil War Round Table, has published numerous articles in Civil War and historical periodicals. His most recent work is the forthcoming *We Are In for It!: The Battle of Kernstown March 23, 1862*. He is a charter member of the Kernstown Battlefield Association and has worked as a consulting historian for the city of Winchester and Frederick County interpreting battlefield property.

Robert K. Krick is the author of more than 100 published articles and nine books, among them *Fredericksburg Artillery* and *Lee's Colonels.* His book *Stonewall Jackson at Cedar Mountain* won three national awards, including the Douglas Southall Freeman Prize. His most recent work is *Conquering the Valley: Stonewall Jackson at Port Republic.*

First printing. Printed in U.S.A.
School and library distribution by Time-Life Education, P.O. Box 85026, Richmond, Virginia 23285-5026.

Library of Congress Cataloging-in-Publication Data
Shenandoah 1862 / by the editors of Time-Life Books.
p. cm.—(Voices of the Civil War)
Includes bibliographical references and index.
ISBN 0-7835-4711-0
1. Shenandoah Valley Campaign, 1862.
2. Jackson, Stonewall, 1824-1863.
I. Time-Life Books. II. Series.
E473.7.S53 1997
973.7'32—dc21 97-3198
CIP

OTHER PUBLICATIONS:

HISTORY
What Life Was Like
The American Story
The American Indians
Lost Civilizations
Mysteries of the Unknown
Time Frame
The Civil War
Cultural Atlas

SCIENCE/NATURE
Voyage Through the Universe

DO IT YOURSELF
The Time-Life Complete Gardener
Home Repair and Improvement
The Art of Woodworking
Fix It Yourself

TIME-LIFE KIDS
Family Time Bible Stories
Library of First Questions and Answers
A Child's First Library of Learning
I Love Math
Nature Company Discoveries
Understanding Science & Nature

COOKING
Weight Watchers® Smart Choice Recipe Collection
Great Taste~Low Fat
Williams-Sonoma Kitchen Library

For information on and a full description of any of the Time-Life Books series listed above, please call 1-800-621-7026 or write:

Reader Information
Time-Life Customer Service
P.O. Box C-32068
Richmond, Virginia 23261-2068

R 10 9 8 7 6 5 4 3 2 1